DATE DUE		

of related interest

Raising NLD Superstars
What Families with Nonverbal Learning Disabilities Need to Know
about Nurturing Confident, Competent Kids
Marcia Brown Rubinstien
Foreword by Pamela B. Tanguay
ISBN 978 1 84310 770 5

A Special Kind of Brain
Living with Nonverbal Learning Disability
Nancy Russell Burger
Foreword by Byron P. Rourke
ISBN 978 1 84310 762 0

Nonverbal Learning Disabilities at Home
A Parent's Guide
Pamela B. Tanguay
Foreword by Byron P. Rourke, FRSC
ISBN 978 1 85302 940 0

Nonverbal Learning Disabilities at School
Educating Students with NLD, Asperger Syndrome
and Related Conditions
Pamela B. Tanguay
Foreword by Sue Thompson
ISBN 978 1 85302 941 7

Employment for Individuals with Asperger Syndrome
or Non-Verbal Learning Disability
Stories and Strategies
Yvona Fast and others
ISBN 978 1 84310 766 8

Helping Children
with
Nonverbal Learning Disabilities
to Flourish
A Guide for Parents and Professionals

Marilyn Martin

Foreword by Michele Berg

Jessica Kingsley Publishers
London and Philadelphia

First published in 2007
by Jessica Kingsley Publishers
116 Pentonville Road
London N1 9JB, UK
and
400 Market Street, Suite 400
Philadelphia, PA 19106, USA

www.jkp.com

Library of Congress Cataloging in Publication Data
Martin, Marilyn, 1952-
 Helping children with nonverbal learning disabilities to flourish : a guide for parents and professionals / Marilyn Martin ; foreword by Michele Berg.
  p. cm.
 Includes bibliographical references and index.
 ISBN-13: 978-1-84310-858-0 (pbk.)
 1. Learning disabled children--Rehabilitation. 2. Nonverbal learning disabilities. I. Title.
 RJ506.L4M37 2007
 618.92'85889--dc22

2006101041

British Library Cataloguing in Publication Data
A CIP catalogue record for this book is available from the British Library

ISBN 978 1 84310 858 0

Printed and bound in the United States by Thomson-Shore, Inc.

Contents

Foreword

The class of learning disabilities referred to as "Nonverbal Learning Disorders" has been studied for over 40 years; however, the term did not begin to creep into the awareness of most educators and parents until the latter part of the 1990s. When I founded the Center for Learning Disabilities at the Menninger Clinic in 1984, our focus was language-based learning disorders. We knew far less about children who had strong verbal output and appeared to read well but had difficulty managing information that was not verbal in nature. Oftentimes, we were not able to systematically identify or to even fully appreciate the challenges faced by these individuals even though, by virtue of being at Menninger, we worked with one of the most well-trained and sophisticated multidisciplinary teams in the country. By the late 1980s the picture was changing. At Menninger we had formed a study group composed of LD specialists, psychologists, neuro-psychologists, a neurologist, and a speech-language pathologist. Together we began to explore the broader realm of learning disorders in depth. I became particularly interested in the students described so aptly by Johnson and Myklebust in the chapter "Nonverbal Disorders of Learning" which appeared in their seminal book *Learning Disabilities: Educational Principles and Practices* (1967). In the late 1980s and early 1990s Byron Rourke's ground-breaking work on subtypes of learning disabilities and his book *Nonverbal Learning Disabilities: The Syndrome and the Model* (1989) gave further credence to the existence of this class of learning disorder.

In spite of the persuasiveness of Rourke's research and the growing clinical interest in nonverbal learning disorders, the type of broad public awareness enjoyed by dyslexia and attention deficit disorders has eluded this low-incidence learning disability. As I traveled the country in the late 1990s and early 2000s speaking on the topic of nonverbal learning disorders, I encountered great interest, great need, and great confusion. Parents and educators clamored for information regarding the nature of this class of learning disorders and more importantly, practical and effective interventions.

In 2007, we remain without consensus regarding diagnostic criteria and Nonverbal Learning Disorder (NLD) continues to be excluded from the DSM-IV. It is not clear if NLD refers to one or to a number of learning disorders that share certain commonalties. Public school systems vary in their approach to identification of students who exhibit characteristics associated with this class of learning disorders. There is scant research concerning what constitutes effective interventions. Many students with this type of learning disorder remain without appropriate services. Fortunately the literature pertaining to nonverbal learning disorders has been growing steadily and we are most likely approaching a break-through in terms of achieving more visibility for this largely invisible disorder.

Marilyn Martin's book *Helping Children with Nonverbal Learning Disabilities to Flourish: A Guide for Parents and Professionals* is an exciting and essential addition to the literature. This is a book written by an intelligent and talented educational therapist who, out of necessity, became an educational sleuth. When confronted with her daughter Sara's mysterious learning difficulties, she began to systematically search for the cause. Why should a child with a flawless rote verbal memory, a keen interest in language, and a Herculean ability to concentrate, struggle with learning math, riding a bike, finding her way around her own home, negotiating social exchanges? Ms. Martin's investigations lead to encounters with educational, clinical, and medical specialists, to conferences and workshops, and to an almost exhaustive survey of the literature. These investigations finally lead to a conclusion that will benefit us all. Marilyn Martin decided that finding the answer to "what can be done?" was ultimately just as important as finding the answer to "what is this?"

The author wisely points out that while every *individual* has a unique nature, the *problems* experienced by individuals with NLD are not unique. Thus we can extract an abundance of good solid information regarding multiple aspects of NLD through this recounting of a mother's attempt to understand and help her daughter. Experiences with Sara are used to bring life to the term "NLD." We are allowed to know Sara in the context of a very real world and to travel with her from infancy to college. As a result of accompanying Sara on her developmental journey, we emerge more able to fully appreciate the complex nature of the trials and tribulations associated with this disorder. This is not a book, however, that simply aims for empathic understanding. This is a book that is intended to provide parents and professionals with a solid overview of the current understanding of NLD. The section that details the developmental picture of a typical child with NLD from infancy through elementary school is invaluable and will most certainly aid earlier identification. Navigation of the territory of adolescence and young adulthood gets equal attention. Ms. Martin tackles the issue of subtle, but potentially impairing, language weaknesses head on. We are cautioned that the label "nonverbal learning disorder" may distract us from attending to the serious difficulties with communicative competencies that are often present but masked by verbal fluency.

Sara's tale is used to also illustrate specific strategies to address specific problems at home and at school. There is no single parent, educator, speech pathologist or clinician that can provide the systematic mentoring needed by children with NLD to overcome all the daily hurdles encountered visually, spatially, socially, and academically. Partnerships between professionals and parents, however, can result in powerful and positive outcomes. Ms. Martin shines in her ability to match interventions to a broad range of problems: examples abound in every chapter. Clear, concise, and detailed explanations are given so that the interventions can be applied skillfully. Chapter 10: A Sampler of Interventions is so comprehensive that I consider it absolutely a "must read!" The problem areas addressed include motor skills, handwriting, spatial confusion, reading comprehension, literal interpretation of words and phrases, and social weaknesses. General principles for developing interventions are outlined. Each intervention is presented in a terrifically useful and usable format that includes the problem, strengths available, proposed solution, how the solution can be generalized, the goal of the intervention, and a very up-to-date and helpful listing of relevant resources. The Appendix discusses how the strategies in Chapter 10 can be combined to form lessons to reinforce multiple learning goals.

Perhaps what I prize most highly about this book is the sense of optimism that is apparent throughout these pages. The pain, despair, and hopelessness that were intimate companions throughout Sara's journey are not minimized but never were they allowed to stifle Sara's strivings to grow and to achieve. This book is, in the end, a rousing call to action. It is a response to the often pessimistic and hence limiting prognoses attached to NLD. The message conveyed is that intelligently designed interventions that are thoughtfully and consistently applied can alter the course of this learning disorder and that children with NLD can become, like Sara, successful adults leading meaningful lives.

I wish this book had been available to me when I started my explorations of this topic. I am grateful that it is available now. I am also very grateful to Sara for her generosity in letting this tale be told and to Marilyn Martin for telling it so beautifully.

Michele Berg, Ph.D.
Director, Center for Learning Disorders
Family Service and Guidance
Topeka, Kansas

Acknowledgements

This book would probably not have been written if I had not enrolled in an innovative graduate program in education at Vermont College. It was there that I had the good fortune to meet my program advisor, Kelley Peters. She made learning such a creative process that, under her counsel and encouragement, my thinking expanded and evolved until I discovered what it was I needed to say.

The personal story in this book would probably have been less sanguine if Sara's brother, John, had not been such a sensitive and generous child. He was truly her "compass" during childhood. For certain, Sara's success and my ability to help her were constantly bolstered by the superhuman efforts of her father and my husband, Josh, who was always available to help when my abilities floundered, my spirits lagged, and my confidence vanished. We would have been in a lot of trouble if he had not been so adept at science, math and compassion.

Sara, I cannot thank you enough for allowing your story to be told and for being the most dazzling daughter. Your mind and spirit are rare and amazing. By helping you, I learned how to help others.

So more than anything else, I want to acknowledge the power of love to transform and liberate.

Chapter 1

Beginnings: Deciphering the Rosetta Stone

The five symbols shown above were originally found on the left-hand corner of a large piece of lavender construction paper. Forever lodged in my memory is the image of my daughter picking up a red fine-tipped marker and carefully forming the first symbol—the one that resembles a "3." It is not the figure she hoped to create. So she optimistically tries again, but the "w" that her pen produces next does not have the vertical serpentine curve of the "s" she so desires. Nevertheless, she forges on, writing her version of an "a," then an "r," and finally another "a."

For 20 years, concealed in a box in my daughter's closet, I have kept this piece of lavender paper with its inscrutable signature. The five symbols were my six-year-old daughter's early attempts to figure out how to print her name. The primitive crudeness of the letters belies the enormous effort that went into producing them. In the previous months, my daughter had risen every day at dawn in an attempt to capture an extra hour that she could devote to practicing her printing. Her most fervent wish was to be able to make an "S" that resembled the letter she saw in books. But despite this extraordinary determination, her ability to write seemed permanently stymied.

"What do you think is going on?" I would ask our pediatrician, Sara's kindergarten teacher, and then finally several therapists and specialists from whom I sought advice. These well-meaning individuals could shed little light on my daughter's predicament. Some prescribed further testing with a different professional; others recommended patience since different children develop at different rates. I followed their advice as best as I could, but found that testing resulted in little practical advice on how actually to help Sara. It was easy to be patient with a child as lovely and motivated as my daughter. However, her desire to write was so ardent that patience seemed like a parsimonious remedy to offer her. Despite the fact that neither her teachers nor her mother could figure out how to help her, the infinite optimism with which she seemed blessed made her face each early morning writing session with steely determination. How long would she keep trying so hard in the face of such intractable failure, I wondered?

The following spring, I sought out a school where Sara could spend her elementary school years and where she might possibly realize her dream to write her name. Her private kindergarten was not part of an elementary school, and her preschool, unlike kindergarten, had not been a good experience for her, so I was sensitive to the fact that the school environment played an important role in her ultimate happiness and ability to function. When I phoned the director of the prospective elementary school, I explained that Sara was a lovely child, very well-behaved and enthusiastic about learning. However, she has had a lot of trouble with fine motor tasks, I continue, picking my words carefully, and her speech is still very difficult for strangers to understand. She has been happy in her current school, but she adjusted poorly to a previous school where she stopped talking for two years. Will any of this be a problem for your school? No, the busy director responds soothingly, but there will be an interview. It will only serve as a formality, she assured me, but a member of the faculty is required to interview each child who wishes to enroll in our school.

I made an appointment for Sara to be interviewed on a Friday afternoon in late April. She wore her best dress and requested that I fashion her brown hair into a French braid. As we drove into the city that spring afternoon, she entertained me by retelling the story her father had read to her the previous evening about a woman who dedicated her life to planting lupine seeds on an island. I could understand every word of her accurate oral rendition of the tale, but I knew that very few other people would have been able to glean much meaning from Sara's words. I wondered about the process of "interviewing" a child whose speech seemed so imperfectly formed.

We arrived early and waited in the hallway for our turn to be interviewed. After a short time, a young woman introduced herself and invited us into an adjoining room. It was a large classroom with slightly worn wooden floors. The front wall of the room was covered with an expanse of blackboard on which a castle scene had been drawn in colorful chalk. Sara followed the teacher silently to the front of the room where the young woman told her a story about a girl whose brother was turned into a bird by an enchantress. Sara listened raptly to the tale. She loved listening to stories. When the story was over, the teacher handed Sara a sheet of paper and some crayons and asked her to draw an illustration of the account. As I tried to sit unobtrusively in the back, the room seemed to become uncomfortably warm. Sara picked up the crayons and drew her interpretation of the beautiful story she had just heard. She handed the paper back to the teacher and then, in response to the teacher's question, explained the meaning of the curious blobs and splashes of color on the page. I heard her relate how a brother and sister trespassed too close to the house of an old woman. In revenge, the old woman turned the brother into a sparrow and locked him away in a room. The plucky sister, though, was able to break the spell and return her brother to his human form. Although Sara's ability to listen and enjoy stories was superb, her capacity to speak clearly was not, so her retelling was virtually unintelligible to the teacher. Since her ability to draw was very primitive even for a six-year-old, her illustration contained only amorphous splotches of red, blue, and green.

Next, the teacher asked Sara to walk across a balance beam, look through a tube that was an imaginary telescope, jump on one foot and, finally, skip or hop across the room. Sara gamely executed all these tasks to the best of her ability. However, she had poor balance, so even though the balance beam on which she was asked to walk hovered only an inch or two above the floor, she fell off repeatedly. Sara did manage to look through the "telescope." Unfortunately, she was unable to relate exactly what it was she viewed through the tiny cardboard opening. She could neither skip nor hop, and had an unusual gait. As she sashayed across the classroom, I watched the teacher's eyes grow big with amazement. When Sara's interview was completed, the teacher ushered us out of the classroom and told me not to expect to hear from the school for a long time. "Is there something wrong?" I inquired. The young teacher remained evasive. "Did I do well, Mommy?" Sara asked me as we got into the car.

Sara finally did gain admittance to this school, and it was there that she spent her elementary school years. To the surprise of many, she thrived and learned and grew. The year that she began first grade was a turning point for her. It was that year, when Sara turned six, that I became so anxious about her emotional state I sought help from numerous well-meaning professionals in the fields of medicine, education, and psychology. I received little advice that could be translated into positive practical ways to help her. In desperation, I decided to learn everything I could about how to help children with learning challenges. As we found solutions for her difficulties, Sara's optimistic nature blossomed, and she discovered there was very little she could not accomplish.

By the time Sara entered high school in 1995, she had made much headway overcoming her difficulties. And in the next four years, she grew in ways that amazed even me. She elected to take the rigorous International Baccalaureate (IB) course of study. To be honest, if I had understood how difficult the program was I never would have allowed her to take it. The IB program was designed for students of families involved in foreign service or working for multinational companies who live abroad in more than one country over the course of their school career, and need to demonstrate they have completed a rigorous standard curriculum and are qualified to enter the best colleges in the world. It has evolved into an international effort to improve school standards. Students must take six reading and writing intensive advanced classes. They must also learn to speak, read, and write one modern foreign language. To receive your "baccalaureate" you need to pass six challenging exams, perform a minimum of 150 hours of community service, and write an extended research essay of 4000 words. In 1999, my daughter graduated second in her class.

Sara was able to succeed in an intellectually challenging program despite the fact that she has a nonverbal learning disability (NLD). In addition, she had been plagued by a severe articulation disorder that was not resolved until she was almost ten years old. When my daughter rose on the night of her high school graduation to give the salutatorian's speech, I am sure the audience saw only a hard-working, capable young woman with a bright future. I saw this too, but I also saw the younger girl whose spoken language was only understandable after years of speech therapy, the girl who became so discouraged and depressed in nursery school that she stopped speaking within the confines of her school walls for two years. I saw the girl who got lost in friends' houses, who struggled to write, to learn math, to ride a bike, to make a friend. I also saw a girl with considerable strengths—a Herculean ability to concentrate, a flawless rote memory, a keen interest in language and stories, native intelligence, and an optimistic and resilient nature. Despite my great belief in Sara's abilities, her academic and personal success in high school was unexpected and unanticipated. NLD is considered a serious and frequently devastating learning disorder, and it is never used in the same sentence with the word *salutatorian.*

After high school, Sara continued to do well. She applied to seven liberal arts colleges that are among the most selective in the U.S. and was admitted to six of them. She graduated with honors from college four years later with a degree in English and Spanish. She currently attends a very challenging graduate program in speech-language pathology at a major medical center. Perhaps more importantly, she is generous, kind, and socially conscious. She is deeply reflective and possesses phenomenal metacognitive skills. When faced with new learning or social challenges, she has learned how to independently apply the principles of interventions and strategies that she learned as a child. She has discovered ways to exempt herself from experiencing the lack of insight that plagues many individuals with NLD, described in the following statement by Rourke (1989): "NLD individuals experience a virtual inability to reflect on the nature and seriousness of their problems...and [have] outstanding difficulties in generating adequate solutions for those problems that they do appreciate" (p.171).

This book relates how Sara transformed herself from that young girl whose existence seemed darkened by learning difficulties into the capable young woman she is today. Sara was lucky. In 1987 when she was six, few professionals were familiar with the strengths and weaknesses of minds like hers. That was nearly 20 years ago, and much more is known today about what constitutes nonverbal learning disability. However, children with NLD still find it problematic to receive the help they need in school and at home to lead fulfilling lives.

When Sara was young, I was often frustrated by how few useful suggestions I could uncover to assist me in developing practical ways to help my daughter live comfortably in the world. Gradually, we encountered professionals who did have expertise in practical ways to help her. Finding these individuals felt like mining for gold, but when I discovered someone who had knowledge that was helpful to us, I was often overwhelmed at their generosity. The remedial process has been truly liberating for both Sara and me. It has introduced me to a whole world of knowledge that has served as a rich training ground, so that I could gain the principles I needed to help many other students in my work at a private school with children who had "mysterious" learning challenges and, several years later, when I opened the private practice I have maintained for over ten years. For Sara, it has allowed her to gain the strategies and skills she needs to live comfortably with her unusual mind, and to accomplish a higher level of achievement than would have been forecast by her early academic history. It is important for individuals with NLD to receive early and effective interventions, not necessarily to enroll in rigorous academic programs like Sara, but so they can reach their full potential and realize their own personal dreams. I share her story with others, not to serve as a blueprint for the course that individuals with NLD should take, but to illustrate the possibility that NLD may be a more malleable condition than the current literature suggests.

At present, the typical prognosis for individuals with NLD is pessimistic. They are individuals who, despite high ability, have difficulty securing independent and satisfying lives. Consequently, parents of children with NLD are offered discouraging predictions about the ultimate chances of their children to become capable adults. My daughter, who is now a young adult, has been able to forge an autonomous and rewarding life despite significant limitations associated with NLD. I include her story as an example of hope and possibility for both parents and educators. Additionally, the journey of understanding that I needed to follow in order to develop effective interventions for Sara, and ultimately for other students, led me to form generalizations and conclusions about the best ways to assist individuals with NLD that may be helpful to other parents and professionals.

I include her story for a final reason. I want to describe nonverbal learning disability not only on a technical or theoretical basis, but also through the language of stories. I hope that by relating my experiences as a parent of a child with NLD, both professionals and parents can experience a more empathetic understanding of this mysterious learning disorder that has the potential to cloud lives and limit happiness.

Many years after Sara picked up the red marker to attempt her nascent signature, my husband had these letters copied and placed into a frame that I still display in my office where I work with children facing learning challenges. Trying to make sense of the markings on its surface set in motion the personal odyssey that is contained in these pages. It is my personal Rosetta Stone.

Chapter 2

What is a Nonverbal Learning Disability?

Nonverbal learning disability (NLD) is a confusing term. Children with NLD are not individuals unable to speak, as one might think. In fact, one of the greatest strengths of individuals with NLD is their ability to understand and use verbal and auditory stimuli. A *nonverbal learning disability* refers rather to the difficulty these individuals experience when they try to process and understand visual, or nonverbal, information. For example, children with NLD typically struggle to recognize familiar faces or to find their way around the everyday confines of their school and home. They struggle with academic subjects such as geometry or geography that require acute visual discrimination. So the child with NLD is someone who delights in words, but despite adequate vision, struggles with making sense of the myriad of phenomena we see with our eyes. The following description of a routine car ride I took many years ago with my then eight-year-old daughter and five-year-old son serves to illustrate how children with NLD perceive their physical world:

> We are on our way to the grocery store. Suddenly as we cross the bridge that spans the expressway, an enormous blimp [airship] clearly comes into view through the windshield. It is a huge airborne advertisement with the word, *Exxon*, tattooed in vivid red letters on its side. "Hey," I say to my passengers, "Look at the blimp up in the sky!" "Where, where?" Sara asks with urgency in her voice, her eyes vainly scanning the sky. "Right up there," her brother replies, pointing his index finger at the gigantic object in the sky directly above us. I know that Sara's mind will not perceive an object even this large and obvious without verbal assistance. I point

directly at the blimp and say, "Look out the window, up in the sky, right there. Look for a giant object that resembles a long gray balloon with the letters, E-X-X-O-N on the side." My daughter scans the sky for at least half a minute. When the slow-moving blimp finally registers in her mind, I hear the frustration drain out of her voice, "I see it," she says in awe. Later at home, she draws a huge blimp in the blue sky. Two primitive stick figures look up at the blob in the sky. A cartoon bubble comes out of the girl stick figure's mouth, and the awkward letters proclaim, "Look at the blimp, John!"

This story illustrates how words are essential for children with NLD. At first, Sara found it difficult to perceive the large unexpected object. However, after she heard a verbal description of what a blimp looked like, and where in the sky to locate it, she finally was able to perceive it. Throughout Sara's childhood, I learned about the power of words to guide her through space. Words became her seeing-eye dog. "I can't find the library at school," she complained to me one day when she was in second grade. "The room that you are looking for is the one with the big panel of green glass on the top part of the door," I would tell her. Suddenly, she was able to find her way in a world that appeared to her as an ever-changing landscape.

Besides referring to individuals who are highly verbal and have difficulty understanding nonverbal information, *nonverbal learning disability* is a confusing term to many people for an additional reason. This confusion results from the fact that individuals with certain other congenital syndromes, neurological disorders, and diseases share some or all of the characteristics of the NLD profile. In fact, many of the assets and weaknesses of the NLD profile are included in the description of eight other syndromes such as Asperger's and Williams (Klin *et al.* 1995). Although NLD shares many features with these other disorders, however, it differs from them and is a distinct type of learning disability. For example, individuals with Williams syndrome, a rare genetic disorder, also exhibit stronger language skills relative to their visual-spatial processing abilities. However, individuals with Williams syndrome may have additional characteristics that children with developmental NLD *never* have, such as distinctive facial characteristics and mental retardation (Rourke *et al.* 2002).

NLD is sometimes called a "right-hemisphere learning disorder" because neurologists theorize that NLD, like the other related syndromes that it resembles, is caused by some dysfunction in the white matter of the right hemisphere of the brain (Rourke 1995). The right hemisphere is responsible for processing "nonverbal or performance information, including the visual-spatial, intuitive, organizational, evaluative, and holistic processing functions of an individual" (Thompson 1997, p.11). Neurologists have come to the conclusion that children with "developmental" NLD have something amiss with the right hemisphere of their brain because these children act like individuals who have had actual injuries to the right hemisphere that neurologists can see on brain scans. For example, children with some forms of cancer, who previously showed no unusual learning patterns before cancer treatment, will often exhibit some typical characteristics of NLD after they receive extremely high levels of radiation that cause injury to the right hemisphere (Rourke 1995). Neurologists do not know for certain that individuals with developmental NLD have actual injury to any part of their brain, but simply hypothesize that they do because their actions sometimes resemble those of people who have documented brain injuries.

The difference between NLD and Asperger's Syndrome

There is particular confusion and controversy about the differences between the labels "Asperger's Syndrome" and "NLD." One way to think about the differences between the two disorders is to recognize that an individual with Asperger's Syndrome has many of the strengths and weaknesses of someone with NLD, but also has additional challenges (Klin *et al.* 1995). For example, children with Asperger's Syndrome typically have "restricted interests," where they become obsessed with unusual interests such as snakes, otters, or plumbing materials which they pursue single-mindedly, often "engulfing the entire family's energy" (Stein, Klin and Miller 2004, p.1459). It is not typical for children with developmental NLD to have peculiar or narrow interests. Children with Asperger's Syndrome also suffer from more profound social difficulties than children with developmental NLD (Thompson 1997). Roman (1998) points out that some researchers have made the controversial assertion that NLD and Asperger's Syndrome exist on a continuum where the "lower functioning children diagnosed with Asperger's may be more properly diagnosed as autistic [and] the higher functioning children diagnosed with Asperger's syndrome may instead be children with NLD who have been misdiagnosed" (p.2).

NLD has only recently received attention in the psychological and educational communities. Johnson and Myklebust (1967) wrote the first detailed description of this profile. They pointed out that in contrast to the typical child with learning disability (LD) who has difficulty acquiring some form of verbal learning (speaking, spelling, or reading), there is a less well-known learner who exhibits the opposite learning profile—namely, strength in acquiring much verbal information but challenges with interpreting nonverbal information (Johnson and Myklebust 1967). Subsequently, Rourke (1987, 1989, 1995), the foremost researcher to investigate and describe this syndrome, developed detailed accounts of the principal identifying features of NLD. To date, there is a dearth of literature that explores which interventions are needed to help students with NLD adapt academically and socially.

Individuals with the NLD profile have always been among us, but because the concept of cataloging their difficulties and categorizing them as a "disability" is new, NLD is not yet a recognized diagnostic category under the federal special education law, nor is it included in the latest version of the *Diagnostic and Statistical Manual of Mental Disorders* (DSM; see Roman 1998). As a result, children with NLD are given other labels such as specific learning disability NOS (none otherwise specified), orthopedically handicapped, or even emotionally disturbed. Unfortunately, these incomplete or inaccurate diagnoses do not allow children with NLD to receive the specific help they need to succeed, nor do they allow educators and therapists to develop appropriate educational plans for individuals with NLD. In addition, the absence of a category for NLD under the federal special education law or in the DSM may also contribute to the fact that NLD is unknown to many teachers, parents, diagnosticians, and psychologists. This ignorance has perhaps contributed to the unforgivable lack of intervention literature and to the grim prognosis that exists in the literature for individuals with more severe forms of NLD. When a child's condition has no official name, parents and teachers of children with NLD receive little useful advice on how to proceed in best raising and making educational decisions for their child or student.

My daughter, Sara, was born in 1981 with a form of NLD that is not part of any other syndrome or disease. NLD is not a difficulty that is manifest at birth. Throughout childhood, the beauty and challenges of the kind of mind with which a child with NLD is endowed gradually unfold. I had never heard the term *nonverbal learning disability* until my daughter was 11 years old, but when I heard a description of this condition at a conference for learning disabilities, I knew immediately that this must be the name for the collection of observations I had been making since my daughter's first year. When I also learned that day that children with NLD are at risk for a host of secondary psychological problems, including a higher risk for suicide, I became a convert to the value of early intervention. For my daughter and me, the journey to understand NLD started in her first year, long before I even knew what NLD was. My first stab at "intervention" was to try to lead Sara out of the spatial confusion that seemed to engulf her emerging motor abilities. For us, the story began like this.

Sara's first year

My daughter's life started out perfectly normally. Her birth was uneventful. When she entered the world on that gray and dismal January afternoon, she showed no telltale signs or omens that anything was amiss. If anything, she hurled herself out of the womb with such alacrity that she was almost born in the hallway of the stark university hospital. She was vigorously healthy with Apgar scores of ten and a rosy color that contrasted with the gloomy winter day and the sterile setting of the delivery room. The medical personnel clucked and complimented my husband and me on our robust offspring, and we absorbed the compliments with the euphoric and narcissistic confidence of brand new parents.

We were sent home 48 hours later, blissfully ignorant of the strange new world we would soon enter. We drove home, taking endless city streets to avoid the expressway with its danger and speed. Like all new parents, we were overcome with love for the small glowing creature who traveled with us. We talked endlessly about her perfection—her nose, her eyes, her tiny toes and fingers, a complete human in miniature. We gazed on the flawless skin and speculated on her unblemished prospects. She was perfection; she was our heart as she led us into a world we did not know existed. It would be a world that is both terrifying and mysterious, but also beautiful—full of figurative impenetrable landscapes of dark forests, enchanted waters, and steep mountains. It is the world of learning disabilities with its own vague labels and jargon—a shifting landscape of little light where families and children enter without a guide, and often find themselves lost. It is a world that no one would choose and from which very few escape unscathed.

That day driving my daughter home from the hospital, I had no idea I would spend the better part of my adult life accompanying her through this dizzying enchanted landscape. I did not know how few signposts there would be as we traveled. I did not know if her story would have a happy ending.

In the first two years of her life, it was almost as if Sara had two personalities, her public persona and her private one. Her private persona was reassuring; she was like all other babies. In her baby book, we recorded that she smiled on schedule at six weeks. We took pictures of her and preserved her likeness in the plastic covers of the picture album. At home in our small apartment, she was a content and placid baby. It was when we ventured into the wider world—to the grocery store, to the park, or for our walks—that those first small stabs of worry would rise in my heart. It was if I were keeping a second invisible baby book where I began to record all the subtle differences I observed.

One of the first entries for the invisible baby book was how Sara's motor development seemed to be subtly different from other children. Around nine months, the babies of friends began to crawl. For the next year, baby after baby, even the most cautious, learned to move in some fashion around their environment. Friends began to "baby-proof" their houses, removing heirloom vases and crystal candlesticks from coffee tables. They secured kitchen cabinets with little locks that kept the household poisons at bay. I did these things too, but there really was no need.

Sara was content to stay in one place. At nine months, she still could not sit up of her own accord. She only had the strength to remain in a sitting position if one propped her up. Since she was not able to explore the world under her own steam, I collected artifacts from the rooms of our home for her to experience. As she sat on a blanket, I brought her blocks, pots, and cardboard books. While the vigilance of other mothers was channeled towards following their children through space to guard them from playing with a dangerous object, mine was centered on bringing objects out of space to my daughter for her to experience. "Just a minute. I am going to the kitchen to get an eggbeater so we can make those soap bubbles bigger. Do you want to come?" If she did, I would pick her up and take her with me.

Sara's motor development never deviated enough from the norm to alarm the pediatrician. She always met the important milestones, quite late, but never late enough to veer completely off the developmental charts in Spock and Brazeleton. However, my list of concerns grew in that second invisible baby book. It wasn't how old she was when she learned to sit, crawl, or walk that alarmed me, but the torturous route that she took to learn these things. Balance seemed very difficult for her. She was not able to roll over until she was ten months old. She learned to pull herself to a sitting position a few weeks later. Both of these tasks remained difficult for her, and she started carrying objects with her wherever she went in order to steady herself. She pulled herself into a standing position right on time though, and cruised around the furniture with ease. As long as she had something to hold on to, she could manage movement more easily.

After she pulled herself to a standing position and could move around a bit, I tried to silence my worry. Actually Sara's lack of movement made her an easy baby to care for. She seemed to have much better concentration than the average child her age. Her lack of movement, combined with an assiduous attention span, made her an easy baby to integrate into adult life. Whereas other friends had temporarily given up restaurants and museums, Sara and I could attend these events. We went to conservatories and museums where other adults were always amazed at the small being who never left her stroller, rarely fussed or cried, and seemed genuinely entranced with Monet or orchids. "How beautiful she is," childless young women would tell me, "This is the kind of child that I want to have!" So I pushed the worry to the back of my mind where it hibernated for a while longer.

It remained there until the particular afternoon in February when I became acutely aware of just how disoriented in space my 13-month-old daughter was. She was playing in her bedroom, out of sight but not out of earshot. Her behavior had, perhaps, lulled me into a false sense of security. I did not need to be as vigilant as most mothers about watching her every move. She did not get into dangerous things. She did not fall down, but since she was rarely quiet while she played, I had only to listen to keep track of her. On this particular day, Sara was in her room seated at a child-sized table. I was working in the living room and could hear the clear cadence of her happy voice as she described what her play told her.

There was just a tiny pause of silence before the first scream. It was not a cry, but a scream from someone who was genuinely terrified. It came again, a panicked scream loud and shrill. It was sound distilled from pure horror and dread. It took only a few seconds for me to go from the living room to gaze down the short, narrow hallway that led out of Sara's bedroom. I expected to see her bloodied. Instead, I saw her crawling down the hallway, her forehead wrinkled as tears rolled down her cheeks, her chest heaving and gasping with sobs. She was crawling, this child who had never even been able to balance on all fours, who had never even rocked back and forth on her hands and knees. She stared at the two walls on either side of her, as if she was afraid they would collapse on top of her. She would stare at the walls, sob and move forward a little. An instinct told me not to pick her up or interfere with her struggle. It was clear that she did not know where she was. Although she had lived in the same apartment for her entire short life, she didn't know where to go next, or even what was next. She was like a superstitious member of Columbus's crew, terrified that she would fall off the edge of the earth. "This way, Sara. This is the living room." The only sounds were the slap of her palms as they hit the wooden floor and her sobs as she moved forward into the abyss of the living room. "This is the dining room," I said as she followed me into the next room. "This is the kitchen," I said as we finished exploring her universe. Sara calmed herself soon after. I, however, was overwhelmed with the knowledge of how disoriented my daughter seemed in space. She was totally lost. She did not know where each room was or how to go from one room to the next in our small apartment. She lived in a world where the possibility existed that plaster walls could suddenly collapse at any moment. My worry came out of hibernation.

Developing the picture: A snapshot of a rare mind
Rourke's model

Rourke (1995) has developed the most complete model of the mind that accompanies NLD. Rourke (1989, 1995) has identified two major subtypes of LD: verbal learning disability (affects reading, spelling, or speaking) and nonverbal learning disability. Most of his work has endeavored to establish an accurate description of the assets and deficits that characterize individuals with NLD. He visualizes NLD as a complex pattern of specific neuropsychological assets and deficits. NLD is different from the better-known verbal LD because the assets and deficits of NLD affect more areas of an individual's life. For example, the deficits commonly experienced by individuals with reading disabilities affect only one academic domain, written language. In contrast, the assets and deficits of individuals with NLD can be grouped into three major areas: (a) neuropsychological, (b) academic, and (c) socioemotional/adaptive. Individuals with NLD typically have outstanding neuropsychological weaknesses in tactile and visual perception, in their ability to perform complex motor tasks, and in their ability to deal with novel material. To counter these weaknesses, individuals with NLD have neuropsychological strengths in auditory perception, rote memory, and the ability to learn simple motor tasks. Because babies with NLD are poor at interpreting the sensations they receive through touch and sight as well as being poor at motor tasks, they react to their environment by curtailing early exploratory behavior. Babies with NLD react to the world in a manner similar to the way Sara reacted to her environment during her first two years. Because they are sensitive to the sounds they hear, they try to learn about the world through listening. They tend to be "easy" babies who remain in one place. Long after more typical babies are spending their days moving about their homes, picking up items to taste and feel, babies with NLD are still content to stay in one place and find comfort in speech.

Rourke (1995) points out that typical babies learn about concepts through exploratory behavior. For example, when a baby picks up and touches a smooth object, and hears an adult label the object "smooth," the baby not only learns the word *smooth*, but also what *smooth* feels like, how *smooth* feels different from *rough*, and how to identify another smooth object. Babies with NLD, because they tend to stay in one place, have limited sensory experiences to form these types of important judgments. However, because they are sensitive to language, they do pick up the word *smooth*. Their neuropsychological makeup encourages them to pay attention to everything that they hear, and to disregard most of the things that they see or touch. Unfortunately, exploring the world through the auditory channel gives babies with NLD a limited knowledge of the concepts behind the words they so easily learn. This limited understanding of concepts later contributes to the individual's difficulty understanding complex language.

Individuals with NLD have other neuropsychological assets and deficits that develop as an outgrowth of their difficulties with tactile and visual perception, and from their strengths in auditory perception. For example, individuals with NLD typically have poor visual and tactile memories. Therefore, they may have difficulty recognizing their own houses or the faces of family friends. For example, my daughter, who could remember everything that she heard, who as a school girl could memorize lines of blank verse for school plays after hearing them only once or twice, struggled valiantly to memorize the information that the world sent flooding in through her eyes. By the time she was in high school, she had learned enough about social conventions to recognize it was often better to pretend to know someone even when she wasn't quite certain of the identity of the person speaking to her. For example, she is in eleventh grade, and we are on our way home. We have stopped to run a quick errand. A pretty woman walks towards us on the sidewalk. You can tell that she knows us well. She is smiling warmly, waving to Sara, and calling out to her. "How are you? I haven't seen you in so long." She asks Sara about school. They talk. "Do I know that woman?" Sara whispers in my ear, when the woman is barely out of earshot. "It's Dee, your old baby-sitter. Do you remember her?" She remembers the person. She remembers the name, but not what the person looks like. This happens to Sara all the time. While doing her geometry homework that night, she stares at a picture of a square. She is studying angles. "The angle is found right on the corner," I explain. "I can't see the corner. What is a corner and where is it in this square?" she demands. She is in first grade. Everyone is required to learn to play the recorder. The teacher sits facing the class and silently moves his fingers covering the correct holes. The children are instructed to watch his fingers very carefully and copy his movements. He does not speak while the class scrutinizes his fingers covering and uncovering the appropriate openings on the instrument's wooden surface. Sara is holding the recorder upside down and blowing into the wrong end as she tries to find the right holes to cover.

However, the keen ability of individuals with NLD to pay attention to verbal detail allows them to become highly proficient at rote verbal memory, language output, and verbal associations. Children with NLD are first and foremost children who love language. They are children who enjoy hearing stories, having conversations, and learning the labels for the objects in their environment. Individuals with NLD have excellent memory for auditory and verbal stimuli, particularly memory for rote verbal information. For example, my daughter does not need to keep a personal phone book because she only needs to hear an important phone number once, and she can store it away permanently in her memory. I remember sitting a few years ago in a parking lot of a grocery store with Sara, now a young adult and home from college on winter break. She wanted to run across the street to buy a sweater she knew was on sale at a clothing store. She planned on paying by check, and I asked if she had her driver's license with her. "No," she replied, "Why would I need that?" I reminded her that if she wanted to pay by check, she would need identification. She knew that, she replied, but you only need to know your driver's license number in order to cash a check, and she rattled off verbatim the dozen digits that appear on the back of her license. "Don't you know yours?" she asked. I laughed and said she could try to buy the sweater, but I thought the store clerk would probably want to see the driver's license for identification. She ran across the street and came back with the sweater in a shopping bag.

Individuals with NLD have marked deficits in psychomotor coordination and spatial orientation. They are awkward people who struggle to learn how to hop, skip, ride a bicycle, or operate a car. They have serious problems with orienting themselves in space. Because they have spatial difficulties, they easily lose their way. They frequently misjudge how far away objects are and consequently break things or bump into them.

Once individuals with NLD enter school, they exhibit a number of academic assets and deficits that affect their ability to do school work. For example, they typically have difficulty with reading comprehension, math, science, and mastering how to write. They excel at single-word decoding, spelling, and rote memory. Although children with NLD have some initial difficulty in learning to read, most become excellent fluent readers by the end of third grade (Thompson 1996b). They are good at verbal tasks that involve well-developed phonological awareness like decoding, encoding, and rhyming games. They have excellent receptive language skills and rich vocabularies. They are capable of a great deal of verbal output. As a result, when they reach middle-school age, they often tend to speak and write in a manner that is too verbose and ornate. This characteristic becomes more prominent as they grow older. For example, Sara composed the following thank-you note as a school assignment when she was in the seventh grade:

> Dear Mom and Dad, I would like to express my gratitude for you sending me to the C. Waldorf School…I really appreciate and enjoy your delicious dinners which you are so kind to work on so hard every single night. I am thankful for astounding summer vacations filled with joy every moment. I appreciate our weekend outings, which are filled with bliss…

In addition to being excellent at recalling verbal information, children with NLD can learn both rote material and how to perform simple motor actions through repetition if they are given explicit verbal directions. The ability to learn simple motor actions through repetition is an important strength for these children when they start school because learning how to form letters and perform other simple motor tasks is initially difficult for them. It is through repetitive motoric action, coupled with verbal instructions, that the young child with NLD learns the necessary sequence of motor movements required to form the letter S or the number 5, to open a door or to zip a coat. Molenaar-Klumper (2002), a Dutch teacher of children with NLD, writes about one of her students:

> To teach Joyce something new, a lot of repetition was necessary. Once she learned something after many repetitions, she could do it almost perfectly. A game was designed, in which she talked herself through her actions. (p.20)

In addition to deficits in visual perception, visual memory, spatial orientation, and motor coordination, individuals with NLD have difficulty dealing with novel stimuli. This deficit makes it difficult for them to deal successfully with changes in their routine, or unexpected events. Because of their difficulty in dealing with novel stimuli, children with NLD struggle to understand how to be mentally flexible. They are individuals who think in concrete, logical ways. They interpret language literally and are confused by open-ended questions. Although they love language and usually have an excellent vocabulary, they grapple with pragmatic and semantic language—how to read between the lines of what people mean when they speak, how to understand gestures, facial expressions, slang, idioms, how to judge when to say a lot and when to say little, how to know when something is funny.

Individuals with NLD are capable of interpreting language and everyday situations in a manner so literal that individuals with more typical minds can have difficulty following their logic. Generally idioms are the most frequent examples cited in the literature to illustrate how students with NLD interpret language literally. However, the literal misunderstandings made by individuals with NLD are frequently more bizarre than simply not understanding idioms. The following example cited by Brown Rubinstien (2005) is an excellent illustration of the kind of literal misunderstanding that individuals with NLD often make:

> Recently I learned of a child who asked his mother to put bottled water in his school lunches. Dutifully, she went out and bought several cases of pure spring water and stored them where she could comfortably pack a bottle each day. As the beginning of the school year approached, her son became increasingly apprehensive about his drinks for school. [The mother] gently reassured him that everything was taken care of. Finally, he was no longer able to contain his anxiety. "But Mom," he worried, "those bottles all say 'spring water.' What am I going to drink in the fall?" (p.69)

Individuals with NLD are particularly prone to interpret situations and words literally when they occur in conjunction with one of their other weak areas. The following example illustrates how an individual with NLD is more likely to interpret a situation literally when his poor sense of spatial distance is already taxed (Berg 1999). A man with an undiagnosed nonverbal learning disability was the owner of a small business, and sometimes responsible for picking up clients at the local airport. Over the course of several years, the man's business associates and family noticed a curious pattern. Sometimes his trip to the airport took the usual 20 minutes, but on other occasions he did not return for several hours. When they questioned him on why the trip to the airport sometimes took so long, they discovered that he found his way to the airport by looking up into the sky, locating an airplane and following it from the road. His mistake of assuming that the best way to get to an airport was to follow an airplane in flight was fed by a literal interpretation of language (airplanes are associated with airports), in addition to his usual spatial confusion.

Socioemotional challenges

Of all the areas that challenge individuals with NLD, it is their difficulty interpreting social cues and developing a sense of social competence that is potentially the most debilitating for them. Because approximately 65 percent of an average conversation is transmitted nonverbally through facial expressions, body language, gestures, and touch, children with NLD struggle to decipher these seemingly mysterious interactions with others (Thompson 1997). The social difficulties that these individuals face put them at risk for a myriad of problems such as social isolation, loneliness, and self-hatred. Because individuals with NLD frequently miss the information that is conveyed nonverbally, they miss much of the implied meaning of a typical conversation. In order to compensate for this weakness, individuals with NLD rely on their strong rote memory and verbal skills to piece together meaning from conversations. Their responses, then, frequently miss the mark and are often inappropriate. Some children with NLD withdraw in unfamiliar social situations rather than risk appearing foolish.

In Rourke's model (1989), he lists social competence and emotional stability as socioemotional deficits of the NLD mind. Without intervention, the social fate for someone with NLD is almost never positive. Rourke (1989) writes, "Unfortunately, the eventual social and personal outcome for those with NLD is almost never a pleasant one. Withdrawal, isolation, and loneliness are common" (p.100). Rourke, Young, and Leenaars (1989) also contend that the deficits inherent in NLD put individuals with this syndrome at risk for internalized psychological problems like anxiety and depression. Rourke *et al.* (1989) believes that the inevitable psychological difficulties that individuals with NLD will develop also predispose them to a higher risk of suicide than individuals with other forms of LD.

The assertion that NLD is a condition that predisposes individuals to a higher risk of internalized psychological difficulties than other forms of LD has received much attention in the literature. Little (1993) reviews the literature that addresses the question of whether children with LD are any more at risk than more typical children in the area of socioemotional functioning. She concludes that there is no clear evidence that children with LD are at more risk for significant emotional difficulties than more typical learners. Students with LD do have more school adjustment problems (e.g., immaturity, being less popular with classmates) than more typical learners, but Little (1993) concluded that these adjustment issues "were more likely a result of failure and frustration, rather than an integral feature of learning disabilities" (p.654). However, Little also states that "there is some preliminary support that individuals with a subtype of LD called nonverbal learning disability are at more risk than individuals with other types of LD to internalized emotional problems" (p.662). Greenham (1999), in a later review of the literature, came to the conclusion that although there is "considerable evidence that individuals with LD...experience psychosocial problems in addition to...academic deficits...convincing evidence has not been provided...to address whether psychosocial problems are the causes or consequences of LD" (p.190). Greenham finds that there is small, but growing, evidence to support that individuals with NLD are at greater risk for psychological difficulties, and that this tendency towards psychological problems is an inherent symptom of the syndrome. Rourke *et al.* (1989), Bigler (1989), Fletcher (1989), and Kowalchuk and King (1989) all present evidence that NLD predisposes individuals to increased risk of suicide. It is important to understand that these conclusions were reached through studies based on extremely small samples. Also, research shows that despite a predisposition to internalizing psychological difficulties, most individuals with NLD do not develop psychological problems, and very few commit suicide (Greenham 1999).

It is essential for teachers and parents to keep the assertion that children with NLD are at risk for serious psychological problems in proper perspective. On one hand, it is crucial to understand why individuals with NLD are at more risk for depression and anxiety than other students with more common forms of LD, so that further studies result in practical interventions to help students with NLD function in their environments in healthy ways. On the other hand, it is essential to keep in mind that few individuals examined in these preliminary studies experienced *any* interventions throughout their childhood. Greenham (1999) points out that further research is needed to answer questions about how to develop protective personality traits such as self-esteem and resilience in children with NLD in order to help insulate them from debilitating psychological problems. Fletcher (1989) reiterates the importance of early intervention as a means of making sure that these psychological problems do not become inevitabilities.

It is essential that children with NLD receive direct instruction in how to function socially. Sara was extremely fortunate that she attended schools, with the exception of one early preschool experience, that were accepting of her social challenges. This acceptance gave her the necessary time to learn social skills at a slow, comfortable pace. Some researchers have found that one of the best times to work on social skills is in high school (Trapani 1990). Since adolescents have a consuming desire to fit in, they are often receptive at this age to the kind of instruction that helps them understand their social milieu. Sara was lucky to attend a high school where her peers spontaneously took over her social education. She entered this high school with many social deficits and graduated with only a few. She was also fortunate to attend a high school that supplied her with "psychological safety" at an age when she was at risk for faltering socially.

Finally, it is important to remember that every person with NLD is a unique individual with his or her own set of personal characteristics. Since NLD is a syndrome that consists of many assets and deficits, no two individuals with NLD are the same. Some people with NLD have moderate problems with social relationships, severe problems with math, and mild problems with reading comprehension. Other people, who also carry the NLD label, present a very different picture because, although they have similar asset and deficit areas, these areas are affected at different levels of severity. In addition, the interplay between asset and deficit areas varies among individuals, resulting in different patterns of strengths and weaknesses. Finally, individuals with NLD have all the same characteristics that everyone else has that make them novel and distinct persons—their own unique temperaments, experiences, interests, and family environments.

The psychosocial assets of individuals with NLD

In Rourke's model (1989) of the assets and deficits of NLD, he lists the following areas under psychosocial and adaptive deficits: (a) adaptation to novelty, (b) social competence, (c) emotional stability, and (d) activity level. Under the column for socioemotional and adaptive assets, Rourke (1989) lists three question marks. By this notation he means to convey that typical individuals with NLD have the kind of mind that makes adjusting to the world in a psychologically healthy way difficult, and that they bring to this struggle no known psychological strengths. However, anecdotal evidence points to a number of strengths of character that individuals with NLD often show, and that are invaluable psychological assets.

One important attribute shown by many individuals with NLD is persistence. Thompson (1997), an educational therapist who has worked with countless individuals with NLD, is struck by their tenacity. Johnson (1987) describes their indominatible desire to work, strong motivation, and persistence. Whitney (2002) describes this persistence and points out that children with NLD will keep trying long after most of us would give up. Their persistence grows out of their strong desire to please. Individuals with NLD recognize when they are off the mark, and they feel this incongruity keenly. They are willing to work for hours in order to master a task. Their persistence and desire to succeed are such strong defining parts of their character that they often are relentless perfectionists. Parents and teachers need to help individuals with NLD curb these perfectionist tendencies without dampening their fierce work ethic.

Individuals with NLD have a tendency to be literal and concrete. As a result, they often appear vulnerable and naïve. However, their propensity to concreteness also predisposes them to follow rules carefully and to develop an unquestioning belief in what teachers and parents tell them. If encouraged to do so, they can develop strong ethical values, although these values will probably mirror the values of the adults around them. This characteristic can help them bond with adults and forge the kinds of relationships that they need to learn about the world. For example, my daughter was an easy adolescent who was not interested in taking risks. If I told her that it was better to ride a bike with a helmet and could give her a logical explanation for this requirement, she unfailingly followed all reasonable limits and rules. One day when she was in college, I was cleaning out a closet in her room and found an old diary entry on a slip of paper. She had written this entry several years before when she was on a retreat with her twelfth-grade class. "It is important for adolescents to rebel," she writes, "so I decided to dye my hair green since I had a free hour this afternoon. I used a kind of dye that is not permanent. Then, I quickly washed it out so my parents wouldn't find out about it. I'm glad that I got rebelling against my parents out of the way today." Should all adolescent angst be dealt with so seamlessly!

The value of a label

Individuals with NLD are first and foremost unique people with their own personalities. In this way, they are as exactly the same, and as uniquely different, as everyone else. When I think of my daughter, I do not think of her in terms of the clinical description of NLD. For example, I have two complex neuropsychological reports about her that I keep in a drawer. These reports are filled with test scores and pronouncements about her abilities and deficits. They are useful in understanding certain facts about her learning profile. However, they do not describe even one tenth of the essential beauty and complexity of my daughter. Many people question if the labels that psychologists coin to describe children like Sara serve any useful purpose. Perhaps these labels are only negative weights that cause people to question their normalcy, their sanity, and even their intelligence. Can someone with a disability actually be normal or sane or smart, we wonder? There is also the concern that a label will cause individuals to feel that something is wrong with them, and that they will live their lives in the darkness created by that feeling. For what it is worth, I have come to find some usefulness in labels. Not because they describe much about my daughter, but because they shed a little light on a perplexing part of her. She and I together could not help but notice that the mind she was given by some odd throw of the genetic dice was not the most efficient one to use in the world in which we live. It is true that if we could have changed the world and made it more closely match her learning style, her "disability" might have vanished. However, my very pragmatic daughter did not want to live in another world. The world that she fell in love with was the one outside her window, and it was this world that she embraced and yearned to conquer. The label did not make her feel that something was amiss. She had noticed the irrefutable fact of her differences long before she ever heard the term *nonverbal learning disability*. When you continuously cannot find the bathroom in your best friend's house, or you cannot print the letter "t" when all your friends are writing volumes, you notice, and you ask questions. It was liberating for Sara that there was an explanation for why certain tasks were difficult. The label contained the "truth that set her free"—free from the worry that perhaps it was the label "stupid" that would best explain the unexpected difficulties she experienced maneuvering her world. We decided to use the label as a beacon. The label shed a little illumination on her predicament, and I could use this understanding to help Sara find a way out of her plight and into the light of a less puzzling world.

Levine (2002) calls the process by which adults help children understand themselves and their minds "demystification." He feels that children with learning disabilities "need and deserve to understand clearly the reasons for their academic problems" (Levine 2002, p.278). Levine (2002) argues that it is both comforting and empowering for children to have the technical language and specific words to describe their assets and deficits. By having this information, children can keep their problems in perspective and not worry that the difficulties they experience are caused by a lack of intelligence or fortitude. Understanding their difficulties can also help children with learning challenges develop metacognitive skills that allow them not only to understand their minds better, but also to understand what kinds of work they need to do in order to help themselves. I know that Sara benefited greatly from understanding her unique mind. Through this understanding, both she and I learned to face the world optimistically, and with a dauntless assurance we could find a way to make her mind work to her benefit.

Compass and courage

One of the more curious attributes of many individuals with NLD is their inability to find their way around. I first became aware of how inexplicably lost in space Sara was during a summer vacation our family took when she was five. We stayed in a tiny four-room cabin on a lake in Wisconsin. The cabin's one small bathroom was prominently located between the kitchen and one of the small bedrooms. "Where is the bathroom, Mom?" she asked me the first afternoon we arrived there. "Right in front of you. Look through that door," I replied, pointing out how the bathroom was located directly in her line of sight. Later that evening and several times a day throughout the week we spent there, Sara would repeatedly inquire where the bathroom was located. Once in the middle of the week, I saw her wandering from bedroom to bedroom and down the small hall that lay between them with a puzzled expression on her face. "What happened to the bathroom, Mom?" she asked curiously, "It was here yesterday."

So I began to wonder what it must be like for her, and how she was going to learn to navigate her way around without any sense of an internal compass? I began to imagine how it would feel to go to the local post office on Monday, but when you needed to return to the same post office two days later, you discovered that you could not remember how to get there. Many people have a poor sense of direction; I am one of them. I never venture to a new place without a map or a set of written instructions. However, Sara's spatial confusion was far more severe and complex than simply having a poor sense of direction. If I were to get lost, I could use visual landmarks to reorient myself. I also have the advantage of carrying in my memory an internal visual map of all the familiar places that are close to my home. After all, I have lived in the same town for many years. My internal memory map of my town is also governed by a spatial logic that helps me follow oral directions. I know that some streets run north and south, and some run east and west. I know that the expressway cuts a wide east–west swath through the southern part of my village. I can close my eyes and see each street laid out in my mind's eye in the exact order that I will find them in reality. So if you tell me that I should visit the new store on Lake Street, just east of Oak Avenue and diagonally opposite the library, I could jump into my car and meet you there with only the assistance of my internal compass.

Our internal compass helps us find our car when we park in huge parking lots and return after several hours unable to recall exactly where it is located. After an initial surge of panic, most of us can usually forage our memory for enough visual images to help us locate our vehicle in a relatively short time. It is not surprising that many of us have difficulty locating our car in huge parking lots where scores of similar cars are parked. However, when Sara was young, she got lost, not only in large unfamiliar places, but also in small well-known places like her own home and school. Her problem was nothing like the problem of someone who cannot locate their car in a huge parking lot, but more analogous to an individual who continues to have difficulty locating her car in a parking lot that she drives to every day, and where she always parks her car in the same place.

Since Sara seemed to lack an internal compass, words became her seeing-eye dog. She was an unflappable child, unerringly cheerful and courageous. If the world, even her home, was an ever-changing landscape, she was a fearless explorer. She would leave the house clinging on to the nouns and adjectives that would guide her to her destination. "Allegra's house is in the middle of the block, and it is the only house with a red door.

Call me when you get there," I would say. When she was seven, she dreamed of walking to a park situated one block north and another block east from our house. She didn't realize that this park was so near that she could see it from our front yard. She did not yet have the ability to translate the directions, "walk one block north, and then turn right, and walk for another block" into action. Her younger brother, however, had an unerring sense of direction. Even though they were separated by three years, he was the same height as she was, and people often confused them for twins. Sara confided her modest dream to him one afternoon. "Wouldn't you love to walk to Carroll Park by yourself and go on the swings?" Her brother responded with a puzzled look. "Why couldn't you? The park is just over there, across the street next to Lincoln School." Sara was very excited to learn that her brother could indeed help her to realize her desire. My son, however, had his own worries. He was only four, and the idea of walking to a park without his mother, to venture out alone to a place where one might meet a vicious dog or a bullying boy, held no appeal for him. My daughter convinced him to give it a try. So one spring morning, my daughter, supplying the courage, and my son, furnishing the compass, set off on a pilgrimage to Carroll Park. I watched uneasily from the window, and I saw Compass and Courage, two children about the same height with their arms around each other's shoulders, each supporting the other. I heard Compass explain every step for his sister, "We'll just go up here to the mailbox, and then we will cross the street, walk past these houses, and there will be the park." Courage did her part and reassured her brother, "I don't think you need to worry. I don't see any dogs. All the children look nice. We'll have fun." Her brother was the first of many guides who talked her through different landscapes.

When Sara was in her second year of college, she decided that she wanted to study in Bolivia. She was a Spanish major and wanted to improve her ability to speak the language. I pointed out that there were other Spanish-speaking countries besides Bolivia—that there were actually Spanish-speaking countries that might be safer and easier to travel in than Bolivia, countries like Spain, for example. But no, my daughter replied, she wanted to go to Bolivia. She had looked into programs in Spain, and none of them was serious enough; students went there to have fun. I pointed out that fun wasn't all that bad. No, she said, she was interested in South America because she wanted to study the impact of the educational system on the lives of certain groups of indigenous people.

Shortly after we had this conversation, I went to the library and checked out *Lonely Planet's Guide to Bolivia*. I read the information about poison insects, corruption, disease, and deadly bus wrecks on notoriously poorly maintained highways. The following sentence from the travel guide gave me the raw material for six separate nightmares: "If you're in need of information or directions, be aware that some Bolivians prefer to provide incorrect answers or directions rather than give no responses at all" (p.93). Friends pointed out that I could just say no, refuse to pay for the trip, and insist that Sara go to Europe. Although I thought about taking this course of action, I realized that I had to allow her to go. Because, after all, the reason why our family had committed ourselves so strongly to making sure that Sara could fend for herself was so she didn't have to say no to the things she wanted in life. We couldn't say *no* because we wanted her to be able to say *yes* to the life she wanted. So she went to Bolivia. She made careful arrangements and went under the auspices of a very responsible group. She got very sick twice and was robbed three times. However, she found her way back home four months later, and she returned unimaginably enriched.

Chapter 3

Side by Side: NLD
and Reading Disabilities

A low-incidence disability

No one knows for certain how many children have the NLD learning profile. However, NLD is currently classified as a "low incidence disability" (Thompson 1996a). Thompson (1996a) estimates that individuals with NLD represent between 1 percent and 0.1 percent of the population. However, Roman (1998) argues that "no clear numbers are available regarding either the prevalence or incidence of the nonverbal learning disability syndrome" (p.13). Roman attributes this lack of knowledge to the fact that the disorder is so new that researchers use different definitions and diagnostic criteria to identify the disability, and that it is difficult to differentiate between developmental and neurologically acquired NLD. Roman indicates that the incidence of NLD does appear to be rising as diagnostic criteria become more standardized, and suggests that the increasing number of premature babies who survive infancy also contributes to the rise in individuals with NLD. Successfully surviving treatment for complications related to premature birth increases the number of children at risk for all learning difficulties.

The fact that NLD appears to be a relatively rare, poorly understood phenomenon is part of the reason that few teachers are familiar with this disorder. As a result, little is known about positive educational interventions, and children with more severe NLD remain at risk for potentially serious psychological consequences (Greenham 1999). At the very least, having no clearly articulated educational plan for students with NLD puts them at risk for school failure. All of this gives parents the message that their children are doomed to experience personality disturbances, behavior and school problems, lonely lives, and little prospect of gainful employment. Effective early intervention could transform this message into a more optimistic outlook.

Dyslexia: A model for the development of useful interventions

One learning disorder for which educational researchers have developed excellent intervention protocols is specific reading disability or dyslexia. By looking at how researchers have developed protocols for successfully teaching children with reading difficulties, and comparing them to what is available for students with NLD, we can learn a great deal about what needs to be developed to help students with NLD lead meaningful and productive lives.

NLD and dyslexia are both classified as learning disabilities. However, they are often described as reverse learning problems because individuals with NLD and dyslexia exhibit an opposite pattern of strengths and weaknesses. For example, dyslexia is a difficulty caused by possible disturbance to the left side of the brain; NLD is caused by some dysfunction in the right hemisphere (Badian 1992; Rourke 1995; Shaywitz 2003). The core deficit experienced by individuals with dyslexia is a weakness in phonological processing. As a result, children with dyslexia only learn to read if they are directly taught through specially designed methods that emphasize the phonetic code of the English language. On the other hand, individuals with NLD usually have excellent phonological awareness and as a result are excellent single-word readers. The majority of children with NLD are early talkers who learn to read spontaneously with little need for direct instruction (Thompson 1997).

Incidence is another area of difference. In contrast to NLD, dyslexia (or specific reading disability) is the most common learning disability found among the school-age population today. Shaywitz (2003) estimates that approximately 80 percent of all individuals with diagnosed learning disabilities have a reading disability. Most students receiving special education in the U.S. have difficulty with single-word decoding and word attack. In the last decade, the number of public school students identified with a learning disability has increased 38 percent; most of them are children who struggle to learn to read (Lyon *et al.* 2001). The large number of students affected by a difficulty in learning to read has created an impetus to discover the most effective ways to teach reading to all children. Consequently, dyslexia is the most studied learning disability. Although some of the research has focused on the neurological underpinnings of dyslexia and diagnosis, much of it has focused on identifying the best and most efficient ways to teach children how to read, spell, and write. In 1965, the U.S. National Institutes of Child, Health, and Human Development (NICHD) initiated a longitudinal study of many students with reading difficulties. This study followed students who were as young as five years of age until they were 21 years of age to determine the best ways to teach them how to read. As of 2005, the NICHD maintained 18 research sites throughout the country dedicated to learning more about dyslexia. In 1997, the National Reading Panel (NRP) convened for two years at the request of Congress to assess the effectiveness of different approaches for teaching reading. After the NRP published its findings, a partnership of the NICHD, the Institute for Literacy and the U.S. Department of Education was formed to disseminate them to both teachers and the general public. The efforts of these groups have made it easier for parents and teachers of students with reading problems to receive sound scientific information on the best ways to prevent reading failure. Although there are still unanswered questions about reading disabilities and many challenges in getting the reading research translated into educational practice, considerable progress has been made in understanding this learning difficulty, and improving the lives of individuals challenged by mastering reading.

The lack of scientific knowledge about the best ways to treat NLD puts individuals with this disorder in particular jeopardy due to preliminary evidence that people with NLD are more at risk for potentially serious psychological problems than individuals with other forms of learning disabilities (Greenham 1999). The little research that exists for NLD tends to focus exclusively on diagnosis, the weaknesses of individuals with NLD, and the neurological underpinnings of the disorder. The narrow focus on these topics has resulted unnecessarily in the message that NLD is a condition that compromises the ability of individuals with this disorder to lead meaningful and satisfying lives. In addition, the lack of scientific knowledge about the best ways to intervene to create an optimal home and school environment for children with NLD leaves parents and educators with few professional resources to obtain practical advice about interventions. Without a more balanced treatment of the characteristic strengths of individuals with NLD as well as better information about how to remediate their weaknesses, parents and teachers are left with a discouraging diagnosis. Moreover, negative outcomes can become a self-fulfilling prophecy due to the lack of active, positive interventions to aid these children.

Although there have been recent advances in the recognition of NLD as a serious disability, more work is needed along the lines of what has been done in the research on dyslexia to determine the best ways to teach children how to read. Several support groups (particularly in California) now exist for parents and professionals to learn about NLD. Good information is also available on several websites. New books are regularly being written by parents to document personal accounts with NLD. However, there is still not a national organization for parents and professionals interested in NLD comparable to the International Dyslexia Association. There have been no longitudinal studies for NLD as there have been for dyslexia, and consequently there are no scientifically valid remediation protocols. Finally, there is no seminal book about NLD written for a nonscientific audience that contains the depth of practical and hopeful information contained in Shaywitz's (2003) *Overcoming Dyslexia*.

Another relative advantage for individuals with dyslexia is that they know what it is like to have heroes and role models. Well-known actors, doctors, and writers with dyslexia have served as symbols of hope to others by showing that a reading disability does not need to be an impediment to a meaningful and satisfying life. Individuals with NLD have few heroes, and are not nourished by the hope that such heroes can bring. Instead, parents find that professionals are often at a loss to think of any professions that would be appropriate for individuals with NLD. For example, five years ago I attended a conference on nonverbal learning disabilities at a major medical center. A parent asked one of the speakers what kind of jobs were a good fit for people with NLD. The speaker was completely flummoxed and answered that he couldn't think of any that would be appropriate. After pausing for several moments, he finally came up with telemarketing as a possible career. I find it difficult to believe that if individuals with NLD were helped to develop their frequently extraordinary verbal abilities in positive ways they would have nothing else to aspire to than a job reading scripts on a telephone. This past year I attended another conference on NLD, and another speaker was asked the same question by an anxious parent. This time the speaker gave a more hopeful response, but still struggled to come up with positive examples of successful adults with NLD, and cited jobs for travel agents and radio announcers.

In order to ensure that a higher percentage of children with NLD possess the capabilities to forge an independent adult life, interventions as effective as the ones developed for children with reading difficulties need to be devised and disseminated to parents and teachers. However, because NLD differs from dyslexia in several ways, designing effective uniform intervention strategies will be challenging. First, dyslexia is a specific learning disability that affects primarily academic learning, particularly reading and writing. In contrast, NLD is a condition that affects a broader range of skills that include academic learning as well as practical life skills and physical abilities. The problems of children with NLD are more global in scope than the difficulties facing children with dyslexia. Therefore, the type of intervention program that is necessary to remediate NLD also needs to be more global in nature than the more linear and sequential programs used to teach students with dyslexia how to read. This is not to imply that it is easy to teach a student with dyslexia how to read. However, it is easier to figure out the steps to take when an individual's difficulty lies in a single area. For example, since research has shown that the core deficit in dyslexia is a difficulty with phonological awareness, researchers have been able to isolate the specific finite skills that individuals with dyslexia must acquire to become proficient readers (Shaywitz 2003). Curricula can then be developed to teach these skills in a sequential and systematic manner. Once students with dyslexia master the skills, they can apply them to reading any word because there are a finite and manageable number of letter combinations and rules to master. If given enough practice, students with dyslexia can generalize what they know about linguistic patterns to new words.

An effective intervention program for NLD will be more difficult to develop because the strengths and weaknesses typical of individuals with NLD are more global in nature, and may fall into several different areas each of which requires intensive remediation. The teacher or parent who undertakes the design of an intervention program can easily become overwhelmed by the seemingly infinite areas that need to be covered across the age span to maximize the learning and adaptive behaviors of a child with NLD. However, if children with NLD are going to have a shot at a good life, it is essential that professionals in education put considerable time into the development of model intervention programs.

Another factor that impedes the development of an intervention program for individuals with NLD is that one of their core difficulties is the inability to apply what they know to novel situations. For example, children with NLD have difficulty with tasks that require fine and gross motor skills. They have difficulty getting their hands and bodies to do what is needed in order to accomplish tasks like riding a bicycle, cutting with scissors, braiding their hair, or using a can opener. They can be taught to do all these things. However, because it is challenging for them to generalize what they know to novel situations, individuals with NLD might learn how to open a particular door, but not be able to generalize principles about door-opening that can be used to open other doors with slightly different doorknobs that require different movements. So for people with NLD, the job of mastering the movements necessary for everyday life is a continually changing kaleidoscope of stimuli they are constantly working to master. For example, I recently visited my daughter who is in a challenging graduate program in speech and language pathology. She won a merit scholarship to attend this program, and I mention this fact to illustrate how capable she is in areas that she has mastered. During my visit, she tells me that she is pretty sure something is wrong with the corkscrew I gave her as a housewarming gift. She tells me it doesn't work and opens the refrigerator revealing a bottle of wine with a corkscrew crudely forced into the cork. She explains that she has seen people in college open bottles of wine; they turn the corkscrew into the cork and then just pull it out. She has pulled and pulled, but nothing has happened. It must be defective, she concludes. Of course, the type of corkscrew she owns has a different mechanism that requires a person to pull down on two raised handles in order to remove the cork. After I show her how to use it, she practices the movements several times, and she has mastered how to use this (and only this) style of corkscrew.

Problems with diagnosis and receiving services

A further stumbling block to establishing effective intervention programs for students with NLD is the controversial use of the IQ—achievement discrepancy formula to determine if students have a learning disability. Currently, there are four components included in most definitions of what constitutes a learning disability (Fletcher *et al.* 2004). The first component concerns the idea of discrepancy, or the notion that in order to have a learning disability individuals must exhibit a discrepancy between their intelligence or potential and their actual achievement (Lyon *et al.* 2001). Schools determine this discrepancy by first administering an IQ test to ascertain the student's intelligence (potential). Then psychologists compare the student's IQ score to the scores that the student receives on individually administered achievement tests that measure achievement in school subjects like math and reading. If there is a severe discrepancy between the student's IQ score and the score on achievement tests, the student is believed to have a learning disability.

The second component to make up the LD definition is *heterogeneity*. Heterogeneity refers to the various domains in which individuals can have a learning disability such as reading, math, written expression, and language (Fletcher *et al.* 2004). The third component is *exclusion*, which means that one cannot have a learning disability if one's learning difficulty stems from some other source, such as a sensory emotional disorder, poverty, the fact that English is not your native language, or poor instruction. The final component that makes up the definition of LD is the concept that a learning disability is *constitutional* or a condition that is hereditary.

This diagnostic approach is problematic because learning disabilities are really an amalgam of different problems, all grouped under one single label. Since there are different forms of learning disabilities, it is logical that each of these different forms needs to be identified using different measures and resulting in varied intervention plans. For example, one potential but yet unrealized benefit of Rouke's (1989, 1995) work in the subtyping of LD would be the possibility of developing different interventions to address different learning disabilities. Students with reading disabilities have difficulty in a specific domain, reading, and need interventions to help them learn how to read better. Students with NLD who are good at single-word reading would not need an intervention program to improve word attack, but would need other programs that address their particular profile of strengths and weaknesses.

The IQ—achievement discrepancy model is particularly poor at identifying students with reading disabilities (Lyon *et al.* 2001; Fletcher *et al.* 2004). Since specific reading disability "accounts for four out of every five cases of learning disorders" (Buka 1998, p.2), it is essential that schools identify and successfully help these students, and this would result in resources left to help children with rarer forms of LD. The first problem with the discrepancy model is that an IQ test is not an effective measure to predict children's ability to learn. At best, an IQ test is only a "gross estimate of current general cognitive functioning and should not be used as a measure of learning potential" (Lyon *et al.* 2001, p.266). Sternberg and Grigorenko (1999) have pointed out many of the limitations of IQ tests, including a narrow definition of what constitutes intelligence and problems with the tests' reliability, particularly for individuals from different cultural backgrounds.

The next flaw in the IQ—achievement discrepancy formula is that the point spread between ability and achievement scores needed to qualify for the label *learning disability* varies from one U.S. state to another and even from town to town (Dombrowski, Kamphaus, and Reynolds 2004). This inconsistency means that a student who is classified as learning disabled in one state could move to a different state and no longer be eligible for special education services. An even more serious flaw with the IQ—achievement discrepancy model of diagnosis is that it makes early identification difficult. Before the age of nine, children do not have enough schoolwork at which to fail. Picture a first-grader who is struggling to make sense of the phonetic code. Her reading problem may be apparent to her teacher and her parents, but she still may score just fine on academic measures because at this age these tests require little reading. In the case of reading disabilities, this "wait-and-see" approach (more accurately described as "wait-to-fail") means that individuals with dyslexia usually are not identified until at least the third grade (Lyon *et al.* 2001). Most authorities agree that individuals with LD stand the best chance of success if they receive help as soon as possible, so a method of identification that makes this course of action difficult does not serve the best interests of individuals with LD (Shaywitz 2003). Unfortunately, individuals who are not identified before the third grade rarely catch up with their peers. However, if all students with reading difficulties were screened and given appropriate intervention in the first two years of formal schooling, it is estimated that the number of students who needed special education services could be cut by as much as 70 percent (Lyon *et al.*, p.260).

The final flaw with using the IQ–achievement discrepancy model for diagnosing reading problems is that many studies have shown that there is little difference in poor readers, whether they meet the criteria for LD or not. Bright poor readers who are often classified as learning disabled usually have difficulty with phonemic awareness. Poor readers with low IQs also usually have difficulties with phonemic awareness. Since the interventions necessary to teach both groups how to read are essentially the same, it seems more sensible to intervene as early as feasible and teach all poor readers how to read regardless of their label. Lyon *et al.* (2001) present a new model of diagnosis and treatment of reading disabilities, a prevention model that does not rely on the results of IQ tests. In this model known as "response to intervention," all children are screened in kindergarten for problems with phonemic awareness. Those identified are given appropriate instruction until they are reading at grade level. Children who still have significant reading difficulties after receiving intensive remediation over a course of the first three grades are deemed reading disabled and then qualify to receive special education.

Although "response to intervention" remains controversial, many experts hope that this approach will cut down substantially on the numbers of children who are labeled "learning disabled" (Fletcher *et al.* 2004). Fletcher also believes that the greatest possible benefit of response to intervention will be a shift of focus away from eligibility "to concerns about providing effective instruction" (Fletcher *et al.* 2004, p.311). Additionally, less money will be spent on costly testing that results in little practical instruction for the student. Fletcher writes that, "nationwide, virtually every student considered for special education receives IQ and achievement tests. This practice consumes significant resources, with the average cost of an eligibility evaluation running several thousand dollars" (Fletcher *et al.* 2004, p.310). Others such as Fuchs *et al.* (2003) are more cautious about recommending response to interventions until more is known about the effectiveness of this approach as a means of identifying children with learning disabilities.

If response to intervention is successfully instituted and does result in reducing the number of children receiving special education services for reading problems, this may indirectly help individuals with NLD. The reduction in the rising number of students classified with LD could potentially allow researchers and educators more time and money to investigate other learning disorders, such as NLD and autism, and to develop educational interventions and diagnostic criteria that could help these individuals lead meaningful lives. Currently, students with NLD who are fortunate enough to be diagnosed at all are rarely identified before the fifth grade (Thompson 1996a). The protocol for identifying NLD is less developed than the protocol for identifying dyslexia, partly because NLD is a condition more commonly discussed in the neuropsychological literature than in educational journals. Therefore, many of the tests used to learn about the abilities and deficits of individuals with NLD are assessment tools that are part of neuropsychological batteries rarely administered in schools. Rourke (1989) contains an appendix of measures that are useful diagnostic tools. Since there is not one specific test or battery of tests that points definitely to NLD, it is essential that reliable assessment is conducted by professionals who are knowledgeable about NLD, and that the assessment is focused "on developing an appropriate intervention plan," not simply on collecting test scores and data (Thompson 1997, p.45).

However, the current first step in identifying NLD, like the first step to identifying dyslexia, begins with finding out the student's IQ. Unfortunately just as there are difficulties with using an IQ test to identify dyslexia, there are also several problems when using this measure to identify NLD. The first difficulty pertains to eligibility for special education services.

When students who are suspected to have NLD are tested using a conventional IQ test, they almost always score *significantly* higher on the verbal section than on the performance section. Since NLD is a disorder that exists on a continuum, individuals with a mild form of NLD may have only a 15-point difference between VIQ (verbal IQ) and PIQ (performance IQ) (Roman 1998). However, it is not unusual for individuals with severe NLD to have a 40 or more point difference between VIQ and PIQ (Roman 1998). Unfortunately, this pattern frequently ensures that many individuals with NLD are ineligible for special education. For example, if an individual has a verbal score of 110 and a performance score of 60, they would have a full-scale IQ of 85. Since a person with an IQ of 85 is not considered particularly bright, a school could argue that the reason this person is doing poorly academically is not because she has a nonverbal learning disability, but because she has low average intelligence. Since there is no discrepancy between intelligence and achievement in this case (she is not bright, therefore she lacks the aptitude to do well academically in school), such a student is not classified as having a learning disability. Unfortunately, this approach does not recognize that children with low intelligence almost never exhibit this pattern of strong verbal ability as is frequently the case for children with NLD. Additionally, this approach does not recognize the possibility that individuals with strong verbal intelligence can be taught how to harness their verbal dexterity in order to learn many of the tasks at which they are naturally weak. In many ways, NLD renders the full-scale intelligence score (which merely averages the extreme VIQ and PIQ scores) meaningless for such students.

An additional difficulty individuals with NLD face with IQ testing is that their unusual minds make it challenging for them to demonstrate their true potential because of their difficulties with novel tasks and interpreting visual materials. When Sara was growing up, our family had our most frustrating experiences with issues surrounding diagnosis. As I'll describe in a later chapter, we were not successful in locating someone who was able to accurately describe Sara's problems until she was 24 years old! Even now, her diagnostic report does not state that she has a nonverbal learning disability since the sole purpose of the report is to allow her to receive extra time as an accommodation on exams in graduate school, and on the standardized tests she needs to qualify as a licensed speech-language pathologist. The psychologist who wrote the report specializes in NLD and has told me that without a doubt Sara has a nonverbal learning disability. In fact, with a 50-point spread between her verbal and performance IQ, and just about every strength and weakness typical for individuals with this disorder, she is a textbook example of NLD. However until NLD becomes an accepted category for both psychologists and educators, no evaluation intended to qualify her for services or accommodations can say she has a nonverbal learning disability, the label that best characterizes her difficulties.

Chapter 4

How to Recognize the Child with NLD at Different Ages

Spellbound by words: The unexpected consequences of replacing physical dexterity with verbal deftness
The illusion of competency

Most children with NLD are not identified until later in elementary school, if they are identified at all. Yet NLD is described in the literature as a disability with serious potential consequences. Why is NLD a condition that parents and educators find so difficult to recognize at an early age when interventions could be initiated that could possibly stem many of the negative effects of this disorder? There are two major reasons why NLD is difficult to identify in young children. First, although children with NLD experience difficulty with many tasks in early childhood, none of their difficulties in any one particular area is so striking that it falls outside developmental norms. For example, children with NLD frequently are late at reaching motor development milestones like walking, but most children with NLD learn how to walk by the time they are two years old. In other words, they are typically late walkers who fall within the normal range of child development. Hence, it is difficult for professionals and parents to judge if the problems experienced by these individuals in early childhood should merit concern. For example, the introduction to a popular website about NLD describes the problems that young children with NLD experience in the following manner:

> parents likely realize early on that something is amiss. As preschoolers, these youngsters probably have difficulty interacting with other children,

with acquiring self-help skills, and are not physically adept, are not adaptable, and present with a host of other troublesome problems that are of concern, *but not alarming* [italics mine]. (Tanguay 1999, reproduced with permission)

The website goes on to describe how children with NLD "bump along" through elementary school, but when they reach middle school, they "rapidly begin to deteriorate" (Tanguay 1999). Suddenly, they get lost, suffer academic difficulties in math, writing, and reading comprehension, and have difficulties getting along with peers and teachers. Unfortunately, this description is not entirely accurate. Children with NLD do not suddenly acquire difficulties such as getting lost in middle school. They have been getting lost in the earlier grades. However, their spatial confusion often goes unnoticed because in most elementary schools, students travel as a group under the watchful eye of the teacher. It is not until the later grades when they are asked to handle more tasks independently that the difficulties they have been experiencing all along reach a crisis.

The second reason why it is difficult to identify children with NLD at an early age is their dexterity with words. Children with NLD typically learn to speak early and eloquently. Then, enriched with their sonorous vocabularies, they enter school only to hit the educational jackpot when they frequently become precocious early readers. Instead of worrying about the NLD student, the adults in their lives often believe that they have a budding genius on their hands. However, as Palombo (1994) points out, the behavior of children with NLD does not usually "match the expectations for a child this bright and verbal" (p.2). When they are not able to measure up to the adults' expectations of a typical gifted student, they begin to disappoint, irritate and mystify the adults in their environments. Whitney (2002), writing about her own experience as a mother of a child with NLD, describes a typical response to her then six-year-old son:

As many parents do, I thought my child was exceptional. By the time Zac was six he was reading at a twelfth-grade level. His vocabulary was better than mine, and he had an amazing memory. I was convinced he was a little genius. However, there were aspects of Zac's development that weren't up to the level of his verbal skills; for example, he frequently fell out of chairs and had difficulty writing. But if you had suggested to me that my golden child had a neurological dysfunction, I would have thought you were crazy. (p.3)

Their verbal strengths often mask the bafflement that children with NLD experience in school. Because the elementary school curriculum of the early grades emphasizes verbal tasks like learning how to read and spell, it is difficult to conceive that students who frequently learn to read early are at risk for academic failure. By not recognizing the confusion that children with NLD feel in their physical environment, adults simply believe what these children have to say and fail to realize the conceptual confusion this verbal virtuosity masks. Children with NLD typically present a deceptive "illusion of competency" (Earle-Cruiskshanks 2000, p.10).

In order to accurately assess the early signs that something is amiss, it is important to have a clear developmental picture of what individuals with NLD are like in their early childhood. Even in infancy, there are definite signs that children with NLD are uncomfortable with many aspects of the physical world (Johnson and Myklebust 1967; Palombo 1994). The following section presents a developmental picture of a typical child with NLD in infancy through elementary school, a time of life when verbal strengths and rote memory skills contribute to the "illusion of competency" (Earle-Cruiskshanks 2000, p.10). I include examples from my daughter's early childhood and elementary years to illustrate how NLD can affect one individual's perception of the world.

I would like to add two caveats. First, there is a huge variation in what is considered "typical" human development. Some babies are quiet and cautious by nature; some are boisterous and daredevils. A few babies walk early at nine months; others do not walk until they are two years old. All these variations fall within typical development. Therefore, it is important to remember that variation itself is no cause for concern, and is actually a reason to rejoice, since it is this diversity that makes humans unique and interesting. However, development occasionally swings too far out of the typical range to allow an individual to function comfortably. In describing my daughter's development, my intent is not to label her as having a condition that is pathological, but only to point out that the mind she was given did not always function efficiently. The signs that something was amiss manifested themselves early in her life. If I had not heeded these potentially damaging indications, they might have festered and impeded my daughter from realizing her best self. It was only by noticing these unusual characteristics that I was able to step in and shine some light on the dark signposts that clouded her perception.

My second caveat is that if there is a wide variation in so-called "normal" development, there is also wide variation in the development and characteristics of children with NLD. There are many characteristics of NLD, and children with NLD manifest them in different combinations and with varying degrees of severity. In addition, children with NLD should not be defined exclusively by the characteristics of a label. They each have unique strengths, foibles, and personalities. Finally, it is possible for children to have more than one unrelated difficulty at the same time. For example, Sara had a severe articulation disorder as well as NLD when she was in elementary school. Finally, children with NLD live in different environments and attend different schools, and these factors impact how they adapt to their challenges.

The armchair traveler is born: The infant with NLD

The most striking characteristic of infants with NLD is their physical passivity. They do not explore their environment by moving around in it, looking at and touching objects in a manner that is typical of even a quiet, placid baby. Exploratory behavior allows infants to experience the objects in their world sensorially and to develop the mental images they will need in order to establish a rich conceptual understanding of words (Johnson and Myklebust 1967). Johnson and Myklebust (1967) point out that although the language of children who have few sensory experiences may sound good, their words often have an empty quality because these children have little conceptual understanding beyond the actual knowledge of the word.

Once infants with NLD learn to speak, they explore their world almost exclusively by asking questions and receiving answers (Rourke 1989). Rourke explains that the approach of typical infants, who experience the physical features of an object before an adult tells them the name, has many developmental advantages over the learning style of infants with NLD. When typical babies explore their environment, they need to employ not only touch and sight, but also complex motor skills, and they also gain experience with novel situations. It is interesting to note that the primary deficits of children with NLD are in the areas of tactile perception, visual perception, motor skills, and dealing with novelty—the very areas they neglect in infancy. Since they are skilled at auditory perception, they prefer to learn about their world through words, to the detriment of other important skills.

Our world, the novelty store

Johnson (1987) reports that it is not unusual for parents of babies with NLD to notice as early as six or seven months that something is "wrong." One of the first differences that children with NLD exhibit is an extreme difficulty in dealing with novel experiences. Green (2002) writes, "the baby with NLD may show little interest in anything new. This child will contentedly play with the same thing over and over, and will react to novelty with alarm and dismay" (p.14). I have already written about Sara's first two years and her unusual motor differences and perception of space. At the beginning of Sara's life, I felt as if I was keeping two baby books—the concrete one with the usual pictures and entries about daily life that many mothers keep, and the second invisible baby book where I recorded all the subtle differences that I observed. In addition to differences in motor development, I began to note how difficult it was for her to comfortably embrace new experiences. Since the world was filled with novelty, we could not avoid it unless we stayed inside all the time. The following story illustrates how I discovered that language could be a powerful tool to acclimatize a child with NLD to a novel experience:

> Even before Sara could understand the exact meaning of words, they were able to calm her and make the unforeseen palatable and inviting.
>
> For example, words became one of my most powerful weapons against the lobby of hat ladies whom we started to meet when Sara was six months old. Our meetings with these ladies coincided with a hat strike that Sara went on when she refused to wear a hat in any type of weather. We soon discovered that many older American women whom we casually passed on our walks had strong opinions on the issue of babies and the donning of hats. These women would stop any hatless baby to explain to her mother with missionary zeal the importance of hats in the whole scope of child raising. The hat ladies were particularly disturbing to my daughter as they bent over the baby carriage and peered closely into her hatless visage. Her extreme distress in response to their innocent attentions only caused them more concern and served as concrete proof in their eyes that she would be much happier in a hat. Since Sara now appeared hatless in public with alarming regularity, she

became a frequent object of their circumspection. As I attempted to navigate around the source of Sara's discomfort, I began to spot hat zealots a block away. My first strategy was to cross the street, but soon we were crossing so often that our walks were a series of obsessive zigzags. I was becoming as anxious as my daughter, until I discovered if I told Sara everything that was about to happen she could better tolerate these intrusions.

"Look, Sara, here comes a lady who wants to discuss hats with us," I would say whenever I would see the earnest stride of an elderly lady making her way towards us. "The lady in blue jeans carrying the umbrella—I promise I will not let her touch you." It was not long before we could stop to discuss the importance of hats with whomever we wished. We could serenely acknowledge that 90 percent of my daughter's total body heat was evaporating from the top of her skull and posed a serious risk of illness. Sara and I came to enjoy these exchanges.

By the time Sara turned two, I had learned through trial and error which techniques would successfully encourage her to embrace the world more readily. Language and rehearsal became the key. Each time she was faced with a new experience, I tried to imagine all the components of that experience, and to identify any potentially disturbing elements. I found that if I could relay to her what to expect in words before she actually had an experience, she could better tolerate any situation. As the years passed, I became more adept at crawling into her mind and seeing the world from her point of view. I also began to see that much of her distrust of novelty was intertwined with her difficulties in understanding spatial relationships and how to find her way around. As she got older and more new experiences required her to find her way through new places, we would always go to the new place and practice getting from point A to point B using extensive verbal description until she was comfortable and able to navigate her own way. With time and many years of practice, she learned how to do these things for herself.

The preschool years: Problems with play, self-help, and the beginning of social isolation

During the ages of three to six years, children with NLD typically have difficulty with self-help tasks like how to use utensils to eat, how to brush their hair, and how to dress themselves. Just as they struggled to learn how to master the gross motor milestones of infancy, they now struggle to learn how to walk up and down stairs, how to skip, and how to operate riding toys. Without direct instruction, they fail to understand how to open doors or simple cabinets. They often have difficulty learning how to play with puzzles, to color or to draw, and so avoid these activities. At the same time, the language skills of children with NLD remain well developed and a comparative strength. Some children with NLD who have exceptional language abilities spontaneously begin to read during this time (Johnson 1987).

The most serious potential consequence for individuals with NLD is social isolation. Unfortunately, their social difficulties start when these children enter preschool and first need to conform to the demands of a social group. Children with NLD are ill equipped to deal with the demands of preschool. Most preschools ask children to grapple with extensive non-verbal materials. For example, children learn to tell stories by using pictures. They might draw pictures to represent a story, or the teacher might ask them to put a series of pictures in a logical order to construct a story line. Preschool is a time when children learn to manipulate materials like zippers, buttons, or doll clothes. Children with NLD, unless they receive explicit help, find all these tasks difficult.

Johnson (1987) describes some typical errors and confusions that pre-school children with NLD make in interpreting pictures. She cites the example of a six-year-old boy with advanced language skills who scored below average on several picture vocabulary tests because he confused the picture of a key for the numeral 6, a mail box for a piece of toast, and a pair of glasses for the numeral 8 (Johnson 1987). Johnson (1987) found that children with NLD had particular difficulty with successfully completing partial drawings, or interpreting pictures that required them to interpret part—whole relationships.

Group play will contain many mystifying elements for children with NLD, since the rules for group play are often communicated nonverbally. For example, pretend games often have idiosyncratic rules that children spontaneously invent and communicate to each other through gesture and facial expression. Nonverbal communication will either be missed or mis-interpreted by children with NLD. Children with NLD will react to their social mistakes by either isolating themselves or unintentionally acting in an inappropriate manner. In time, this kind of behavior will cause others to avoid them, resulting in further social isolation. Preschool children with NLD rarely receive the necessary verbal rehearsal they need from adults to help them clarify classroom rules and routines (Johnson 1987).

For Sara, the most difficult years were during preschool. For her, it was like an alien environment where every activity seemed designed to test her weak areas. When she began her second year at preschool, she refused to utter one word inside the walls of the school building. She never complained or acted out in the classroom. At first, she simply endured nursery school with stoic mute patience; in time, she came to bear it with the hopelessness of a condemned prisoner.

At Sara's nursery school, cutting with a pair of small children's scissors was an activity with status. Her classroom had a special station where there were little cups of scissors and piles of colored papers printed with different patterns. The children were instructed to cut along the lines as best as they could. They would then have the privilege of pasting their "cuttings" onto a piece of construction paper. It was Sara's age group, the almost six-year-olds, who could cut the best. Although there were others who could not cut straight or particularly well, Sara was very conscious that she was the only child who could not hold the scissors in any effective fashion.

She started to practice using a pair of scissors at home. My efforts to reassure her about the difficulty of cutting with scissors fell on deaf ears. Although she spent considerable time practicing how to operate scissors, her efforts went unrewarded until one Saturday morning. That particular morning she sat at our kitchen table staring at a pair of scissors and a piece of paper with the penetrating concentration of someone in a trance. She would prefer, she told me, if I did not speak to her for a while, and no, she did not need any help at the moment. I left her alone, silently checking on her periodically. For nearly three hours, she sat immobile, her eyes locked on the scissors. Finally, she picked up the paper and scissors and cut a thin strip. "There," she said, "Now I can cut like the other kids." She left the room without triumph, but with a grimness and lines of fatigue on her face.

I do not know what the act of staring down the scissors cost her. But it was soon after this incident that her attitude about school changed from stoicism to despair. Grimness began to seep into her demeanor and, for the first time, discouragement and defeat. Perhaps she realized that school was too difficult and that the tasks asked of her by the teacher were going to be mastered at too high a price. She started to spend the whole school morning sitting on a chair facing the classroom doorway. There was no point in participating in school, she explained to me, because she was too stupid and different from everyone else. She was a "Dumbo" like the elephant in the movie. She would wait until I came to fetch her; she would evaporate into the air.

Soon after the incident with the scissors, I took steps to provide Sara with intensive interventions, and her situation in school began to improve. She learned to master the tasks that were difficult for her. The confidence that this mastery brought gave her the confidence to believe in herself and to trust adults. By strengthening her weak areas and capitalizing on her strong areas, she has been able to avoid the grim fate that individuals with NLD often face. For Sara, preschool was the low point in her life. Although her problems did not disappear, every subsequent school experience was an improvement over the one that went before it. Unfortunately, this gradual improvement is not typical for the majority of students with NLD. Without interventions, the interplay of their weak and strong areas causes them to experience continually more devastating difficulties in academic, social, and adaptive behaviors.

Early readers who disappoint: Elementary school years

Because NLD manifests itself with different degrees of severity in different individuals, many children with NLD do not have as difficult a time in pre-school as my daughter. In addition, many children with NLD have extraordinary vocabularies, are voluble, and frequently learn to read at an early age. Any worries that parents previously harbored suddenly evaporate when their highly verbal child hits the educational jackpot of elementary school. Because a typical elementary school curriculum emphasizes tasks that require rote memory, verbal dexterity, and strong phonemic awareness, it is difficult to recognize good readers as children at risk for academic failure. Volden (2004) describes the language displayed by typical children with NLD as "an abundance of verbal output along with precocious vocabulary development and complex grammar, [so] parents, clinicians…and many researchers interpret this to mean that language development is advanced" (p.134).

A more careful analysis of their language reveals many difficulties with comprehension that are already apparent in the elementary years. Many of their language difficulties result from a weakness in interpreting what they see. Because they frequently misinterpret what they observe, they will habitually answer questions and give explanations that contain bizarre verbal responses. Johnson (1987) cites the example of a seven-year-old boy with NLD who was shown a picture of a burning house surrounded by three firemen holding hoses. The child shared with the teacher that he thought the picture showed people having a birthday party because the men were holding birthday candles. However, when the teacher simply pointed to the "relevant objects in the picture such as the firemen and the source of the flame he immediately corrected himself" (p.136). Children with NLD often have difficulty interpreting other visual media such as TV programs, movies, comics, and advertisements. If they listen carefully, teachers and parents will frequently hear similar bizarre verbal summaries given by children with NLD when they discuss the plots of TV shows or movies.

An additional language problem that will emerge in the elementary school years is difficulty with semantic language, such as a reliance on literal and concrete interpretation of words. As a result, children with NLD are often overly naïve and trusting because they believe whatever they are told. Students with NLD struggle with the pragmatics of language, in part because so much of pragmatics is conveyed through nonverbal means such as gesture, tone, and facial expressions. Some students with NLD speak in a monotone because of motor difficulties.

A characteristic language strength of most children with NLD is excellent phonological awareness, an asset that translates into good single-word decoding. Since one of the most important tasks we expect students to accomplish in the first three grades is to learn how to read fluently, the ability of many students with NLD to accomplish this task so effortlessly lends much credence to the "illusion of competency" (Earle-Cruiskshanks 2000, p.10). However, some children with NLD do have initial problems with early reading. Thompson (1997) hypothesizes that this is because reading is a novel task for a young child, and many children with NLD deal so poorly with novelty that all new experiences are initially challenging for them. Many children with NLD respond well to teaching methods (e.g., Wilson, Lindamood-Bell LIPS) that are actually designed for children with dyslexia because these methods are heavily rule-based. Children with NLD, even those with initial difficulties learning to read, usually become excellent readers of words by the end of third grade. Due to their excellent rote memory abilities, they also develop accurate spelling, another highly prized skill in elementary school.

One difficulty that young grade school students with NLD develop is in learning how to print. Due to their weaknesses in the area of visual perception, they have difficulty understanding how to identify the salient components of a letter. They have trouble understanding and judging the size and spacing of letters on the page. In addition, they are poor at connecting a verbal label such as *straight, curved, diagonal* to a mental picture unless they are explicitly taught how to do so. Difficulties with fine motor tasks also make it challenging for them to use writing implements. With considerable practice, most students with NLD can acquire very serviceable handwriting. However, if these students do not have the opportunity for intensive handwriting practice, their writing will remain permanently arrested at the level of a young child.

The difficulties that children with NLD exhibit in performing arithmetic computations first become noticeable in elementary school. They have difficulty lining up numbers correctly on the page and confuse the meaning of mathematical signs. They struggle to understand quantitative concepts such as the difference between an inch and a mile, estimating, and how to reason their way through word problems. They try to over-rely on their rote memory by memorizing facts and rules that they attempt to apply to all mathematical situations. Rourke (1989) feels it is highly unlikely that students with NLD have the ability to progress beyond the fifth-grade level in both mechanical arithmetic and mathematical reasoning. However, recent research by Forest (2004) refutes this claim. Forrest (2004) found that children with NLD are capable of performing well on many kinds of mathematical tasks, particularly on number tasks where children can use their excellent verbal skills. Currently, there is no research that investigates the effects of remediation or intervention to help students with NLD learn how to use their verbal skills to better understand mathematical and scientific concepts. A grave danger of Rourke's (1989) estimation that the math abilities of students with NLD are arrested at a fifth-grade level is that his prediction could discourage teachers from developing methods to enhance the mathematical thinking of students with NLD. Sara, who has a severe form of NLD, has been able to learn to reason mathematically as measured on standardized tests and in practical applications that she uses in school. Math has been a difficult subject throughout her entire school career, but she has had the benefit of considerable remediation in the area of math and science, and is successfully functioning in a graduate program that requires substantial course work in subjects such as statistics and neuroanatomy.

Elementary school is a time when the social difficulties of children with NLD become further exacerbated. At a time when their peers begin to grapple with acquiring a more sophisticated sense of humor, the student with NLD has difficulty understanding and recognizing sarcasm or teasing (Johnson 1987). Additionally some individuals with NLD have difficulty understanding another person's point of view, and this deficiency makes them appear narrow and egocentric to their peers (Johnson 1987). They frequently relate better to adults than to their contemporaries because adults are easier to engage verbally and their responses are more predictable (Palombo 1994).

If nothing is done to help students with NLD early in life, they frequently reach a crisis in middle school. As the school curriculum becomes more complex, students can no longer rely exclusively on their rote memories to get them through their schoolwork. For the first time, they are expected to travel independently to different classes, and suddenly their spatial disorientation is spotlighted. Later in high school, the increased emphasis on mathematical and scientific concepts results in further academic stresses. Finally, their social resources are sorely taxed by the psychosocial demands of adolescence, which are challenging for all individuals.

One way that educators, physicians, and psychologists can create an environment where children with NLD receive effective early intervention is to understand their profile. One of the first misunderstandings about nonverbal learning disabilities is that we should only heed behaviors if they are alarming. Repeatedly in the literature, parents describe how professionals dismissed their early concerns about their children. Thompson (1997) sums up this common experience when she states, "early consultation with a school psychologist or family physician typically only serves to dismiss or minimize a...parent's worries" (p. 2). To many professionals, the early behaviors exhibited by children with NLD are simply not alarming enough to merit concern. However, learning disabilities in general are relatively subtle difficulties; they are in no way like physical ailments that may herald their presence with truly alarming symptoms. For example, the core problem that causes people to struggle with reading is simply a difficulty in isolating and manipulating sounds within words, a particularly inconspicuous behavior that sets off few alarm bells. Yet reading problems are the most commonly diagnosed form of LD. Because research has provided guidelines to help us recognize the subtle behaviors that might lead to possible reading failure, educators are able to identify students at an earlier age who will struggle to learn how to read, intervene before they fail, and prevent them from developing the truly alarming condition of illiteracy.

Professionals need to learn how to "read" the behaviors of young children with NLD as deftly as they judge the behaviors of children with verbal LD. We have learned to intervene on behalf of students with reading disabilities because we understand that these students are at risk for academic failure. Students with NLD are also at risk if they are not helped, and they are additionally at risk for potentially serious psychological consequences. A recent study found that 41 percent of students with NLD were misdiagnosed as emotionally behaviorally disabled (Mooney 2004). This unfortunate situation will not change unless professionals become familiar with the characteristics of individuals with NLD and learn to hear the alarm bells ringing at an earlier age.

Learning to navigate: Adolescence

Adolescence, that bridge between childhood and adulthood, is a precarious crossing for students with NLD. Many of the developmental goals of adolescence such as developing abstract thinking skills, launching a sense of purpose, securing an independent identity, and establishing satisfying personal relationships with others, will place a strain on their weak attributes. If adolescents with NLD are to cross safely into the world of adulthood, they will need the guidance and protection of empathetic and knowledgeable adults.

Individuals with undiagnosed NLD, who enter high school without the benefit of prior intervention, are particularly vulnerable to psychological and academic failure. By the time they reach middle and high school they have been inundated with "so many experiences in which others respond to them in ways that do not make sense to them [that] they have learned to live with and to expect disconnection" (Vacca 2001, p.26). "How do I get to the gym?" they ask. "Go down there," the well-meaning teacher points off in the distance. "Then turn right, and go down the hall and up some stairs, and you will see it. You can't miss it." Unfortunately students with NLD will miss the gym every time because this set of directions makes no sense to them. If they find the courage to ask a question about a novel they had difficulty understanding, they might be instructed to watch the movie. Gradually, they learn to ask few questions and consequently give even more frequent responses that make no sense to adults. When Sara was in tenth grade, she went to a math tutor who helped her with geometry. This kind and intelligent woman recognized Sara as an excellent student and never realized how geometry functioned as a type of intellectual Chinese water torture for my daughter. Before Sara left to go to her weekly tutoring session, she would invariably ask me to clarify certain basic concepts for her, such as which diagram depicted a larger angle and why, the location of the angles in the diagrams, which side of the number line contained the negative numbers, and so on. "I need to get oriented before I work with Mrs. B.," she would say as she went out the door. "After all, there are some questions I could never ask her. She would think I was nuts!" Because NLD is a life-long problem, all students with this learning disorder will find the demands of adolescence challenging and, at times, exhausting. The greatest gift they can have is someone who understands their unique way of perceiving the world.

"You can steal the shirt right off their back"

One afternoon when Sara was in the tenth grade, she returned home from school with a perplexed expression on her face. Her new watch was gone, she said. She had looked everywhere, but it was nowhere to be found. Sara regularly lost things when she was a teenager. Between September and November of that year, I had driven at least a half dozen times to the lost and found office of our public bus company to collect backpacks, books, and wallets that she had inadvertently left on the seats of different buses. Because of her extreme difficulty with visual-spatial organization, it was not easy for her to keep track of her possessions, particularly in high school when she was responsible for transporting so many books and papers between school and home. Frequently, I would actually see her holding a missing item in her hand as she frantically searched for it, unaware that the object of her desire was already in her possession.

However, this missing watch incident was different. She lost this watch because she, like most individuals with NLD, was unusually naïve and trusting. After school, Sara took a public bus home. However since most of the passengers on the bus were students that she personally knew from her small, private high school, and since the social environment at her school was warm and protective, we felt she was completely safe traveling back and forth on this bus. She usually sat with girls whom she knew well, but this week, she related to me, another girl whom she didn't know well made a point of sharing her seat. The other girl, J., liked to discuss Sara's watch. She complimented her on its appearance, asked a lot of questions about its value, and inquired about how the band worked. On the day of the watch's disappearance, Sara said that shortly before J. exited the bus, she reached over and admired the watch on Sara's wrist. It was immediately after the young woman's departure that Sara noticed her watch was missing, and although she searched the floor and between the seat cushions, it was not to be found. Did the young woman, who never again elected to sit next to Sara on the bus, literally steal the watch right off her wrist? I will never know for sure, but I imagine that she sat next to Sara for several days, biding her time. Because motor tasks were difficult for Sara, the opportunity to remove the watch would present itself on one of the many days that Sara neglected to securely fasten the clasp on the band.

Because children with NLD interpret situations in the most literal ways, they often fail to comprehend the motivations and intentions of others. It is particularly difficult for them to understand the concepts of deception and dishonesty. Thompson (1997) writes that they do "not intuitively understand the concept of lying and therefore [do] not question or evaluate the information [they] receive from others. This leaves [them] defenseless against the deception and mockery of the more cunning individuals [they] encounter" (p.131). Because of this vulnerability, adolescents with NLD need more protection than the average teenager. In addition to being vigilant about securing their safety, adults who care about them also need to simultaneously shore up their defenses, so that they can eventually learn to protect themselves from negative influences. Since we do not want them to remain defenseless, we need to give them supervised opportunities to deal with deception and manipulation. The watch incident actually turned out to be an opportunity to fortify Sara with knowledge about why some people choose to harm others, and how individuals can protect themselves from deception. Shortly after the incident with the watch, I had her answer the phone regularly to talk to solicitors, so she could build up a repertoire of experiences on the different forms of deceptive techniques used by salespeople. Whenever I received an unbelievable offer in the mail, she and I dissected the letter, looking for flaws in the writer's argument so she could begin to recognize the skewed logic of deception. It took many years of intensive practice, but today Sara has a sophisticated understanding of the "rules" of urban living.

The circle of friendship

Thoreau wrote, "the language of friendship is not words but meanings" (1989, p.222). Adolescents with NLD struggle with making sense of the hidden agenda that successful social interactions require. They struggle with such fundamental social tasks as how to initiate, enter or end a conversation. They do not always understand humor or recognize when to apologize. By adolescence, the social perception, interpersonal skills, and sophisticated semantic language skills needed to form and maintain friendships is indeed complex, beyond the abilities of many children with NLD. In addition, teenagers with NLD are keenly aware of their limitations in this area and suffer because they know they inhabit an area outside or on the periphery of any circle of friendship. This characteristic, the awareness of the tragedy of their situation, is a one of the differences between NLD and Asperger's Syndrome. Because individuals with NLD desire the very social acceptance that seems inaccessible to them, they frequently experience anxiety, frustration, poor self-esteem, and discouragement, in addition to social isolation. They know they are doing something wrong; they simply cannot figure out what is wrong with their actions or how to correct their behavior.

The sadness that individuals with NLD feel concerning their social ignorance can, however, be used to their advantage. Because they desire social acceptance, they are grateful for any help they receive to improve their social functioning. Although the social arena is a complex labyrinth of interrelated interactions, teachers and parents can pull apart the individual skills their students need, help them to understand these skills using sensitive, direct oral language, and provide opportunities for intensive practice.

When Sara entered high school, she had only a rudimentary understanding of how to hold a meaningful conversation with an unknown peer. It was particularly difficult for her to figure out how to "keep a conversation going." Although the stereotype of an individual with NLD is someone who is highly verbose, many people with NLD are quiet around casual acquaintances because they cannot discern a good place to enter a conversation. Other conversational skills that elude them are how to initiate or end a conversation. These inadequacies often result in them saying very little in the presence of others. They may have a lot to say, but their timing is off. They cannot figure out an appropriate place to insert their words into a running conversation so they keep their thoughts to themselves. The following is an example of a conversation which Sara had repeatedly during high school:

Peer: "What school did you go to for junior high?"

Sara: "Waldorf." (drops eye contact and looks away)

In this short exchange, Sara failed to realize many things about the nature of conversations. At the most concrete level, she did not realize that by giving a short one-word answer and then exhibiting the body language of dropping eye contact and looking away, she was effectively ending a conversation that had hardly started. She failed to understand how awkward her abrupt response made the other girl feel. The other girl was motivated in asking her this question, not because she was really interested in the name of Sara's former school, but because she wanted to be her friend and elicit information to see if they were compatible. Sara was at a complete loss on what words to use to transform this terse unsatisfying exchange into one that allowed her to connect in a satisfying manner with the other person.

Because individuals with NLD interpret language in such a literal and concrete manner, they will not figure out how to establish fulfilling friendships without explicit instruction. Not all adolescents with NLD would respond to the inquiry about the name of their former school with a one-word answer, as was Sara's habit. Others might answer with an outpouring of information about their school, but in this outburst of words, they would still fail to notice the reciprocal nature of conversation. Teenagers with NLD fail to discern that conversations function like a dance. In order to formulate an appropriate response to another's question, they must learn to follow their partner's words and successfully evaluate the important clues conveyed by tone, body language, intent and circumstance.

Turning up the volume: The increasing novelty of the school environment

Typical American middle and high schools are crowded places, teeming with variety and change. Seventy percent of American high school students attend a school with an enrollment of more than 1000 students; 50 percent attend a school with more than 1500 students (www.hoover.org/publications/digest/30629666.html, retrieved January 29, 2007). In addition, in most middle schools and in practically all high schools, students receive daily instruction from many different teachers. It is not unusual for a high school student to visit ten different classrooms in one day, each with 20 to 30 different students. Students are given about five minutes to travel from class to class, their movement strictly monitored by bells. Many students with typical minds find the variety that high school offers an exciting change from the more protected environment of elementary school. In theory, the departmentalization of high school allows students to receive instruction from teachers who have special knowledge about the subject matter they teach. Larger schools can offer a smorgasbord of stimulating classes, appealing extracurricular activities, and exciting social opportunities.

But for teenagers with NLD, this novelty stretches them in unproductive ways. It leaves them standing naked, no longer clothed by the "illusion of competency." The spacious architecture of a typical high school building with its long intersecting corridors, multiple floors, various gyms, labs, and libraries presents too great a spatial challenge for many with NLD. They become highly anxious about finding their way to their classes and can get into trouble when they are repeatedly tardy. When Sara was in eighth grade, she and a friend spent one day visiting our local public high school to see if it was a suitable place for them to spend the next four years. As I dropped her off that morning and watched her disappear into the doors of the building with 3000 other adolescents, I was thankful that she would spend the day under the protective tutelage of her friend. Without her friend's assistance, she never would have got past the front door. When I picked her up later that morning, she told me that the only thing she could figure out about the layout of the school was that there were many staircases, and it appeared you walked up some of them and down others.

If older students with NLD are troubled by the spatial diversity of a typical middle and high school, they are even further stressed by the variety of humankind that vies for their attention on a daily basis. Every hour they need to adjust to the different personality and teaching style of a new teacher. Even though their social skills are rudimentary and their ability to form friendships underdeveloped, they find themselves trying to relate to a constantly changing sea of peers who are beginning to relate to one another in more sophisticated ways—romantically, by phone conversations, by forming mysterious cliques, by wearing fashionable clothes, and developing friendships based on common interests and experiences. Because of their difficulties with pragmatic language, individuals with NLD are not adept at conversations, particularly telephone conversations. They rarely have the ability to decode independently the social logic of romantic friendships or cliques. Because of their difficulty with spatial concepts and motor skills, they are at risk for fashion faux pas that leave them open to ridicule. For example, it is not unusual for teenagers with NLD to regularly put their shoes on the wrong feet, their shirts on backwards, or to place buttons in the wrong buttonholes. They are poor at personal hygiene tasks such as taking care of their hair and, if not monitored, can appear at school looking very unkempt. For adolescents, appearance is very important, and they judge each other based on conformity to the current fashion. Teenagers with NLD often cannot figure out the current rules of fashion unless these conventions are explicitly pointed out to them. When they appear in school acting and looking strange, they are at increased risks for bullying, social isolation, anxiety, and sadness.

Entering the intellectual boxing ring: Grappling with abstraction, moral ambiguity, and complex thought

Although individuals with NLD struggle academically in the earlier grades, they have particular intellectual strengths that allow them to be successful at reading, spelling, and memorizing information. Since developing these very capacities is one of the major goals of the elementary school curriculum, younger children with NLD are often successful academically in certain valued subjects. However, in high school as the texts they are exposed to become more complex, their difficulties with semantic language make it increasingly difficult for them to understand what they read. For the first time, they are required to master subjects such as biology and chemistry, which require them to explain hypotheses, theories, and abstract concepts. How different science was in elementary school when they could rely on their rote memories to learn the required factual information about more concrete categories such as plants, animals, and heavenly bodies! The labs included in high school science classes emphasize not only their intellectual challenges but also their motor weaknesses. Mastering new tasks, such as working with Bunsen burners, dissecting frogs, and combining chemicals in test tubes, requires careful verbal instructions and practice. When Sara came home after the first day of high school, she spent an hour practicing how to light a match so she could function in her biology labs. In addition, the complexity of the visual representations introduced in high school science class adds another level of frustration for students with NLD. The spatial logic of complex graphs and charts will not be obvious to them unless it is carefully explained, and they are given many opportunities to practice this new knowledge.

The spatial and academic challenges of science pale compared to the new challenges presented by high school math. Math, always a difficult area for these children, suddenly becomes so abstract and visually challenging that it is no longer feasible for them to use their rote memory to adequately understand important mathematical concepts. A subject such as geometry not only taxes their weak ability to form abstractions, but also sorely tries their poor spatial abilities, and requires them to make judgments based on dimension, size, and proportion with *little or no verbal information*. We assume that all people can tell from simply looking at several pictorial examples of angles which one is larger, or which angle is *obtuse, acute,* or *right*. We assume that it is as clear as day that because a 30-degree angle looks like this (<), the visual representation of a 210-degree angle must logically look like this ()). Higher-level math is difficult for students with NLD because so much information is communicated without verbal mediation. The teacher might say, "Look at the two angles on the top of page 13. The first one is an acute angle because it is smaller than 90 degrees. An obtuse angle is one larger than 90 degrees." These sorts of exchanges are complete gibberish to students with NLD. However, if they are taught higher math in a way that allows them to code the necessary principles into language, and then are shown the logic behind these principles, they are able with varying degrees of success to master many important mathematical ideas.

Not only is the abstractness of the academic material increasing in high school but the volume of written work also multiplies. Students with NLD who never learned to master handwriting or keyboard skills do not have the ability to write fluently, and do not have the physical ability to produce masses of written work. In addition, the kinds of questions these students are required to write about no longer deal exclusively with concrete ideas. In English class, these former stars at early reading discover that the ability to comprehend challenging text requires more skill than a facility at decoding the words. As they grapple with the new demands of understanding Shakespeare, Dickens or Melville, they struggle not only with comprehending the literal meaning of the text, but also with making sense of concepts such as metaphor, symbolism, and character motivation. At a time when typical adolescents work at developing a personal sense of morality, students with NLD are potentially stymied by their concrete, literal sense of right and wrong. They struggle to understand the ethical ambiguity of human action because they view the world through their rule-based eyes. Without assistance, students with NLD are plunged into an academic arena in which their particular type of mind is poorly equipped to cope.

They even struggle with extracurricular activities and the elective subjects that high schools typically offer to students as a way to add some rest and recreation to a busy school schedule. For the student with NLD, many familiar elective subjects such as art, music, driver's education, and physical education are not a respite but further sources of stress. For example, gym class puts enormous stress on the motor difficulties of these students. They are generally poor at running, throwing, activities that involve balance, and activities that involve catching and hitting balls. They are particularly poor at motor activities that require the execution of more than one of these skills at the same time or in quick succession. Therefore, traditional organized sports such as softball, soccer, and basketball present significant challenges for them. In addition because of their spatial challenges, they often do not realize the logic behind the rules of the game.

Unless specifically instructed, they often do not discern which team they are on, or even that there are two distinct teams. When Sara was in seventh grade, her class spent a lot of time playing basketball. It was not unusual for her to attempt to make a basket and occasionally score points for the opposing team because she wasn't sure which basket belonged to her team. She was lucky her school did not emphasize athletic competition, so she never suffered any ridicule for her mistakes. Her teammates simply pointed her in the right direction.

Although organized sports are challenging for students with NLD, they are able to become surprisingly adept at physical tasks if someone verbally describes each component movement and then gives them ample opportunity to practice. They need a mind-boggling amount of practice in order to become proficient at any complex physical activity. However, the effort can be worthwhile if the activity they master is one in which they have an interest, and it gives them opportunities for positive social interactions and a sense of personal competency. When Sara was in high school, she attended a two-week summer program where she learned to play volleyball. She did not play on a formal team, but the ability to play a sport, even in a rudimentary fashion, gave her confidence. Her father taught her how to rollerblade, and she spent hours traveling many miles while clocking the requisite practice needed to master this skill. Because driving a car was so difficult for her, her rollerblades became her adolescent "wheels." At first, she fell, her knees bloodied from their frequent contact with cement. Sometimes, I would be driving through the streets of our town running some errand, and unexpectedly come upon her. Through the car window, I would see her clinging onto a fence for dear life as she tried to skate down an incline. She practiced, and she learned.

Art is another difficult extracurricular activity for students with NLD. Unless they are given specific help at a young age, and many opportunities to improve their artistic ability, their drawings will forever resemble the artwork of a young child. Since children with NLD can benefit from connecting words to drawings, there are advantages for them when they improve their artistic skills. One medium that gives teenagers with NLD the opportunity to connect words with pictures, without emphasizing their poor drawing skills, is photography. They will need specific verbal instructions on how to operate a camera, how to focus, and how to think about the composition of a meaningful photograph since they will not intuitively figure these things out. *Because pictures do not move* as scenes in the real world do, photography gives individuals with NLD the opportunity to capture and discuss visual images without any time pressure. In addition, they can return to the same image over and over again to discuss new features and make new observations. When Sara was a teenager she enjoyed making scrapbooks of vacations using either photographs or postcards. She pasted the visual images into the pages of a blank book and would write captions under each picture describing the scene in the photograph. "This is a picture of John and me standing on the bridge overlooking Niagara Falls. We are wearing yellow rain coats and black boots because we are going on a boat that sails right next to the gigantic falls." For individuals with NLD, the world moves too quickly. They do not have the natural ability to learn from the quickly changing images that come flooding into their field of vision. Life is a film that is being played too rapidly for them to glean much understanding. By isolating visual images (pictures) and giving them the opportunity to write words that match the images in the picture, we give them the extra time they need to process and code these images into words. Photography can also help them learn how to form judgments. As they develop more proficiency with the camera, they need to make choices about what kinds of images to capture. Photography can also be used to develop their social skills. Sara created other scrapbooks that contained photographs of schoolmates. She wrote important information underneath each snapshot.

> Here is T. She is a funny girl who makes up stories. She told everyone she has a twin sister who lives with her grandmother. My mom doesn't think this is true. I am not sure. I will have to listen and see if she gives any clues that prove she is making this up.

Musical activities are also challenging for most teenagers with NLD. They tend to have poor rhythmic abilities, which makes it challenging for them to play in a group. In addition, they struggle with the physical dexterity needed to play many musical instruments. *The Right Instrument for Your Child: A Practical Guide for Parents and Teachers* by Atarah Ben-Tovim and Douglas Boyd (1985) is an excellent resource for helping parents and teachers to acquire the necessary information to assist youngsters with NLD to find an appropriate musical outlet. Based on the information offered in this book, Sara began playing the clarinet in the fifth grade. She never completely conquered her difficulties with rhythm but learned to play well enough to participate in chamber groups and bands while she was in high school and college.

Learning to drive a car is one extracurricular activity that is particularly challenging for adolescents with NLD. This is true for several reasons. First, the complex motor movements needed to successfully drive a car are difficult for them to execute. In order to drive, you need to be able to smoothly synchronize the movements of your feet on the pedals with the movements of your hands on the steering wheel. A second reason that driving is so challenging is that you need to be skilled at quickly interpreting a constantly shifting visual landscape in order to make instantaneous decisions about what to do—should I stop, slow down, speed up, or turn right? For example, a driver in the U.S. needs to be able to look at an oncoming car and in a split second decide if this vehicle is far enough away to allow for a safe left turn. A third reason driving is so difficult for people like Sara is that not only do they need to interpret novel and constantly changing visual images quickly in order to determine which motor movement to execute, but they also need to use this visual and spatial information to form more complex decisions about situations that don't conform to the usual patterns, such as a jaywalker or an oncoming car that is behaving erratically. Driving puts stress on many of the weakest areas of individuals with NLD—the ability to deal with novelty, the ability to interpret visual fields, the ability to execute complex motor tasks, the ability to interpret spatial information. Driving also demands that the driver do all these things rapidly and smoothly; individuals with NLD, if they do manage to master these tasks, execute them slowly and awkwardly.

None of this would really matter if driving were not potentially a matter of life or death. In order for individuals with NLD to learn anything, they need many opportunities to repeatedly practice a skill. They need to make mistakes and be verbally set straight by another person. If they are going to become competent drivers, they need to practice driving at 60 miles an hour on urban expressways and repeatedly change lanes. The best individual to teach someone with significant NLD how to drive is probably someone with nerves of steel and a strong sense of fatalism. Unfortunately, neither my husband nor I fit the bill.

Sara did not learn how to drive in high school. Since NLD exists on a continuum, I am sure there are some individuals with NLD who are able to become competent drivers. However, driving placed extraordinary stress on Sara's weakest areas. She eventually received a driver's license when she was in her twenties, but has never become a skilled driver. As an adult, she depends on public transportation to get around. Compared to the current typical high school experience of many students with NLD, Sara led a charmed existence in secondary school. If I count her blessings, I can gauge the increments of her success. Hard work was her daily bread and, through its stark medium, she has fashioned most things of value. But she has had her disappointments. She cut her long hair because she could never learn to braid it. Although she is excellent at finding her way around on public transportation, she is more earthbound than she wishes. She yearns for the freedom of the automobile.

Finding a niche

A study conducted by Mississippi State University in the U.S. concluded that extracurricular activities help students develop both academically and socially. According to the study, high school students who participate in after-school activities build "social capital" by regularly interacting with adults who value education and who nurture the personal assets of the participants. Students with NLD desperately need to build "social capital." However, because of their weaknesses in social acumen, motor development, visual-spatial perception, and semantic language, they seldom experience the satisfaction of being a successful member of a social group. At first glance, they are unlikely candidates for the varsity baseball team, the art club or the school orchestra. However, by carefully reflecting on their strengths and weaknesses, it is possible for students with NLD to play a musical instrument, participate in a sport, or create artistic works.

Students with NLD do best in extracurricular activities that do not emphasize competition. Keep in mind that the main purpose of extracurricular activities for students with NLD is to supply opportunities to practice social skills in a structured environment with rules and goals that can be easily articulated verbally. They are more likely to be successful in activities that emphasize verbal aptitude. For example, they frequently have facility in learning foreign languages. School clubs, camps, and programs that center on acquiring a foreign language can be a satisfying experience for these students. Carefully structured opportunities to perform service work give students with NLD the chance to practice reflection, empathy, and ethical values. Students with NLD who have been fortunate enough to receive sound writing remediation before high school often have the ability to write for the school newspaper. Some students with NLD have the ability to participate in theater. They frequently have an extraordinary ability to memorize lines of dialogue with little effort. However, they are often poor at producing facial expressions and coordinating the bodily movements necessary to portray a role on stage. They may be better suited to other theatrical undertakings such as developing a radio program.

Chapter 5

A Constructive Diagnosis and Remediation Plan

Developing a method of remediation
What we know

There is little information in the literature that spells out in detail what an ideal intervention program for individuals with NLD should look like. Little (1993) states that "no large-scale studies have been reported, and no statistical relationship has been demonstrated between nonverbal learning disabilities…and effective treatments" (p.662). Consequently what little information exists about effective intervention strategies is based on the clinical experiences of educators and related practitioners.

Most of the literature on intervention argues that an appropriate educational plan for students with NLD needs to recognize and build on the strengths of these students as well as taking into account their challenges, in order to teach compensatory skills that shore up the weak areas. In addition to focusing on academic growth, effective intervention plans for students with NLD need to emphasize social skills, developing a sense of personal competency, and increasing their ability to match the right coping strategy to the appropriate situation (Earle-Cruiskshanks 2000; Foss 1991; Matte and Bolaski 1998; Thompson 1997). Telzrow and Bonar (2002) give short succinct recommendations that could easily be included on an Individualized Education Program for students with NLD who are attending a public school.

There is a growing literature written by parents of children with NLD that describes their efforts to increase the adaptive, social, and academic skills of their children (Burger 2004; Tanguay 2001; Whitney 2002). Accounts by Tanguay (2001, 2002) describe ways to help children with NLD learn how to master everyday motor skills, encouraging parents to seek guidance by reading about related disorders and seeking appropriate parenting advice listed in useful bibliographic materials.

Two of the most detailed articles containing specific intervention recommendations are Foss (1991) and Volden (2004). Foss (1991) identifies elements that she feels should be included in all remedial lessons for students with NLD. These elements are first helping students learn how to use their relatively strong verbal skills to analyze and mediate difficult tasks or situations, and then teaching them how to associate the verbal and nonverbal aspects of a task (Foss 1991, p.139). Teachers should first use explicit direct instruction to verbally mediate tasks for students, with the ultimate goal being students acquiring the ability to verbally self-direct their own learning. Foss (1991) gives specific examples of how to reach this goal in the areas of clarifying language concepts, developing verbal reasoning, increasing comprehension and written output, and social understanding.

Volden (2004), writing from the point of view of a speech-language pathologist, deals exclusively with how to develop interventions to improve the language deficits of students with NLD. Although language is a relative strength of individuals with NLD, weaknesses in two areas of language—namely, semantics (understanding content) and pragmatics (understanding function)—impede their ability to reach their full potential. The subtyping of learning disabilities has resulted in a model that establishes two separate, mutually exclusive categories of learning disabilities, verbal ones and nonverbal ones. Volden (2004) argues that there may possibly be more overlap of strengths and weaknesses than currently exists in the descriptions of these two subtypes. Volden feels that one unfortunate consequence of Rourke's work on the subtyping of learning disabilities has been a "reduced emphasis on systematic investigation of the communicative profile, with clinicians and researchers alike ignoring the [language difficulties of students with NLD] because of a label that identifies the problem as 'nonverbal' and therefore implies that the difficulties lie outside the linguistic domain" (p.134). Volden then includes an excellent description of the strengths and weaknesses of the language of typical individuals with NLD, and outlines how clinicians should proceed in designing appropriate language interventions. She states that until research validates which interventions are clearly beneficial for students with NLD, those who wish to design intervention strategies should remember the following advice:

> Clinicians are reminded that clinical practice has always benefited from relying less on categorical labels and more on detailed and careful descriptions of developmental status…to date, there is still no substitute for carefully describing a child's abilities: comparing those to what we know of the sequence of typical development; and intervening directly where a child's performance disadvantages him or her, relative to his or her peers and/or his or her environment. (Volden 2004, p.138)

The power of observation

Since there is little empirical research to guide the developer of positive interventions for children with NLD, the ability to make meaningful observations about children's behavior takes on added importance. Levine (2003) has written extensively on the value of observation in developing a useful individual learning profile for students who struggle with learning. He believes that the current system of diagnosing learning disabilities generates little more than an empty label, and that these labels rarely result in positive suggestions for remediation. He believes that labels put too much emphasis on deficits, and too little emphasis on strengths and possible talents. Additionally, labels cast children with LD as having permanent pathological conditions that are immutable to change. Levine suggests a new model based on careful observation.

In Levine's model (2003), he recommends that educators "become knowledgeable about neurodevelopmental function and variation" (p. 18) so that they are equipped to make meaningful observations about the student's memory, motor abilities, language, and attention. If teachers observe a student who is struggling, they should develop an intervention plan that is specific to that student's learning profile. Levine is not opposed to psychological testing. In fact, he encourages teachers to turn to school psychologists to get specific information about the individual student's strengths and weaknesses. However, the ultimate purpose of gathering this information should be to develop useful instructional strategies. Because the ability to make meaningful observations requires considerable skill, Levine (2003) has established a not-for-profit institute to provide professional development for classroom teachers so they can learn the best ways to observe students based on an understanding of neurodevelopmental principles. The goal of this training is to develop positive interventions to enhance student learning.

Levine's model (2002) does not use specific diagnostic labels to develop intervention programs for children with learning challenges. Levine is opposed to the use of labels for several reasons. First, he feels that labels are imprecise and group too many students with different problems into one category. Instead of labeling the disorder, Levine believes there is more value in labeling the learning difficulty that the child is experiencing. For example, instead of labeling a child who finds it difficult to learn to read as "reading disabled," Levine recommends that teachers label the specific reason why the student is struggling with reading. For example, the teacher could state that this child has difficulties learning to read because he or she has difficulty perceiving the individual sounds in words. A second reason Levine opposes labels is because he feels that labels over-simplify children and reduce their complex natures to the narrow confines of a single word. Some individuals identify so strongly with their label that they define themselves totally in that light (e.g., I am a dyslexic). Finally, Levine (2002) points out that there is a danger that labels "signify that you may have only one problem. For example, a school…may [be] forced to decide if a student" (p.328) has either a learning disability or a behavior disorder. This kind of rigid choice implies that these categories are mutually exclusive, and that it is impossible to have both an emotional and a learning disorder.

One potential weakness of Levine's intervention model is that it relies heavily on the observation skills of classroom teachers. In an ideal world this approach could be highly successful, but currently the majority of teachers do not have a sufficient level of knowledge about learning disabilities and the corresponding intervention techniques to understand how to act appropriately on their observations. Levine recognizes this problem by offering professional development through his organization, All Kinds of Minds. Unfortunately only a small number of teachers have the benefit of his professional development.

Levine (2002) is eloquent in his critique of labels. Without a doubt, a broad label like *learning disability* has little practical value because it lumps too many divergent difficulties under one name. However, Levine may be overlooking the potential value of attempts by researchers to develop a model of subtypes of different forms of learning disabilities. By studying learning disabilities in depth, as the U.S. National Institutees of Health (NIH) has done for reading disabilities and Rourke's lab has for NLD, researchers have developed neuropsychological and cognitive profiles that can, if used in conjunction with common sense and careful observation, help clinicians and educators develop effective interventions. Although it is important to acknowledge that we are all individuals with unique strengths and weaknesses, it is also important to recognize that as human beings and members of the same species we all share certain tendencies. For example, by studying many individuals with reading problems, researchers have determined that most of them have exactly the same core deficit that is impeding their ability to learn to read (Shaywitz 2003). This information can help teachers when they observe that a student is struggling with reading. Instead of seeing each example of reading difficulty as a different and unique problem, teachers can first check to see if their student is experiencing a likely difficulty with phonemic awareness. Each *individual* has a unique nature, but each *problem* is not unique. Labels like *dyslexia* and *nonverbal learning disability* can be useful as meaningful semantic categories if they are well defined and if everyone agrees on the definition.

Sara's "unwritten baby book" contained the nascent collection of the observations that I used to help design interventions for her. I certainly did not consider the things that I did to help her when she was a baby as formal interventions. I acted at first instinctively; I helped her move around and acclimatize herself to strangers and new experiences because it seemed a natural outgrowth of the love that I felt for her. However, as time passed, and the problems that Sara presented became more puzzling and complex, I found that love and instinct were simply not enough to adequately help her. I realized that I did not have enough knowledge about learning difficulties and human development to answer the questions that were multiplying in the unwritten baby book. I sought the advice of experts. By the time Sara was six, I had consulted with three pediatricians, a pediatric neurologist, the staffs of two preschools (one was a lab school for a small university and the other was a Montessori school), a private speech and language pathologist, and the learning disability team at our local public school. The day that we went to see the pediatric neurologist was a turning point. Our experience went like this:

We went to see the well-known neurologist because Sara wanted to learn how to print the letter *T*. We hoped that the learned man could shed some light on her predicament. She was six and very keen on learning how to write. Lately, she had got into the habit of rising early and spending an extra hour before school practicing her letters. "It's not going well," she confided to me. Recently, she had received a birthday invitation addressed in the hand of a friend from her class. The letters of her name, *Sara*, were spelled out in the other child's impeccable handwriting on the front of the envelope. My daughter was deeply impressed. "How do you think she does it? Look at her *S*. It is perfect!" The ability to form legible letters eluded my daughter, even though she spent considerable time practicing, trying out different writing utensils and different types of paper in hopes of finding the key to unlock her difficulty.

So we traveled into the city that gray winter day, and the three of us, my husband, my daughter and myself, found ourselves in the waiting room of a well-known pediatric neurologist. I carried with me the invisible baby book. By now its entries had grown long and singularly more baffling. I had spent the previous evening transcribing its entries from my memory into cold print. *She learned to speak at the appropriate age, but most people cannot understand anything she is saying. She cannot count to ten, although she can tell me how many objects I have if I show her four things. All motor tasks are difficult if not impossible.*

The doctor ushered us into an examining room. He was not terribly interested in the invisible baby book, and implied that I was spending too much time composing it. He took a medical book from a shelf and held up a page for Sara. "What letter is that?" he asked her. "A *T*," I heard her bravely answer. She knew the names of all her letters and had for some time. "And that one?" the esteemed doctor asked. "An *S*, a *G*, an *E* and an *M*," Sara answered. The doctor quickly reached his conclusion and told us, "She is smart, you see; she knows all her letters." The last thing the doctor did was to measure the circumference of Sara's head with a tape measure. My daughter, usually so compliant, hid under the examining table, and when the doctor tried to exit the room, she leapt out, grabbed him around the legs, and tried to trip him. He was correct in pointing out that she was intelligent.

When we got home that day I decided that we would consult no more experts. I realized that we could spend our entire lives in the waiting rooms of various medical and educational experts. We would get off that train now. I also realized for the first time that I had an invaluable asset that was missing in the experts we consulted. Unlike them, I was cognizant of the important fact that I knew nothing about how to help my daughter. Because I recognized my ignorance, I knew that I had a lot to learn and was willing to do so. I also decided that evening that if someone as prominent as the pediatric neurologist whom we had just consulted knew nothing about my daughter's condition, then I need not worry about doing a bad job if I decided to take a more active role in directly helping her. Even if the amount I would be able to help my daughter learn turned out to be meager, it would have to be greater than the amount she would gain by following a road dictated by ignorance. So started a great adventure.

Sara went on to accomplish much more than I could have ever dared imagine that evening. Her accomplishments are her own; she forged them out of her own will and drive. The things that I did only aided her. I did not necessarily make life easy for her, but only helped her to use her time and energy in constructive, positive ways. I once heard a psychologist say that every day in the life of a person with NLD is like running a marathon. This comparison is only a slight exaggeration. For Sara, intervention has allowed her daily race to be more joyous and meaningful, not necessarily shorter.

Special children need special parents

I am not suggesting parents of children with NLD become their children's teacher. It is the job of the school to educate our children, and it is the role of researchers and psychologists to figure out the most effective interventions and diagnostic tools to aid our children. However, the lack of awareness and consensus about effective ways to diagnose and intervene on behalf of individuals with NLD has left parents of these children in a difficult catch-22 position about how to proceed in best developing a strategy to assist their child.

The first piece of advice most parents are given when they have a child with a suspected learning disability is to have their child tested in order to get an accurate diagnosis. The rationale behind this advice is that it is easier to develop effective interventions to help struggling children if their problem is properly categorized and defined. The second reason is to ensure that a child receives special help in a public school. In order to be eligible for special education, students must have a diagnosis that both seriously affects their educational performance and also falls into one of 13 recognized categories such as autism, specific learning disability, deafness, or serious emotional disturbance. For example, children who are diagnosed with a reading or writing disorder would be eligible for special education because they fall into the category *specific learning disability*. Children who seriously act out in school might be diagnosed with the label, oppositional defiant disorder, and would be placed into the category, *serious emotional disturbance*. Children who are diagnosed with attention deficit are usually classified into the category, *other health impaired*. Because NLD is not currently a recognized diagnostic label, children with the NLD profile are usually classified into one of the following three categories depending on the diagnosis they receive: (1) specific learning disability; (2) other health impaired; (3) serious emotional disturbance.

The diagnostic labels attached to individuals with NLD are problematic for several reasons. Labels frequently take into account only one of their challenge areas. Some labels are too wide-ranging in scope. Other labels are just inaccurate. An example of a label frequently given to children with NLD that is too narrow is "disorder of written expression." Although writing is commonly one of their problem areas, this diagnosis does not come close to describing all the areas in which they will need intervention and assistance. NLD is also sometimes narrowly classified as a developmental coordination disorder. Again this label only describes a single area of difficulty for students with NLD. Most children with NLD have difficulty with motor tasks, but this label does not take into account their extensive academic difficulties, their social challenges, or their problems with language.

Children with NLD are regularly diagnosed with the broad label LD NOS (learning disability none otherwise specified). This vague and amorphous label yields little useful information to help educators plan remedial interventions for these children. Since most students with LD are individuals with reading difficulties, it is not surprising for students labeled as LD NOS frequently to find themselves placed in remedial reading programs along with the other students with more common forms of learning challenges. Unfortunately, remedial reading programs that focus on single-word reading are not the kind of intervention that most students with NLD require.

Children with NLD are also given labels that are patently inaccurate. Because many of their difficulties, such as getting lost, misinterpreting social skills, and misunderstanding language, frequently go unrecognized, they sometimes react and cope by acting out, becoming anxious, or responding strangely. When they are then treated as if their behavior is their primary difficulty and not a result of other stresses, the opportunity to see them clearly is lost. Therefore, individuals with NLD can find themselves labeled behavior disordered. Because there are similarities between the profile of individuals with NLD and those with Asperger's Syndrome, children with NLD are sometimes misdiagnosed as having Asperger's.

The value of a diagnosis and obstacles to obtaining an accurate one

It is worth advocating for a diagnosis that most accurately mirrors your child's major challenges and allows her to receive the kinds of educational services she will need in order to function successfully in school. Of course, in a perfect world it would be best if children with NLD were labeled with a precise term that accurately described their specific strengths and weaknesses. However, until NLD is recognized as a discrete and separate diagnosis, the best parents can do is to be pragmatic. In order to ensure that your child receives the breadth of services she requires, make certain the language of the report accurately describes your child's strengths and challenges in a precise and detailed manner, regardless of what label she receives. This information will help school personnel design a meaningful educational plan.

It is also important to keep in mind that the most useful category for your specific child can change over time depending on her current educational needs. For example, if the purpose of the evaluation is to establish eligibility and to develop an educational plan for an elementary student in a public school, the category *specific learning disability* might be the most appropriate since this category would allow the child to receive more specific educational interventions that focus on academic weaknesses than the category *other health impaired*. However, if the sole purpose of the evaluation is to prove that a high school or college student is eligible to receive extra time on standardized tests, either category might suffice. In no circumstances do you want your child to be placed in an inaccurate category. For example, unless your child really has bona fide behavior issues that are the primary reason for her learning difficulties, you probably do not want her classified as behaviorally disordered because this label will not allow her to receive the kind of educational interventions she needs.

Try to procure a diagnosis for your child as early in her school career as possible, so she does not experience years of academic and social frustration. Currently, it is unusual for these children to be recognized before the fifth grade, and this situation makes it unlikely that they will receive any early intervention. Since early intervention is the key to the successful functioning of children with other forms of LD, it makes sense that children with NLD would also benefit from earlier intervention in areas that are challenging for them. The earlier a child is identified, the better are her chances of receiving the amount and intensity of help she needs to build a strong learning and social foundation. However, because of the lack of consensus on nearly everything about NLD—its definition, what tests to use to diagnose this difficulty, what interventions are needed, the prognosis, and even the existence of such a problem—parents can only do the best they can to ensure that their child is identified early. Please keep in mind that any accurate diagnosis and ensuing interventions at any age are better than none at all.

Finally, books and articles written for parents often point out that they will be more likely to receive good advice and an accurate diagnosis for their child with suspected NLD if they seek out the services of a clinician who is knowledgeable about this problem. Although this is good advice, most parents who are seeking an evaluation do not suspect NLD; they only know something is amiss with their child. The reason they are seeking the evaluation is to find out what is wrong, so how can they possibly know what is wrong before they receive the results of the evaluation? Perhaps the first quality parents need is an appreciation for the absurd.

Even though parents still face enormous difficulties in obtaining both an accurate diagnosis and constructive practical suggestions to help their child, there is more accurate information available to parents and professionals than when Sara visited a neurologist in 1987. It is essential that parents access this information, because they will need to be informed in order to take a leadership role in advocating for their child to ensure that she receives the depth and breadth of help required over the course of her entire education, including higher education. Understanding NLD will aid parents in making thoughtful decisions about their child's school placement. Finally, being informed will help them create the kind of home and family life that enhances their child's psychological and cognitive development.

Before families can schedule an evaluation to obtain a diagnosis, they need to come to the realization that their child's development is deviating far enough from the norm to merit concern. Parents seem to arrive at this conclusion in different ways. Sometimes they rely on their own observations and hunches. In this case, parents are frequently the ones who are the impetus for seeking out an evaluation. For other parents, the idea that their child may have unusual problems with learning is something they have never considered. In this case, a teacher is frequently the first one to notice that the child may have unusual difficulty with certain learning tasks.

Listen to your instincts

Why are some parents so good at noticing the learning difficulties of their children, while others parents need to be convinced of this fact by someone else? The first reason is that children with NLD frequently seem more adept than they actually are because of their relative verbal strengths. The second reason is that NLD, like many learning disorders, exists on a continuum from mild to severe. It is logical that children with more significant NLD will deviate more from the typical and will more easily elicit concern from those who love them. Children with mild NLD will be easy to miss because their learning will deviate less from the typical.

Parents who find themselves in the position of being the first to observe their child's differences and the first to initiate the possible need for an evaluation frequently find their concerns dismissed by professionals. In this case, it is important to listen to your instincts. Parents may not know a great deal about learning disabilities but they are experts on their own child. Most parents have an instinctive sensitivity to their child's moods, challenges, and strengths that they can tap into to form good observations about their child's learning and developmental progress. Listen to that voice, and trust your hunches. If you feel there is something amiss about your child's development, ask questions and carefully investigate your concerns, particularly if you see a pattern of difficulty that progresses or persists over time. Many parents of children with NLD have felt that something was amiss early in their child's development, but were unable to put their concerns into words because of the amorphous quality of the early signs of NLD. One way to make your concerns more concrete is to keep a journal where you record all the instances in your child's life that make you uneasy. In this way, you can gather many specific examples of your child's behavior to refer to when you talk to professionals. For example, instead of saying that you are worried because your child seems clumsy, you can cite specific examples of your child's awkwardness to illustrate how pervasive your child's clumsiness is in her daily life. Keep in mind that many professionals are not particularly adept at asking the kinds of questions that help ferret out relevant information, so the more specific you can be in articulating your concerns by using particular examples and patterns of behavior, the more successful you may be in getting them to take your concerns seriously.

When parents who have believed something is wrong with their child over a long period of time finally receive an official diagnosis, they often feel relieved and vindicated. They have an official name for their child's difficulties; a legitimate means to discuss their child's educational and psychological needs with school personnel, friends, and family members. An official diagnosis can put clear limits on the seriousness of their child's problem. Before, their unchecked imagination might have made parents worry that their child's problem was more serious than it actually is. Now their worries can take a concrete form; they can move beyond simply worrying about their child and start to do constructive things to help her. They can also feel vindicated because someone finally agrees with them.

Another reaction: The child with NLD and high verbal intelligence
However, for many parents the process of learning that their child has NLD takes the opposite course. The news hits them as a startling unexpected pronouncement. This experience is particularly true for parents of children with mild forms of NLD, and of children with NLD who have superior verbal intelligence. Young children with NLD who also have superior verbal abilities frequently have many of the characteristics of gifted children. They frequently dazzle their parents when they speak at an early age using complex sentence structure and sophisticated vocabulary. It is easy to understand why such parents would feel their son or daughter is

more destined to become a poet, academic or politician than someone at risk for learning and social difficulties. When their child then learns how to read early and well, the parent is even more convinced of their child's exceptional abilities. Finally their incredible rote memory seems to give even less credence to the idea that there could be something amiss.

For example, I was utterly captivated by Sara's ability to commit certain kinds of information to memory at an early age. When she was very small, she entertained her brother in the car by reciting all the verses of his favorite nursery rhymes, poems, and songs verbatim. I cannot count the number of times she saved me having to look up the telephone number of a friend: "'You don't remember that number, Mom?,' she would ask perplexed, as she rattled off the necessary digits. 'That surprises me; you call them a lot.'" It was only because she had such striking difficulties with social situations, new experiences, and spatial tasks that the warning bells went off for me when she was so young. In many ways, I was lucky that she had an additional difficulty, a severe articulation disorder, which is not typical of NLD. Because she had such difficulty speaking clearly, her precocious verbal abilities were frequently masked. In addition, the articulation problem was a concrete tangible problem that was difficult to deny.

Since parents typically see their child in the best possible light, they are often caught off guard when a teacher points out their child's difficulties with handwriting, math, motor tasks, and social relationships. The process of readjusting their perception of their child as highly capable to someone who is vulnerable and at risk is painful. Parents who are shocked to find out their child has significant challenges need to remember that their original perception of their child was not wrong, only incomplete. Your child still has the same wonderful gifts of verbal dexterity and a great memory. Discovering that she also has challenges and how to deal with them will allow your family to see beneath the "illusion of competency" and learn how to nurture your child in a way that truly recognizes who she is.

The evaluation for a school-aged child: Private or public sector?

Parents can choose to have their child with suspected NLD evaluated at their local public school or seek out the services of a private evaluator. Public schools in the United States are required by law to provide free evaluations to any child residing within the district who has suspected special learning needs. Children who reside in the school district but who attend a private school are also eligible for free evaluations. As more educators and school psychologists become knowledgeable about NLD and its unique characteristics, it is sometimes possible for parents to obtain the help their children require through the results of public school evaluation. The many advantages to a school evaluation include the following:

- *Cost*: This option may be the only one available to many families since the cost of private evaluations can range from several hundred to several thousand dollars.

- *Acceptance*: School districts differ in how well they work with professionals in the private sector. Some districts will only accept the results of an evaluation conducted by their own school personnel.

- *Minimizing the number of necessary tests*: Even when a public school accepts the results of an outside evaluation to establish eligibility, the school usually requires the child to undergo additional testing conducted by school personnel.

What is the main purpose of a public school evaluation?

The main purpose of the evaluation is to establish "eligibility." Public schools in the U.S. are required to follow the federal special education law, and the law states that before a student can receive special education services it must be established that this student does indeed have a condition that seriously interferes with his or her learning. The child's learning problem needs to be severe enough to be thought of as a *disability*. Most students who are eligible for special education are those whose test results show they have a learning disability (a discrepancy between potential and actual achievement).

Unfortunately, many parents will find it frustrating to try to secure an accurate diagnosis and the breadth of services their child needs solely on the basis of the results of a typical public school evaluation. In theory, the results of the evaluation are not only supposed to establish eligibility for special education, but also to pinpoint the areas in which the child needs specific help, such as reading or speech. If the results of the evaluation do show that your child has a learning disability, the next step in the process is for a team of professionals who work at your child's school and who have potential expertise and insight into your child's difficulties (e.g., the school psychologist, your child's teacher, the special educator, speech-language pathologist, and occupational therapist) to meet and discuss the best way to proceed in designing an individualized education plan (IEP) for your child. In this way, children with LD are required to receive a written individualized education plan that is carefully designed to capitalize on their strengths and bolster their weaknesses. In theory, the IEP is supposed to be a custom tailored document that addresses all the individual learning needs resulting from your child's specific learning disorder.

Who administers the different tests that are part of the evaluation in public schools?

Usually a school psychologist administers an IQ test as the first step in an evaluation. The purpose of this test is to establish the child's intelligence (potential). A teacher with a specialty in learning disabilities usually gives a number of individually administered achievement tests to measure the child's grasp of traditional academic areas such as reading, writing, and math (ability). Since the law states that students need to be assessed in all the areas that are difficult for them, students will receive different tests depending on their particular challenges. So reading specialists, speech-language pathologists, and occupational therapists might also be involved in the evaluation process. If all the members of the team decide that the child does indeed have special needs, the team then meets again to write a plan that outlines the special services the child will need in school.

Potential disadvantages to public school evaluations for students with NLD

There are a number of disadvantages to public school evaluations, particularly for children with NLD. Some students with NLD, particularly those with high verbal intelligence, simply do not qualify for special education under the criteria set up under the special education law. How could this be, you might wonder? First, many children with NLD do not show a discrepancy between potential and achievement in the early grades because they frequently excel in subjects such as early reading, and therefore can score quite high on certain achievement tests. In the later grades when the school curriculum puts more stress on their weak academic difficulties in reading comprehension, math, and science, it is easier for them to exhibit a discrepancy. However, most parents do not want to wait until their child has failed before they start receiving help. So, this situation makes it challenging for parents who feel that something is seriously amiss with their child's learning to procure help for them at an early age before their children find themselves in serious academic difficulty.

The second reason students with NLD sometimes do not qualify for special education is because of the unique way they score on IQ tests. Individuals with NLD usually have a significant difference between their ability to deal successfully with verbal and nonverbal tasks. Remember that IQ tests consist of two main sections, verbal and performance. In order to determine an individual's IQ, the evaluator averages the two different scores on the verbal and performance sections to get a number known as the full-scale IQ, which is supposed to indicate the person's potential. Our children are usually good at the tasks on the verbal section, tasks that ask them to demonstrate their abilities in using and understanding words. They are usually not as adept at the kind of tasks they are asked to do on the performance section, which require them to interpret pictures and visual patterns, and notice visual details. Therefore, they may receive very different scores on these two sections. Most people with typical learning patterns receive about the same score on both sections. Even children with more typical learning disabilities such as reading disabilities usually receive similar scores on the verbal and performance sections. When children with NLD receive a relatively high score on the verbal section and then a relatively low score on the performance section, their full-scale IQ can appear quite low. The school then might conclude that the reason for the child's difficulty is a lack of intelligence.

The first scenario, where children with NLD are not identified because they do not score poorly enough on achievement tests, is common. The second scenario, where children are not identified as having a learning disability because of questions about their potential, is probably less common.

Private evaluators

Frequently, the public school is not the best place to get accurate information about the learning profile of a child with NLD. Remember the main reason you are seeking a diagnosis is practical—you want the evaluation to result in information to help you better understand your child's unusual learning profile, so you are equipped with the right knowledge to make sure she receives the concrete help she needs in school and at home. If you are not happy with the results of your child's public school evaluation, you can seek out the services of a private evaluator either as a second opinion or to gather more relevant information to assist you in understanding your child's educational needs. You can also decide to use a private evaluator as your first choice to conduct the evaluation and then present this evaluation to your child's school.

Choosing a diagnostician

When you seek out a competent individual to help you understand your child, keep in mind that many professionals are skilled in administering tests. You are looking for someone who is skilled, not only in giving tests, but also in interpreting them. Particularly in the case of NLD, a relatively rare learning disorder with few agreed diagnostic criteria or educational protocols, it is essential that the individual who assesses your child is a flexible and creative thinker who is adept at administering tests and coming to diagnostic conclusions, and also at translating the results of the tests into practical educational interventions for home and school. The evaluator should be someone who takes the time to carefully consider the information you have about your child, to answer your questions, and to take your concerns seriously. Finally, you are seeking someone who will be able to establish a good rapport with your child and endeavor to ensure that the evaluation is a positive experience for her.

One professional who is likely to be familiar with NLD, and who also has the training to interpret a wide array of diagnostic tools, is a neuropsychologist. Parents may want to seek out the services of this professional to conduct an initial evaluation of their child with suspected NLD for the following reasons:

- NLD is most often discussed in the neuropsychological literature and the term, *nonverbal learning disability*, was coined by a neuropsychologist. Therefore, parents may have the best luck finding someone familiar with NLD in this field. It is also possible to find neuropsychologists who specialize in this disorder and are familiar with individuals with NLD who have been successful. In addition, neuropsychologists are familiar with the differences between NLD and other disorders, such as Asperger's Syndrome.

- Neuropsychologists tend to use a wider range of tests than is typical in most educational evaluations. For example, they frequently give tests that try to measure visual-motor abilities, sensory-motor integration, and spatial reasoning. Since NLD affects so many different areas of a child's life, it is important that the evaluation takes into account more than their academic functioning.

- Neuropsychologists try to pinpoint the exact reason why individuals struggle with certain tasks. For example, a good neuropsychologist would not only conclude that someone has difficulty forming letters, they would also try to figure out exactly why this individual was struggling at this task. Was it because the individual had trouble with visual perception, or with the necessary physical motor movements, or both? It is easier to design effective interventions when one understands the reason why a task is difficult for a person.

How to get the most from a private evaluation

Before you take your child for an evaluation, take time out for self-reflection. Because you know your child so well and also because you have had years of dealing with her challenges and quirks, you have much valuable information to help any professional. However, parents are often not very good at translating their intuitive understanding of their child into clear analytical language that will help a professional. In turn, many professionals are poor at asking the kinds of questions that would help them elicit the information they need from parents. Parents can maximize the value of the testing experience for themselves and their child if they prepare for the evaluation. The following are ideas that may help you get the most from a private evaluation. Questions to ponder before the evaluation include:

- What is the purpose of the evaluation? What do I hope to accomplish for my child by having her evaluated?

- Since my intuition is telling me that something is different about my child, what are some specific examples I can think of that are concrete evidence of my hunches? (Get in the habit of becoming a good observer of your child's behavior. It is a good idea to write examples down of specific incidents where you were troubled by your child's behavior and keep these observations in a journal. If anyone asks you why you think your child is literal or clumsy, you will have specific examples.)

- What are my greatest worries about my child?

- In the past when I tried to seek help for my child, what has happened? Why were these experiences unsatisfactory? What can I do this time to make sure that I receive a reasonable explanation for my child's difficulties?

Many diagnosticians will meet with parents before the evaluation to explain the diagnostic process and to answer any questions you may have. It is a good idea to write your questions down. In addition, you can use this meeting to assess the personal style of the evaluator and see if this is someone with whom you think you can work.

Potential questions to ask the diagnostician before evaluation include:

- Have you ever evaluated other children with a similar profile/difficulties as my child?

- How is the testing you will administer different from the testing my child would receive at his or her public school? How is it different from the testing that a private school psychologist would administer?

- Do you write a report where you summarize your results, and how long will it take to receive the report?

- What kind of information do you include in the report?

- Do you include a section that outlines specific educational interventions for the school? Suggestions we can use to better help our child at home?

- If you recommend private tutoring, speech therapy, occupational therapy, and so on, do you have the names of individuals who are qualified to implement the suggestions in the report?

- Will you help us communicate with my child's school? Would you be willing to attend my child's IEP meeting and explain the report to his or her teachers? How can your report help us establish eligibility for special education and the services and accommodations my child needs?

- Have you ever worked with the staff at my child's public school?

- We are looking for a private school for our child. Are you familiar with private schools in our area that might fit my child's needs?

- How do you recommend we prepare our child for the evaluation? How do you make the child feel comfortable? How do you explain the results of the evaluation to them?

- Will any one else in addition to you be involved in testing my child?

- Do you meet with parents after the evaluation? Do you explain the results of the evaluation to an older child?

- In the unlikely event that we do not agree with the diagnosis or with some of the conclusions that you reach about our child, how would you handle such a situation?

Questions to ask after the evaluation include:

- Based on the test results, do you think our child will be eligible for an IEP? Do you feel our child will be able to receive all the help he or she needs through the school? If not, what private services should we consider?

- Would it be better for my child to be classified as LD or other health impaired? Why do you feel this way?

- What kinds of technology could possibly help him or her academically?

- My child attends a private school. The teaching staff has indicated they are willing to work with us to make the school environment a good place for our child. What kind of information and suggestions do they need?

- What accommodations will he or she need?

- How should I explain the results of the evaluation to our child?

- Since you feel my child has a nonverbal learning disability and that label is not used in my child's school, what alternative label would you recommend and why?

- How can we best help our child's social development?

- What kind of school would be best for his or her academic and social development?

- How can we explain our child's difficulties to his or her siblings?

- What extracurricular activities would you recommend for our child?

The IEP

Once it is determined that your child is eligible for special education, a team of professionals meets to write the IEP. Many parents find IEP meetings intimidating and overwhelming. However, keep in mind that you have been dealing with your child's unusual way of seeing the world from birth and probably have developed effective ways to manage many of her baffling behaviors. If you are able to consciously articulate the techniques you have developed intuitively, this information can be of great use to the IEP team. You also may have a better understanding of the range of your child's difficulties than some teachers who are more familiar with children with language learning disabilities. You can use this knowledge to make sure that your child's IEP contains interventions in all areas of need—spatial and motor tasks, academic learning, semantic language, and social development. Finally, you can be the voice that reminds the IEP team not to be fooled by your child's verbal dexterity.

If you have been fortunate enough to find a private diagnostician who is knowledgeable about NLD and your child's learning profile, invite him or her to the meeting to present the findings of the report to the team. Including another knowledgeable voice, particularly in the case of a less well-known disorder, can help the team better understand your child's educational needs. The following are suggested dos and don'ts for parents to ensure that the IEP meeting results in a good educational plan for your child:

- If your child has two parents, make sure both parents attend the meeting. If you are a single parent, bring with you to the meeting a trusted friend who knows your child. You will feel more comfortable and less "outnumbered" if you attend with someone who cares about you personally. In addition, the second person can take notes and will be someone with whom you can later discuss the proceedings of the meeting and clarify any questions you had about what you heard.

- Do your homework. Learn all you can about the eligibility and the IEP process before you attend the meeting. The intervention appendix (Chapter 10) includes many books and articles written for parents about IEPs.

- Be respectful of the school staff. It is important to be assertive about getting what you need for your child. However, you are more likely to accomplish this goal if you learn how to be a good listener, keep your anger in check, and make your points without resorting to emotional confrontations.

- Some school districts work beautifully with private professionals; some do not. If you want to include the input of private practioneers at the meetings, remember to inform the school before the meeting. Also, photocopy the report for each member of the team and give it to them well in advance of the meeting so they have time to read it.

Sara's diagnosis story: Novelty as a possible wild card during assessment for individuals with NLD

When Sara was growing up, our family searched futilely for someone who could accurately explain why she had so many mystifying learning challenges. I first publicly voiced the question, "what is wrong with my child?" during a routine pediatric exam when Sara was 13 months old. I asked the same question every subsequent year as the list of tasks she found challenging multiplied and intensified. I turned to many different professionals to see if they could furnish a reasonable explanation for Sara's difficulties. They all tried to supply an assessment of our situation, and though I reflected long and hard on what they told me, none of their explanations ultimately rang true. For example, when Sara adjusted poorly to her Montessori school, the principal and her teacher urged me to see a speech therapist, Dr. A., who was also a psychotherapist. The principal believed Sara's difficulties with pronunciation and other tasks were psychological and that they were caused by my inability to "let her go" and to accept the reality of her problem. When I inquired exactly how they would describe Sara's problem, they said they believed Sara's difficulties stemmed from a lack of intelligence. "We need to accept our children for what they are," they reminded me. "Not all kids are bright. Sara has many other positive qualities."

So I made an appointment to see Dr. A. even though I saw no lack of aptitude in my daughter. As usual I brought the unwritten baby book and related my observations to Dr. A. She was interested in its contents and complimented me on my careful record-keeping. However, she concluded after several months of visits that Sara's difficulties were caused by a "separation problem." She believed that if this problem were resolved Sara's other learning difficulties would also disappear. I went home that afternoon and reflected on what Dr. A had said. Was I really overprotective? Certainly, other people, both professionals and friends, had suggested that this might be the case. I hoped that if I were unintentionally guilty of interfering with Sara's development, I would have the maturity to accept this fact and do something about it. I certainly could understand why someone might perceive my daughter as unusually clingy for a child of her age. Even after attending the same school for two years, Sara was still uncomfortable there. She also stuck very close to me in social situations, always asking me questions about what was going on. In addition, she related poorly to other children.

However, I noticed she always agreed to go to school without a fuss. She was clearly unhappy there, but her discomfort did not seem to stem from being parted from me. When she spoke about school, she mentioned her distress at not being able to master the tasks she was asked to do, or to figure out a way to make herself understood, or to join in the other children's games. I particularly felt others underestimated how confused she was spatially and how much of her reluctance to leave my side was caused by her inability to find her way around. "I can't find anything in the room," she would tell me. "You get in trouble if you don't put stuff back where it belongs, so I am afraid to work with things." Then there was the difficulty of the doorknob. Sara could not figure out how to open the door at the main entrance to her school despite the fact she had been shown many times. She worried the whole way there that she wouldn't be able to get into the building. I always had to get out of the car to help her open the door, and parents were not allowed to do this because such actions held up the line of cars dropping off other students. Her teachers believed Sara refused to open the door because she was deliberately feigning helplessness to gain my attention. I, on the other hand, believed Sara could not figure out how to carry out the motions required to open the door.

So I decided to reject the separation anxiety hypothesis, and at my next meeting with Dr. A. asked her to consider the possibility of another explanation for Sara's school problems. To Dr. A.'s credit, she did consider other possible ways to explain Sara's difficulties, but she was not willing to drop the idea that her primary problem was psychological. She visited Sara at school and brought a large baby doll with her. By this time, Sara had stopped speaking at school, so Dr. A. tried to convince Sara to speak with the doll. Sara informed me later that school was difficult enough without having to deal with a weird lady who was unaware of one of the cardinal rules of Montessori school: you weren't allowed to bring toys to class.

I stopped seeing Dr. A. shortly after she made the school visit. A month later, I transferred Sara to a small parochial school where the day before Sara's arrival the teacher told the class that God was sending them a new girl who would speak in school only if everyone was very nice to her. In this friendly environment, Sara spoke constantly from the very first day.

However, I had learned a disturbing lesson. Once a professional, such as Dr. A., has reported her findings to other professionals, such as the staff at Sara's Montessori school, a mere parent such as myself was rendered essentially powerless to challenge her verdict. In fact, I discovered that by disagreeing with the results of her evaluation, I was unwittingly supplying further proof of being "in denial" and an obstruction to my daughter's progress. The truth had been stated, and there was no room for discussion. So, like Sara, I learned the value of silence in some situations. I learned to voice my concerns about Sara's learning difficulties only to those whom I trusted.

As the years passed, I became adept at answering a more important question: "What can be done to help my child overcome these challenges?" As I successfully figured out practical ways to help her accomplish difficult tasks, I watched her reap the benefits of my assistance. She turned doorknobs, rode bicycles, participated in other children's games, spoke clearly, and wrote stories. I concluded that finding an answer to the question, "what can be done?" was more important than discovering the answer to my original question, "why was she having these difficulties in the first place?"

However, my desire to find an answer to the *why* question never completely disappeared. When Sara was eight, I began designing remedial programs for other children with learning difficulties. I could not help but notice how different were the challenges faced by the majority of children with whom I worked. Most of them had specific difficulties in one academic area, such as written language or math reasoning. A few had serious issues with social skills. Very few had the breadth of challenges Sara faced on a daily basis.

When Sara was 11, I attended a session at a conference on dyslexia where I heard a learning specialist describe the profile of someone with a nonverbal learning disability. I know now that the presenter was giving a synopsis of Doris Johnson's well-known article, "Nonverbal Learning Disabilities," which appeared in 1987 in the journal *Pediatrics*. As I listened to the presenter's words, I was struck at how perfectly my daughter's development matched the description of an individual with NLD. After the session was over, I remember wishing I had more concrete evidence to verify my hunch. I yearned to be able to say: "My daughter has a nonverbal learning disability," because I longed to understand why she had such difficulties.

Sara was a young adult before we found a psychologist who could accurately label her difficulties. However, until NLD becomes an accepted category for both psychologists and educators, no evaluation she receives can state that she has a nonverbal learning disability, the label which best characterizes her difficulties. Fortunately, the accuracy of her diagnosis is not particularly important at this point in her education, since its sole purpose has been to grant her the accommodation of extra time on examinations in graduate school and on the standardized tests she must take in order to qualify as a licensed speech-language pathologist.

Still, acquiring access to a precise label for individuals with NLD might fortify them against the dangers of misdiagnosis, from the possibility that someone could attach a label to their condition that is not only inaccurate but also potentially injurious. In an effort to receive an accurate diagnosis, Sara faced a significant stumbling block when she was young. The following account describes this most distressing chapter in our family's attempt to secure a meaningful education for her.

I relate Sara's disturbing experience with assessment for the following reason. I want to suggest that any label an individual receives by undergoing a battery of psychological and educational tests should only be considered accurate if that individual deserves this label both under testing situations and in authentic real-life situations. An extreme example from my professional practice can serve to illustrate this point. I once worked with a student who had a significant reading problem. After several years of special help, his reading improved so greatly that at the end of fourth grade he decided to read all the volumes of *The Chronicles of Narnia* aloud to me.

Subsequently, his parents took him to a psychologist who gave him a battery of tests to assess his progress. My student unexpectedly performed poorly on these assessments, and the psychologist came to the conclusion that he was virtually a nonreader. The psychologist then recommended my student undergo a very intensive remedial program to help him learn to read. I told the psychologist that I believed the results of the evaluation did not correctly describe my student's actual reading ability. I did not question the results of the tests. My student had indeed scored poorly on them. Since he could clearly read quite well in real-life situations, the key consideration should have been to identify why he did so poorly in a testing situation rather than conclude that he was unable to read. However, the evaluator did not agree with my point of view because he believed in the infallibility of his assessments.

I recorded my student reading a page of *Prince Caspian* and played the tape at the IEP meeting where the psychologist presented his findings. On the tape you can hear my student fluently reading a long portion of text he had not previously seen. Even in the face of this evidence, the psychologist would not revise his opinion that my student was only capable of reading at a first grade level. Luckily, my student's parents did not place him in the remedial program recommended by the psychologist, and in time my student got over his test phobia and was able to read well in both test and real-life situations.

I have found in my practice that the way students perform in test situations in most cases does mirror their real-life abilities. However, in the rare cases where there is a discrepancy between what an individual can accomplish in reality and under test situations, it seems to me that what someone can do in real life is the truer measure of their abilities. In a way, I do believe tests are infallible. Individuals clearly score well or poorly on a particular assessment. What is sometimes tricky is to figure out the reasons why someone scores poorly. In most cases, it is because the person actually has trouble performing the task that the test measures, but in rare cases there is a different reason.

In an effort to find a definitive answer to that nagging question of why Sara struggled with certain tasks, I arranged for her to undergo a formal assessment. In the process, I unintentionally opened up a can of worms and exposed her to an untenable situation. Sara was one of those individuals who did poorly on an important test for reasons that were difficult to discern. We found ourselves marooned in a place where there was only truth or falseness, and no shades of gray.

Sara's personal experience with evaluation

The year Sara turned 14, she left the imaginative world of the Waldorf school to attend a small Catholic girl's high school. She had visited many high schools the spring before her freshman year, trying each school on like a potential pair of new shoes. This school seemed to fit the best. Its small size would allow her to receive the personal attention she needed. In addition, the school's simple layout would make it possible for her to find her way to classes with a minimal amount of practice. Sara felt welcomed by the teachers and other girls. I remember picking her up inside the vestibule of the building after her first visit. She smiled brightly as we walked down the sidewalk towards the car. "This is it, Mom," she said. "I can do this."

To gain admittance to this high school, she would be required to take an entrance exam. Because her unusual elementary school did not value psychometrics, it would be only the third achievement test she had ever taken. We went to the bookstore and bought *Mastering the Catholic School Entrance Exam*. Every afternoon as fall darkened into winter, Sara practiced answering questions from the manual, learning about the importance of number 2 pencils and how to fill in tiny circles with just the right amount of shading. We found out she did well on this third foray into the world of psychometrics in a letter the Catholic school sent her. *Dear Sara, we are pleased to inform you…of your acceptance into T.'s Freshman Honors (pre-International Baccalaureate) program…* We were then admonished to take the time to consider how truly challenging the International Baccalaureate (IB) program was going to be, an academic dragon that was designed to slay even very smart girls. *Send us your first-born. Enter the lion's den.* If we were sure that our daughter was up to the challenge, we were told to send in money by a certain date.

We were not sure at all, so my husband and I made an appointment to meet with the principal and several other members of the school's staff to try to explain that although Sara was bright and capable in many ways, she also had challenges. Since our family is Jewish, we also figured that while we had the attention of the school personnel we would inquire about how they thought a non-Christian would fair in their midst. The principal was enthusiastic about the opportunity to have a Jewish student attend the school. She promised to respect Sara's religious perspective. Two Muslims and a Buddhist were already enrolled at the school, she told us. She was not as enthusiastic about the prospect of enrolling a student with a learning disability. The school preferred not to accept students with learning disabilities, she explained. The staff was not in a position to allow any accommodations, nor could they offer any special help to students enrolled in the International Baccalaureate program. However, the principal pointed out that the results of the entrance exam indicated Sara should be successful in the IB program. "Why don't you let her try it?" she advised. "If the program turns out to be too challenging for her, she can drop down into our much less taxing regular college preparatory program."

So we decided to take the principal's advice even though she understood little about Sara's challenges. I took her to be measured for a plaid skirt and a red sweater, and Sara began the International Baccalaureate program. If the principal and her teachers knew little about NLD, I was just as ignorant about the rigors of IB. That first day when we stood in line waiting for our turn to be measured by the kind Irish woman who would supply the school uniforms, I had no idea about the intensity of remediation I would be required to develop in order to help my daughter get through the next four years. "You don't have to do this," I would say every year for the next four years. "I want to," Sara would always tell me, "as long as you can show me how." She didnt care how hard it was if I could weave a safety net and show what to do to get out of this forest.

By the beginning of tenth grade, her hard work was paying off. She was doing well despite her struggles with math and science. Her life revolved around mastering the academic demands placed on her. She studied all the time, sometimes six or seven hours a night. Luckily, the structure of the IB program also gave her opportunities to have meaningful social experiences, so she was gaining social acumen as well as academic understanding. She still needed extensive assistance in order to master geometry and chemistry, but she was functioning with considerable independence in literature and Spanish. I was so consumed by the challenge of developing ways to help her "find her way out of the forest" that I didn't even realize how well she was doing academically until I received her first quarter report card in the mail. In the fall of tenth grade, she was ranked seventh in her high school class of 200.

It was ironic that the results of a test allowed Sara to participate in this difficult academic program. Sara's testing history was unusual. She had little experience taking the norm-referenced achievement tests like the Terra Novas or the Iowa Test of Basic Skills that are ubiquitous in American schools. She had taken the Iowa's once in the sixth grade and again in seventh grade because many of her fellow students at the Waldorf school planned to attend public magnet high schools where they were required to submit scores from this assessment. Her class had practiced taking model test questions to get ready for the actual exam.

But Sara's testing history was particularly unusual for a 14-year-old child with a learning disability because she had never taken an IQ test. She had taken only two batteries of psychological tests—one administered by her speech pathologist and the other by a learning clinic—and neither of these test batteries had included an intelligence test. For American children with any kind of learning disorder, taking an intelligence test is a rite of passage, the most characteristic way to obtain a diagnosis, acquire an IEP, or receive the standard accommodation of extra time for exams. By the time most children with any form of LD enter high school, they usually have accumulated a thick file of evaluations, a set of purported psychological fingerprints, written by psychologists, neurologists, educators, and assorted therapists. In contrast, Sara's file was thin and anemic, containing only the tiny allotment of tests needed to procure the outside help we had sought to supplement our own remedial program. Sara had never taken an IQ test because I had been able to develop effective ways to help her learn through careful observation and research. When I did not have the expertise to help her, I sought out other professionals to fill in the gaps. For example, a speech therapist helped her overcome an articulation disorder and later helped with pragmatic language. Her speech therapist did not need to know her intelligence in order to help her with these tasks, and neither did the Lindamood-Bell Clinic, where she studied reading comprehension, semantic language, and visual-motor processing for several hours a day during one summer. Most children with learning disabilities take an IQ test because it is an established part of the process they need to undergo to receive a label that qualifies them legally for special education services in a public school. Since Sara did not attend a public school, the information an intelligence test would have yielded did not have any practical advantages, so I never had her take one.

In addition, the idea of Sara taking an intelligence test made me uneasy. She was clearly intelligent, so there was no rational explanation for my apprehension. However, some intuitive sixth sense advised me not to muddy the water for her, now that all was going so well. Perhaps I was not able to quiet those vague misgivings because my experience with professionals had not been particularly positive. It was difficult to forget her early school experiences before I began to translate the observations of the invisible baby book into action. Certainly, our family had been fortunate to find several professionals who took our concerns about Sara's learning seriously. These individuals were supportive of my efforts to assist my daughter because they saw first-hand how the work I did with Sara augmented her learning and furthered her independence. They also understood that I only devoted so much time to helping her because I had looked for outside assistance and could find very little constructive help for her. However, as I recalled the many conversations I had with educators and psychologists over the years, the general consensus was that it was inappropriate, even damaging, for a parent to teach her own child. *Perhaps this is true in many cases, I would say in my defense. But for us, things seem to be working out. She is so happy and successful because of the extra work we have undertaken. Yes, yes, they would smile and then drop eye contact. I was deluded and overprotective. I had unrealistic expectations and cared too much about academic achievement. Sara would soon burn out. I lacked proof that she even had any difficulties. The evidence gleaned by my own senses was not enough.*

However when Sara turned 14, I decided it was time to beef up her records. In a year, she would need to take the SATs for the first time and, in order to qualify for the extra time that would be her legal right if she were identified as a student with a disability, she would need her difficulties measured, quantified, and distilled into clinical language. With trepidation, I made the appointment to have Sara tested. Because she had such an unusual mind, I worried about how she would interpret some of the curious tasks she would be asked to undertake. However, I considered how well she had been able to function in a rigorous academic program, and this knowledge gave me courage. In addition, the diagnostician with whom I arranged to administer the necessary tests was someone I knew and trusted. She was eminently qualified to administer the measures that Sara would soon receive. She supported our "home" intervention program and understood why Sara had attended unusual schools. She wisely pointed out that there was no need to reveal in the body of the written report the controversial fact that I had overseen most of Sara's remedial work. The diagnostician would simply write, *Sara's parents engaged her in intensive therapy over the years, making significant progress,* and list the details of the interventions. I quieted my worries and convinced myself that the results of the evaluation could only mirror what I already knew—that Sara was a very intelligent child with an unusual learning profile.

So I felt few misgivings on a lovely morning in October when I drove Sara to the first of her three appointments. We drove for an hour. "Tell me again about these tests?" Sara asked. "You have to go three times, today and the next two Saturdays," I replied. "Will they be hard?" "Not hard, but sometimes strange, with pictures and puzzles. More like the tests you took at Lindamood-Bell." "Tell me again how these tests are going to help me?" she wanted to know. I left her at the office of the diagnostician. I said goodbye, good luck.

Six week later, I received a thick manila envelope in the mail. The report was ponderous—almost 20 pages. Its purpose was to capture Sara's mind in words and numbers, to describe her strengths and weaknesses, to measure her mental powers, and to chart an educational course for her future. The centerpiece was the Wechsler Intelligence Scale for Children – third edition (WISC-III), a measure that is widely regarded by psychologists as both reliable and valid. Reliability means that if you complete this assessment instrument when you are ten and then again when you are fourteen, you should receive about the same score both times. Intelligence then is not like money. If you work hard, you can't make more.

The assessment is valid because psychologists believe intelligence is tangible and that the assessment instrument accurately measures this tangible concept. They believe an intelligence test is a good predictor of academic and job success because it primarily measures an individual's academic learning, the ability to acquire knowledge by reading books and absorbing facts. The questions ferret out what you know about things outside your typical everyday experiences. They have only one correct solution, and allow only one way to arrive at this solution. People who have a knack for answering these kinds of questions typically get "As." They can learn how to practice law and medicine; they rise to the top.

The WISC-III, the edition of the assessment administered to Sara, consists of two portions—the verbal section and the performance (nonverbal) section. Both of these sections contain five distinct subtests. The verbal subtests ask individuals to demonstrate their verbal comprehension ability by showing how much general knowledge they have about the world and social situations, and if they understand why two concepts are alike. The performance section requires individuals to interpret nonverbal stimuli such as pictures, mazes and puzzles, and to demonstrate their nonverbal problem-solving ability. The child receives a separate numerical score for the verbal and performance sections of the assessment. These separate scores are then averaged together to calculate a child's full-scale IQ. If a child receives a score of 100 on either the verbal or performance section or for her full scale IQ, she is exactly in the middle range, which means half of all children will score better than she did, and half will receive lower scores.

Children with NLD typically score higher on the verbal portion of the WISC-III than on the performance section. Although it is not unusual for individuals with typical learning profiles to exhibit small differences in the scores they receive on the two portions of the assessment, it is unusual to have very large differences. Some children with severe NLD have significant differences, as much as 50 to 75 points, in the scores they receive on the two portions of the assessment. For example, in an extreme case, a child with NLD can have a verbal IQ of 130 (superior range) and a performance IQ of only 50. Other children with severe NLD have average verbal ability but very low ability to answer the questions on the performance portion. When this happens, the individual is left trying to function with an uncomfortable imbalance of abilities. They are like a chair with two very long legs and two very short legs.

Intelligence tests have recognized flaws. For example, they are not considered to be reliable for children under the age of seven. Also, if children who were not exposed to reading materials or rich oral language during early childhood are placed in "enriching" programs, their IQ scores sometimes go up ten points or so. The test does not pretend to measure how well a creative individual can form new and original thoughts or ideas, nor does it gauge one's inner drive and tenacity. In addition, the assessment is poor at measuring the kind of practical intelligence individuals need to figure out solutions to everyday problems like how to retrieve the keys you accidentally locked in your car. However, for the most part, IQ tests are considered objective soothsayers. As I would repeatedly be told over the next decade, *the test doesn't lie.*

I was standing by the front door when I opened the manila envelope. It arrived on a Saturday. It was still autumn. Sara was upstairs in her room reading *Moby Dick* for the second time. I consider myself an intelligent person, and it has always been my understanding that if something doesn't lie to you, it will tell you the truth, and this truth should mirror reality. I opened the envelope and began to read about the girl who was upstairs in her bedroom reading such a difficult novel.

The intelligence criterion for establishing mental retardation has changed over time. Today most authorities claim that an individual has mental retardation if their IQ is less than 70–75. While Sara sat in her bedroom reading *Moby Dick*, I read about how she must be a delusion, a fantasy daughter. Her IQ hovered only a few points above the cutoff separating the wheat from the chaff—the border that separated the so-called dull from the rest of us.

I could not reconcile this information with what I knew about my daughter. I remembered teaching her how to read when she was seven. I had decided to learn a new complicated reading method to try with Sara because she was not learning successfully when I used other approaches. We had waited by the window, watching a brown delivery truck make its twice-daily route down our street. "When will it get here?" Sara asked. "It is coming in a big box from Texas. The brown truck will bring it," I reply. "Do you think it will really help me?" she inquires. I cannot know for sure. Several days later when the UPS man walked up to our door with a large package, she saw him as he got out of the truck. "It's here," she shouted. We unpacked the carton and looked at its ponderous manuals.

Months later we were working on an exercise from the box. Our work was going well, and we quickly finished what I had prepared for the day. "Let's do more," Sara said. "I do not know how to do the next step. I need to read more from the manual and figure it out," I told her. She decided to go and play for a while with her brother John. She instructed me to call her when I was ready to do the next step. The afternoon darkened into dusk. My children had become absorbed in their play. Toy figurines were arranged in elaborate scenes on the stairway. I heard laughter. Through the corner of my eye, I saw them race by dressed in costumes. They had traveled to an enchanted realm, and I did not want to call Sara back to the dominion of her labors. However, I remembered how she returned of her own accord, her long hair in disarray, her cheeks flushed, propelled by her own sense of personal purpose. "Weren't we supposed to get back to work, Mom? Have you figured out what to do next?" We worked another hour. Her brother, dressed as a knight, waited on the stairway for his lady. My daughter had become adept at this journey. She had learned how to integrate labor into childhood.

The report in the manila envelope does not dispute that Sara has been successful. I call my friend, the diagnostician, and ask her how it is possible for a child who is flourishing in such a difficult academic program like the IB program to have so little of what we measure and define as intelligence. I tell her there is something wrong with this picture—something doesn't add up. She has an explanation. The reason Sara is so successful is due to all the extra work we have done. I acknowledge that the interventions in which Sara has been involved have helped her mightily, but I am not a miracle worker. Sara could not have progressed as far as she has without my assistance, but at the same time, I could not have helped her as much as I did unless I was working with rich raw material. My friend stands by her report and the validity of her measures. Tests are objective, and apparently they leave no room for questions about incongruity, for reality checks, for doubt, for common sense. My friend congratulates me on how much a family can accomplish.

I put the report in a drawer. I do not tell Sara about the message of the report. She is 14 years old and spends all her time on self-improvement. She does not need the extra burden of integrating the concept of *absurdity* into her self-image. I do not send the report to the College Board. Sara takes the SATs with the same time constraints as everyone else. She does fine, but not as well as expected. In school, she does incredibly well for a girl who, according to the assessment results, is not terribly bright. She graduates second in her class and receives her IB diploma by taking many difficult exams. She gets the highest score possible on her history and English exams.

I learn that the test that never lies also spreads rumors. When Sara appears again at breakfast with her shoes on the wrong feet, when she struggles with the can opener, I worry that the test is correct and that I am wrong. I watch it plant a tiny seed of doubt in my mind every time Sara struggles with the tasks of everyday life. I worry that I am pushing her too hard. I do not believe the gist of the report, but I cannot totally dismiss its results until I can figure out a rational way to explain the parts that make no sense to me. If the report can cause me occasionally to doubt my daughter's intelligence, then I recognize it has the power to do this to others who know her less well. When Sara leaves for college, she does not take the report with her. She will try to tackle the demands of college without the benefit of accommodations. She reasons that she was able to function well in high school without any extra help from her teachers. Yes, this is true, I concur. Then I consider the daily assistance she has received at home for so many years—how the work we do is so seamlessly intertwined into the fabric of our lives she does not even recognize it as support. I believe it is possible that this work will give her the power to tackle her processing and perceptual challenges independently, but I am not convinced that she will be able to work as quickly as college will require.

Sara has been away at school for almost two months when she calls me frantically. She needs the report, she says. She cannot function without extra time. She took her first exam in Freshman Studies, a great books course, where students are required to read classic literature such as works by Plato, Shakespeare, and Faulkner. The exam consisted of three essay questions on the Plato readings. Sara tells me she had time to complete only the first essay and part of the second. The instructor liked what she wrote so much that he took off no points for her completed work. However, she received a "C" for her overall grade because she completed only half of the required questions. She has a scholarship that she can only keep if she maintains a certain grade point average. She is afraid she will lose her scholarship at this rate; English is her best subject and if she cannot get a good grade in this class, what will happen to her in other classes that are more challenging for her?

I call my friend the diagnostician. We come to an agreement. She agrees to modify the report by omitting all the incriminating numbers that point to my daughter's feeble mental powers. I re-read the cryptic words of the new document, which only reveal Sara was administered the WISC-III. The report discusses how some tasks on the WISC-III were difficult for her relative to other tasks, but these observations are not backed up with the currency of numbers. Although the report is over 20 pages, Sara's mind is shrouded in the obscurity of verbiage. The test that never lies has been reduced to the test that prevaricates, and it is this incomplete document that I mail to Sara. After she delivers it to the appropriate office at her college, she can begin to take her exams with extra time. A representative from the learning disabilities office calls Sara and asks if she would like another student to take notes for her. She declines; she wants only the extra minutes to do all the work.

It is snowing the next time she takes another essay test for her great books course. This time the essays she needs to develop interpret the words of an ancient Chinese philosopher. She writes late into the afternoon. The other students leave their blue books on the wooden desk of the instructor. She watches them sled down the hill outside the classroom on cafeteria trays. "It was hard to watch," she tells me later. "I missed the first snow." It is dark when Sara leaves her exam book in the professor's mailbox. He returns them graded a few weeks later. Sara is rejuvenated when she receives an "A."

Time passes, and Sara is in graduate school. The words of the report are only good for five years. Soon she will need another report if she wants to continue to receive extra time to complete the timed examinations that she needs to pass. When I attend conferences on learning disabilities, I go to further my professional knowledge, but I also have a private reason. I am on a pilgrimage, a quest to discover someone who can illuminate the inexplicable results of my daughter's report. When I attend sessions on NLD, I feel as if I am secretly auditioning psychologists. I hang on their every word, searching for some kind of logical explanation for Sara's diagnostic experience. I ask questions about the reliability of intelligence tests. I learn that one of the sacred bedrocks on which psychologists base their thinking is the belief that there is a social construct called intelligence. They also believe that their training gives them access to infallibly calibrated measures by which it is possible to calculate the degree of brilliance that shines in each of us. By October of Sara's first year in graduate school, the five good years of her report have almost run out and if she doesn't file a new one soon she will forfeit her right to extra time. She calls me from Boston. "Should I find someone here to do the tests?" she wants to know. "My work is really hard. I couldn't do it without extra time. I am getting nervous." I assure her that I have everything under control and that I will contact someone shortly to whom she can go for new testing. In reality, I do not feel comfortable about any of the diagnosticians with whom I have spoken about Sara's situation.

A few weeks later, I attend a conference about nonverbal learning disabilities. One of the most respected experts on NLD is speaking in the morning; another less well-known individual is scheduled to speak on NLD in the afternoon. I am required to attend these lectures to fulfill the requirements of a graduate course. As I drive to the conference, I intend to stay only for the morning session to hear the expert speak. I am too busy to give up a whole day to hear information I already know.

It is fortunate I decide to stay to hear both speakers because I receive two gifts that day. As I listen to the first speaker describe how individuals with NLD process novelty, I am able for the first time to extrapolate a reasonable explanation for why Sara's score was so inexplicably low the first time she took an IQ test. Suddenly not a modicum of doubt remains in my mind that her intelligence is rock solid and her accomplishments are clear manifestations of this aptitude. I am so exhilarated by this flash of insight that I decide to stay for the second half of the program. My decision is rewarded because 15 minutes into the afternoon session, I have discovered someone who really understands the complexity of NLD and who can possibly liberate Sara from the judgment of the test.

Later that evening, I send an email to the psychologist who I believe can help us. He writes back the next day and asks me to phone and give him more information about Sara. After I have described Sara's academic accomplishments and contrast them to her inexplicable scores on the IQ test, the voice on the other end of the telephone utters the words that I had waited five years to hear, "But that is ridiculous."

A few weeks later, my husband flies to Boston and drives Sara to another New England state where the psychologist lives. This time I decide to give Sara a little information about the fateful test she is about to take. Since I am not a psychologist, I do not have access to any actual IQ tests. Although I have read many psychoeducational reports that have included a student's IQ scores, I have never seen an authentic intelligence test, nor am

I familiar with any actual questions which appear on them. However, I know from my work how to interpret the results of these measures in order to design effective remedial interventions for individuals like Sara.

So I decide to design an "IQ test overview." Of course, I am unable to give examples of any specific questions and would not want in any case to provide information that could give her an unfair advantage or might be construed as cheating. So I only attempt to familiarize her with the design and format of the assessment. I want simply to neutralize the novelty of the tasks she will soon be called on to perform. I phone her in Boston and tell her about the verbal and performance sections, about what each subtest is trying to measure, and which subtests will be timed. I remind her to scan the entire picture for any question that requires her to interpret a drawing or diagram and not just to focus on one part.

The results of this evaluation arrive in a manila envelope the day after Thanksgiving. Sara will receive her own copy at her apartment in Boston several days later. I take the envelope into a room and shut the door. It is several minutes before I can will myself to tear open the flap of the envelope and take out the yellow paper. My hands shake as I read how in the nine years that elapsed since the first evaluation, my daughter has apparently undergone a transformation. She still has the huge point spread between her verbal and performance IQ, typical for individuals with NLD, in Sara's case over 50 points; but this time, her verbal intelligence is estimated to be so high that only 1 percent of the population has more. I look into the mirror of this report, and it is no longer the distorted funhouse mirror of the former report. This report mirrors the reality of my daughter's mind—that Sara is a very bright person with a problem and that this problem is called a nonverbal learning disability. It is a Thanksgiving filled with thanks—*I thank you for these pronouncements, for these words, thank you.*

A possible explanation: The role of novelty in comprehension

I will never know for certain why Sara scored so poorly on the first IQ test. However, I believe the difficulty Sara has always had dealing with novel situations, questions, and ideas greatly interfered with her ability to answer accurately the questions posed on the test. Unlike other tests she had taken prior to the first IQ test, Sara received no explanation that would have prepared her for the unusual nature and purpose of some of the test questions. For Sara, explanations and practice are effective ways to neutralize the "newness" of an unusual experience or an original idea.

It is important to understand that the difficulty individuals with NLD have with novelty is more complex than simply being uncomfortable when faced with new experiences, such as going to a party or changing schools. Certainly these individuals have difficulties when they encounter uncommon social situations or changes in their routine. But children with NLD also have great difficulty processing new intellectual material. They struggle with familiar academic material when it is presented in unexpected ways. For example, one of the reasons these students find it difficult to understand what they read in depth is because they struggle to transform previously mastered information into new original thoughts. They have great difficulty forming generalizations, making inferences, or drawing new conclusions. They do not have a knack for molding the words on the page into brand new hypotheses or forming concepts when faced with surprising ideas. Original thought is new and startling. Consequently, they try to compensate for these difficulties by relying on rote learning and memory.

As Sara learned how to read and comprehend complex material more successfully, she simultaneously improved her ability to contend with original ideas. However, she still struggled to demonstrate her understanding of a concept when she was confronted with a new situation like an exam with an unfamiliar format. Throughout high school, college, and graduate school, Sara learned to use practice and preparation as an antidote to novelty, particularly when preparing for examinations. As long as she had the opportunity to understand the purpose of the test and to experience some prototypical items, she tended to score well.

Sara found she needed to undergo more preparation than a typical student if she wanted to make sure she scored well on an exam. She needed extensive preparation not only for standardized exams but also for the more everyday tests she experienced as part of her high school and college courses. For example when typical learners study for a test, they make sure they have a thorough grasp of the material the test will cover, such as the reasons for the civil war. If they have a thorough knowledge and understanding of the required material, they expect to perform well on a fair exam. Sara needed to have the same systematic command of the test material as anyone else. However, she required a "test overview" and the chance to practice questions that followed a similar format to the actual questions that would appear on the test. Fulfilling this prerequisite is one of the reasons why Sara had to study so much longer and harder than her peers. She needed first to master the subject matter, but then she needed to study the test. Practice was how she neutralized the novelty. Invariably when she was required to take a test "cold," even when she knew the material well, she tended to score poorly. Conversely, if she had the opportunity to practice model test questions in addition to acquiring a command of the subject matter, she almost always scored exceptionally well.

It is important to understand that Sara did not need to practice identical test questions to those that would appear on the test, or even questions about the topic the exam covered. First, she needed knowledge about the topic. For example if she was taking an exam on the causes of World War II, she would first learn all the historical information pertaining to the topic. Because she has such a remarkable rote memory, she frequently would simply memorize massive amounts of factual material about battles, generals, and dates. Next, she would find out information about how the test would be constructed, such as the number of multiple-choice questions and how many required essays there would be. She would then write all the information about World War II she had memorized on cards, and would manipulate this material in her mind to figure out which information was most important and why. She would classify the information into categories and ask herself questions about how to form generalizations and inferences. After she had a good grasp of the "big picture," she would then start to imagine which parts of this information would make good multiple-choice questions or topics for essay questions. She would frequently make up her own prototypical questions and practice answering them. When she was young, I would assist her with this process. However, as she matured, she was able to accomplish her preparation independently.

Some of the standardized exams Sara experienced throughout her school career allowed her to "prepare" by taking practice tests that contained questions similar to the ones she would face on the "real" test. In this way, she could take a test and experience few unexpected questions. For example, she spent one to three hours a day for six weeks preparing for the Catholic school entrance exam when she was in the eighth grade. She prepared extensively for the SATs and for her six IB exams. When she was 22, she devoted several months to carefully familiarizing herself with the format of the Graduate Record Exam, a standardized entrance exam required for admittance to some graduate programs. She received average to very high scores on all these tests.

Perhaps most students would perform better if they practiced as diligently as Sara did. However, most students, as long as they have a reasonable grasp of the required material, would probably not fail an exam simply because they lacked knowledge about the kind of questions that would appear on the exam paper. More typical learners still score close to a true reflection of their ability without this kind of information. Sara, on the other hand, cannot function well in a testing situation without this kind of knowledge.

It is probable that the first time Sara was administered the WISC-III, she was overwhelmed by the novel format and questions on the assessment instrument. It is true that she was eight years older the second time she took an IQ test. Certainly, it is possible that maturity increased her ability to function more successfully in a testing situation. Second, she took a different version of the Wechsler Intelligence Scale during each of the testing situations. The first time she was administered the WISC-III, a version of the Wechsler test that is designed for children. The second time she was given the WAIS-III, the Wechsler Adult Intelligence Scale. Finally, different diagnosticians administered the tests on each occasion. Perhaps the second diagnostician was more skilled than the first tester, or Sara for some reason felt more comfortable with the second psychologist.

Although any of these circumstances might have negatively impacted Sara's ability to function in the first testing situation, I do not feel they are compelling enough reasons to explain fully why her IQ score increased so radically the second time. If she was so swayed by these kinds of environmental factors, I feel she would not have been able to score well in other testing situations where she experienced similar stresses. For example, she was only 13 when she took the Catholic school entrance exam. The test was administered by proctors in a large room in an unfamiliar school to more than 100 students, none of whom Sara knew. At the time of this experience, she had only taken two other standardized tests, neither of which was machine scored, so this testing experience was the first time she needed to fill in an electronic answer sheet. In addition, the two other times she took a standardized test, she took them in her classroom at the Waldorf school with familiar classmates and teacher. She actually scored higher on the Catholic school entrance exam where the testing environment was more "novel" than at the Waldorf school. The difference between the two testing experiences was that Sara prepared more thoroughly for the Catholic school entrance exam. She was cognizant of the format of the exam and the types of questions she would need to answer. She knew that she would have to write a short persuasive essay. Four years later, she took a series of extremely rigorous exams in order to qualify for her IB diploma. The seven exams that Sara was required to take each lasted from two to four hours. Many of the questions required the examinee to write extended essays. The math exams did not contain multiple-choice questions, but instead required the students to show the actual mathematical steps they took to arrive at a particular solution. Sample IB tests were not available to Sara, but her school was conscientious in making certain that students were well versed in the types of questions that would appear on the test. For example, Sara knew which of the novels they had studied that year would appear in questions on her English exam. She knew that the questions on her history exam would concentrate on the Cold War. She understood the purpose of the exam, how long the test would take, and its general format. She also had many opportunities in the months before taking a particular IB exam to practice answering questions and writing essays that were similar to the ones she would be required to complete during the exam. So when she sat for these high-pressure exams, she was not troubled emotionally by the stress of taking such complex and lengthy tests because she knew what kinds of questions she would be asked to answer. She received the highest score possible on her history exam and the lowest passing score on her biology exam.

Generally, the diagnostic process is better at ferreting out an accurate picture of an individual's intellectual strengths and weaknesses than it did in Sara's case. However, I sometimes wonder what Sara's life would be like today if I had believed the results of the first report. Even more tragically, what if she had received an IQ test at an earlier age when she was even less adept at dealing with novel ideas. Almost certainly, any score she received at a young age would have been incredibly low. Would I have been more inclined to accept unquestionably the results of such a report before I had personally helped her mine her "diamond in the rough" abilities and seen her steely determination cut through every difficult task set before her? Would I have made different educational choices for her?

I believe that the diagnostic process has limitations, and that children with learning disabilities would be better off if these limitations were recognized. It seems to me that a diagnostic report should always mirror reality and when it does not, as in the case of my daughter, it is the duty of the clinician to figure out why. The reason I did not have Sara retested immediately after we received the first report was because I found it difficult to find a psychologist who could offer a reasonable hypothesis to explain the incongruity of Sara's experience. I was told repeatedly that psychoeducational tests were objective measures that do not lie. No one I questioned felt there were any unique aspects of nonverbal learning disability that could possibly skew the results of an IQ test. I needed at least a hypothesis about why Sara might have had so much difficulty the first time. I probably would not have ever bothered to have her tested again except that she so desperately needed to be granted extra time on examinations in graduate school in order to complete her studies.

I also waited so long to have her retested because I was afraid the results could possibly shake Sara's confidence in her abilities. I felt justified in not revealing the results of the first report to her because she was a minor when the report was written. As she got older, I realized she would ask about the results of any new report—she would read the words that could possibly cause her to question her own intelligence. The power of the test is indeed great. I knew that if it could shake my own confidence in her abilities, it could easily do the same for her. After all, individuals with NLD are very trusting; they believe in the power of authority and in the literal truth of what they read.

After we received the second report, I let Sara read the original one. In the end, it served as a meaningful learning experience for her. Ironically, she studied the format of intelligence tests in her graduate program shortly after she took the second test. Based on her own experience, she understands that tests are useful tools but have limitations. This insight is valuable for someone who is entering a profession where she will need to administer tests and interpret psychoeducational reports. But most of all, her experience has endowed her with a rare empathy for others. She knows that sometimes it is essential to look below the surface and that the truth is not always obvious. She knows firsthand how unexpected and startling the results of remediation can be. She has been there.

Chapter 6

The Importance of the School Environment

A picture of a model school

Most children with NLD attend public schools. One reason many families choose public school for their child is financial. Children with NLD frequently require extra educational services such as speech and occupational therapy as well as special education. Since the cost of private services is high, many families feel that the public school supplies the environment where their child can receive the most outside help and therapy without putting the family under financial stress. They believe they can best serve the needs of their child by working to modify the educational environment to ensure that his or her needs are met. Many families also prefer public schools because they feel their child can benefit socially from attending school with familiar neighborhood children and siblings. In addition, public schools, particularly elementary schools, are frequently located in close proximity to the student's home, making it easier for the child to learn to navigate.

However, some families find it difficult to meet the needs of their child at public school because the challenges of NLD are so different from those faced by the majority of the other children who qualify for special education. Families may find that most school special education programs are designed to cater to the needs of this larger population, particularly students with reading disabilities. In addition many of the needs of the student with NLD are environmental. For example, children with NLD function better in small, structured environments with a limited number of teachers. Parents may find meeting the needs of their child with NLD particularly challenging during middle school and especially high school when the sheer size of most public schools, the number of teachers with whom the child comes into contact each day, and the changing of classes become an overwhelming experience. As a result, some families choose public school for the elementary years, but a private school for the high school years.

No matter what arrangement you choose for your child, it is important to keep in mind that an ideal school for children with NLD should meet their unique social, emotional, and academic needs. An ideal school should also be committed not only to accommodating their learning style but also to furthering their social development by designing rewarding social opportunities for them, furthering their cognitive development through language, and encouraging them to become independent by teaching them how to find their way around and how to master the physical demands of their environment such as opening doors. For example, an ideal school would do more than supply an aide who leads students with NLD from class to class. A model school would also be committed to teaching students how eventually to accomplish this task independently by supportively talking them through their school journey, and giving them adequate opportunities for supervised practice. In addition, the staff of an ideal school would be committed to understanding the unique profile of this kind of learner and the importance language plays as a conduit for learning.

The importance of the school environment

I feel that there were four main reasons why Sara has been able to overcome many of the challenges presented by NLD. First, she received many educational interventions starting at an early age. Because these interventions successfully taught her how to write, think mathematically, and function socially she never experienced the kind of failure that is common for students with NLD. The second reason for her success is that both the schools she attended and our family carefully cultivated her language development and taught her how to connect what she said with what she saw. The third reason is that she grew up in a supportive family. The final reason is that she attended schools that furthered her development.

I learned how important the school environment is to children with NLD by the educational mistakes I made. Sara had two negative school placements. Interestingly, both of these were lovely schools with stellar reputations in our community. As a matter of fact, they both had a long waiting list of families who hoped their children would gain admittance. When Sara was accepted at the first school she ever attended, other parents were envious at our good fortune. However, her experience at this pre-school was negative enough to be described as damaging. Sara attended this school for three long years. I did not yet have the confidence simply to remove her from an educational environment that was clearly not working for her. I needed to learn the hard way that a good school for Sara was not necessarily the high status school with the best reputation, the most beautiful building or the richest academic program. I have many photographs of Sara at the high-powered school. In each photograph, she looks deeply out of place, like a deer caught in the headlights. The camera captures the habitual vacant expression she donned each time she walked through the school door. After Sara left this preschool, she attended a less coveted pre-school with dark basement classrooms and a program that emphasized play and socialization. She was transformed there, and a photograph of her at this school reveals a smiling relaxed girl holding hands with her teacher and another child. Her first school was a good school in the abstract, but it was a bad school for her. By observing the differences between the two schools, I began to understand what Sara required. I also realized how much her psychological safety depended on the school environment meeting certain criteria. She, like most people with NLD, simply did not have the ability to adapt easily to environments that were not supportive of her challenges. As a result, she could not learn well in those places. I found that I learned the most about Sara's needs when she was in schools where they were not met. For example, Sara left the Waldorf school in the sixth grade to try out a private school located nearer to our home. However, she returned to the Waldorf school a year later when the new school proved to be too socially difficult for her to navigate.

A picture of a model school for children with NLD

When Sara was ready for first grade, I spent many months looking for an appropriate school for her. I remember spending one morning sitting next to a life-size statue of the Virgin Mary, while I observed a small alternative

parochial school where all six grades worked in one room. I talked to officials at our local public school and even had Sara undergo some evaluations
and speech therapy there. Because she had a happy experience at her
Lutheran preschool, I took her kindergarten teacher's advice and considered a local Lutheran school where they only agreed to let Sara enroll in
their program if she repeated kindergarten. If you had asked Sara what she
wanted from a school, she would have told you that she wanted a nice
school, a place where she could be happy. She would particularly like to
learn how to read. She would go to any school, she told me, except one like
her first school, where she could not find anything and the kids were mean
to her. "I trust you, Mom," she said to me when I returned from observing
yet another elementary school. "I know you will find a great school for
me."

I wasn't quite as confident and was beginning to doubt that I would
ever find a school where Sara could thrive. By the spring of kindergarten, I
had narrowed her choices down to two schools—our local public school
and the Lutheran elementary school. Our local public school had many
advantages. It was right across the street from our house, and I liked the
idea of Sara making friends with children in our neighborhood. If she
went to public school, there would be no extra tuition, and she would not
have to travel far. However, our local public school seemed rigid. When I
spoke with the principal, she told me that they had a number of special
education programs designed to meet the needs of children, and Sara
could attend one of them. When I mentioned that I had understood special
education was intended to give each child individually what was needed,
she told me they wouldn't deviate from their programs. When I showed
her some samples of Sara's writing and tried to explain to her how much
she had improved when we used certain techniques, the principal made it
clear that she didn't think it was a very good idea for me to help Sara with
learning.

Since I wasn't ready to give up on the idea of public school, I decided
to let Sara start speech therapy there for her articulation disorder. By doing
this, I was hoping to give Sara a trial run and to have an opportunity to
evaluate how well this school could help my daughter. At this time, she still
attended her private kindergarten. I took her to the public school across
the street from our house where she took a number of tests to see if she
qualified for speech therapy. Since her ability to speak clearly was quite

poor, she easily qualified, and the school speech-language pathologist scheduled her for one 30-minute session a week. As we made the short walk from our house to the school to attend the first session, Sara ran ahead of her brother and me. When I told her that there were teachers who had special training to teach kids how to speak clearly, she became very excited. "Let's go right now," she said. The school speech-language therapist was a kind man who met us in the corridor as we entered the school. He took Sara by the hand and told us to wait in his office while he collected the other children in the group. Twenty minutes later, he returned with a group of four other children and told us to come back to get Sara in a half hour. When we returned later, he told us that Sara's problem was indeed severe. "Had we considered private speech therapy in addition to this?" he inquired. "I cannot give her the time she needs," he continued. "I have too many children to work with." Sara was the only child in the group of five children with a severe articulation disorder. One of the other children had very mild articulation issues, one had autism and the other two had various language issues. In addition, it took the teacher so long to collect all the children from their classrooms that there usually was only ten minutes remaining for instructional time. As I listened to the teacher explain the situation, I realized that under these conditions Sara would be a very old woman before her speech would be clear enough for anyone to understand well. She needed more intense help that was individually geared to her problem. Sara only attended two sessions of speech therapy at our neighborhood school before I enrolled her in individual private therapy. Three years later, after undergoing 312 hours of well-conceived therapy, Sara stepped onto the stage at her school to play the role of a Norse princess and also to make her debut as an articulate individual.

Finding the Waldorf school

There was nothing convenient about the Waldorf school; it was located an hour from our house in the middle of an industrial stretch of road in the nearby city. However, when a friend called and asked if I wanted to go to an orientation session, I went because I had visited every other school in the area close to our home, and each one seemed like a place where other children, not Sara, could thrive.

The building where the Waldorf school was housed looked like something from a Dickens novel—an old decrepit brick building with a heavy

THE IMPORTANCE OF THE SCHOOL ENVIRONMENT

front door that opened into a small vestibule. Directly behind the vestibule, a steep narrow staircase ascended up to a long hallway. A dozen classrooms were located along this single corridor. The floors of the classrooms, the hallways, and the stairs were all covered with a coating of dirt. Children of all ages trooped in and out of the building, their feet shod in rubber boots, their hair sparkling with tiny misty raindrops, their cheeks pink from the air. The school and the children had the slightly messy look of child's play. There appeared to be little separation between the outside world and the inside world. Children brought in sticks and collections of leaves and deposited them in corners of classrooms. Rocks and crystals were displayed on tables. The disarray of the school was magnified by the numerous art projects in progress throughout the building. Sinks were filled with glass jars containing richly hued liquid paint and large wooden paintbrushes with black bristles. Menageries of tiny animals modeled from beeswax were set out in scenes and rows. Wooden and tin boxes of vividly colored crayons were everywhere. The children themselves were boisterous and noisy, but deeply involved with each other and the tasks at hand.

This school seemed to contain many of the elements that I believed would help Sara learn and find a social place. I was at first put off by the physical condition of the building, particularly the long narrow staircase where children scampered up and down pell mell with no regard for who had the right of way. I could see Sara, who still walked up and down staircases awkwardly and retained the habit of younger children who don't alternate their feet on each step, falling and breaking her neck. When I asked a teacher if anyone had ever fallen down the stairs, she replied that only once a few years ago did someone actually fall and fracture an ankle.

I realized no school would be perfect. Despite problems with the physical plant, large class sizes, and the emphasis on motor tasks, I decided with some trepidation to send her to this school because it had so many other positive elements. In truth, I was getting desperate because I had investigated so many schools, and none seemed to be a place where Sara was going to thrive. In addition, I discovered that many private schools, including the Waldorf school, were reluctant to accept children with learning differences. In the first chapter, I described Sara's interview at the Waldorf school, and how the school was hesitant to allow her to enroll in their first grade. However, I was able to convince the school to allow Sara to enroll "on probation" when I assured them that I would either supply or make sure she privately received any "extra" remediation or therapy she might need. I don't think they ever regretted their decision for she adapted beautifully to the school.

I remember driving her to school on the first day of first grade. She sat in the back seat of the car with her brother. She was wearing a pink dress with white smocking just purchased for the occasion and a new pair of sandals. Her hair was braided into two long plaits. She was both excited and apprehensive as we made the long drive into the city. I helped her open the heavy front door of the building. She grasped the railing of the steep stairs and concentrated on making her way up, as dozens of other children swarmed around her, laughing and calling out to each other.

I will never forget her face as she descended the same steep staircase several hours later. Halfway down the stairs, she looked down at me, paused and mouthed the words, "I love it here. It is so much fun and I love the kids. It is the best school ever. It is going to be great!"

For Sara, the Waldorf school supplied many of the elements that children with NLD need in order to develop to the fullest. For example, although the school environment stressed her visual spatial challenges, it supplied the high level of consistency that she needed. She had the same teacher for eight years. The children in her class in first grade stayed with her for all eight grades. The classroom schedule was also consistent and predictable. Because the children and teacher made a commitment to stay together for so many years, much attention was given to making sure each child developed a positive social identity within the group.

The philosophy of the school held that ritual and repetition were important for all children, so each morning a child was chosen to start the day by relating what had happened in class the previous day, and then the teacher verbally relayed what activities the new day would bring. By listening to a review of the daily schedule verbally, Sara was able to develop a clear picture of what had transpired and what to expect next. In addition, each year Sara's class celebrated a series of holidays and festivals that formed a backbone of consistency to the events of the year that aided her both socially and in having a way of understanding time and space. Finally, the curriculum was highly structured and heavily language based, with an emphasis on story-telling, play acting, and learning foreign languages. In addition to emphasizing language and connecting language to art and other visual images, the curriculum was designed in a way that the children repeated a similar activity (or "block") for several weeks before moving on to a new topic. This in-depth study of one topic gave her the time and opportunity for the extensive practice she needed to master a task. All these elements, coupled with outside interventions like those contained in Chapter 10 allowed Sara to develop academically, socially, and emotionally.

What kinds of school environments best serve children with NLD?

What should parents look for when trying to find the most appropriate school? The first principle is to be open-minded and flexible, and to consider the unique needs and strengths of your child. Parents know more than anyone else about their own child. By the time your child is ready for school, you have been dealing with her unusual mind for many years and probably have developed many effective methods of helping her cope. You can use this knowledge to help evaluate a school and decide if it can provide the right environment for your child. When trying to locate a school for a child with NLD, keep in mind that you are seeking an environment that meets the needs of the whole child, not just one that supplies remediation for your child's difficulties. You want a school that recognizes your child's strengths as well as her challenges. You also want a school that does not perceive NLD as an immutable condition, but one that understands how far children with NLD can progress if given the right kind of help.

The answer is not that all children with NLD should attend a Waldorf school. It is important to keep in mind that there is never only one perfect school or program. For one thing, the quality and consistency of programs vary from school to school and even from classroom to classroom in the same school. Families also need to take into account their own personal values, financial situation, the time they can give to transport children to school, and the needs of other family members when choosing a school for their child. However, the Waldorf is an example of a school that did have certain essential elements that in conjunction with intensive private remediation allowed Sara to flourish despite having significant learning challenges. What are these essential elements that children with NLD need?

Visual-spatial elements

Because children with NLD are plagued by visual-spatial difficulties, the physical layout of a school should not compound these difficulties. A great deal of the anxiety children with NLD experience comes directly from their inability to find their way around, to keep track of their possessions, or to recognize important people and to draw conclusions based solely on visual input. These students will only learn how to deal more effectively with space if someone explains clearly in words the logic of how spaces are constructed—for example, our building has two floors; the first floor has rooms with the numbers ranging in the 100s; the "1" in the number tells us it is on the first floor, and so on. Chapter 10 contains many suggestions on how to help children with NLD improve their understanding of visual-spatial concepts. However, it is easier to learn to navigate in a simple space than in a complex one. Children with NLD in a small building with a simple layout will still need verbal instructions, but such an environment is easier to describe and easier to master. In addition, children in the earlier grades frequently can get by without much knowledge of the physical layout of the school because they usually travel in groups with the teacher. However, this situation is not ideal because these children should start early to practice and master finding their own way around so they do not fall apart in the later grades when the physical environment is even more demanding. An ideal school would meet the following conditions:

- A small building with a simple, logical layout, few floors, and few rooms on each floor.

- If the rooms have a numbering system, it should be clear and logical.

- All classes occur in one classroom or only a few.

- Few doors. Doors are confusing to children with NLD because when they enter and exit different doors they find themselves in unexpected places in the school.

- A limited number of places (lockers, desks, closets) in which to put books, coats, and so on; preferably one place to keep all books and one place to store everything else. These storage areas should be in the classroom and in close proximity to each other.

- The school should be decorated in the minimalist style. Visually busy environments are difficult for these children to process. They become exhausted and confused when asked to deal with too many visual distractions. It also takes them a long time to process unexpected auditory stimuli. It is difficult for them to judge what is visually or auditorially important and therefore needs their attention. For example, they often do not "hear" announcements on loudspeakers, or respond quickly enough to bells that indicate the end of a class period. They always respond best to verbal instruction from a caring individual.

Novelty

These children struggle with all kinds of novelty, not only new places and unfamiliar people, but also unexpected ideas and ways of thinking. Again, they need to learn how to deal more effectively with the concept of the unexpected but will only do so with careful, sensitive exposure to new situations. A school environment that emphasizes regularity and consistency is the best environment for them to learn how to deal better with unexpected circumstances. Key elements are:

- Limit the number of teachers; have one consistent main teacher.

- Small classes. If not feasible, assign the child to work with a small group of children.

- A daily schedule that varies as little as possible. For older students, semester changes are difficult because they result in a new schedule with new classes. Limit class changes as much as possible.

- A highly structured environment where students know what to expect—not an open classroom setting where students are left to make their own decisions about what they should be doing and with whom.

- A "strong" teacher who gives clear oral directions about what is required and what is expected. A teaching staff who are knowledgeable about NLD or interested in gaining that knowledge.

- Some elementary schools now have classes where students spend two to three years with the same teacher and children.

Sometimes these are mixed age groups. This arrangement has potential benefits for children with NLD.

- Commitment to preparing students with NLD for any changes in their routine (substitute teachers, field trips, change in schedules, etc.)

- Commitment to carefully exposing children to new ways of thinking about a problem, giving them opportunities to practice new concepts, and finally making sure they have opportunities to demonstrate they understand concepts through verbal expression.

Social elements

These children need richly structured social experiences carefully monitored by adults who recognize their vulnerability but also take advantage of their keen desire to understand how to function socially. Key elements are:

- An atmosphere that encourages tolerance and cooperation.

- An atmosphere that downplays competition (particularly athletic), and downplays sophistication and fashion (or requires uniforms).

- Opportunities to socialize in small groups with adult interaction.

- Experiences with play are very important, but they need help deciphering the rules of play.

- Structured social activities with a clear purpose, not hours of unstructured free play.

- Older children need assistance in finding social and extracurricular activities.

- Speech therapy for pragmatic language. Help with starting, maintaining and ending conversations, how to speak on the phone, and so on.

- No tolerance for bullying.

Language

Language is both a strength and a weakness for these children. An ideal school for them would be rich in language and also supply assistance in the areas of language where they are weak. Key elements here are:

- Commitment to using words to explain almost everything.
- Provide opportunities for students to participate in language-rich activities such as foreign language, vocabulary building, story telling, theater, and so on.
- Provide speech therapy for semantic language.

Academic

An ideal school should have the staff who can assist the students with the following academic areas as needed.

- Writing: penmanship, using a keyboard, use of technology, written expression.
- Math: learning how to line up numbers in columns, understanding number concepts, understanding geometric concepts, interpreting word problems.
- Reading comprehension and upper level thinking skills in all subject areas.
- Science.
- Geography.
- Maps, graphs, visual organizers.

An ideal preschool

Currently, few children with NLD enter preschool with their challenges recognized. However, many parents have already observed troubling differences in their child's ability to perform certain kinds of tasks and to function well in new social situations. Consequently, an ideal preschool for children with NLD will have teachers who are open-minded, flexible, and respectful of parents' observations. Since one of the ultimate goals for these children is to prevent them from falling too far behind academically and socially, it would be best if children received assistance in their weak areas before they enter middle school with many of their problems deeply entrenched and intractable. One of the unusual characteristics exhibited by individuals with NLD is their ability to master seemingly impossible tasks if they receive enough practice. However, the amount of practice they need to master a task is vast. If they do not receive this practice they will stay arrested at a very low level of development. Therefore, an ideal preschool for these children would recognize the areas in which they are struggling, have the skill to communicate effectively with parents in order to learn what kinds of techniques are working well at home, and to aid families in developing additional constructive procedures to assist their children.

Preschool is an ideal time to begin to help these students because many of their challenges—such as difficulties with fine and gross motor tasks, social conventions, interpreting pictures, and learning how to print—are areas that are usually covered in school at this age. The biggest difference between children with NLD and more typical preschool children is that they do not learn by many of the common techniques used in preschool. Children with NLD do not easily figure out how to do things by watching the teacher or other children unless these demonstrations are accompanied by language. It is almost impossible for them to work out the social rules of the classroom by mere observation. They do not learn very effectively by doing, through intuition, or by discovery. They need to attend a school that is committed to *verbally* explaining the steps of all tasks and social routines, giving them ample opportunities to practice a skill until it is mastered, and then checking to make sure they have learned the salient points by talking to them.

A comparison: Two preschools

Since both preschools attended by Sara were good environments for more typical children, what were the elements in each that either hindered or helped her learning and social development?

By the time my daughter turned six she had attended two preschools. Both schools were "good" schools. The first, a popular and well-respected Montessori school, was disastrous for her development. Here, her challenges were magnified. The second school, a traditional religious preschool and kindergarten that served as a lab school for a small college, allowed her to grow. Here, Sara's challenges associated with NLD did not hinder her ability to function as greatly as they did at the first school.

The contrast between Sara's ability to function in these two schools was striking. As I watched my daughter wither in one school and flourish in the other, I learned important principles about how to choose an effective school environment for students with NLD. I learned the hard way that the most impressive school environment is not always the best for children like my daughter. For example, I was sure Sara's first school would be a wonderful experience because it was the most impressive preschool in our area. What I saw when I looked at Sara's Montessori school was a school housed in a lovely building that was immaculate, light and welcoming. The classrooms were organized in an orderly fashion. The school had its own spacious grounds where the children could play. However, to Sara, it was a huge maze in which she could never find her way. In addition, this preschool was part of a larger private elementary school that had six grades and enrolled at least 250 students. The school perceived the preschool experience as the beginning of a child's academic life, and the curriculum emphasized independence, academic accomplishments, and cooperation among different age groups. What I saw as a rich social environment, Sara experienced as a place with too many confusing social variables for her to find a comfortable niche. I saw a school that could supply the stimulating intellectual substance from which I felt a child like Sara could benefit, but in reality, Sara could never figure out how to make sense of the academic activities or perform the tasks, such as buttoning, cutting with scissors, or using tools, that were designed to make her independent.

In contrast, the classrooms of the traditional preschool were dark because they occupied the basement area of an older college building. The classrooms looked like a larger, grander version of a playroom in someone's house with the same commercial toys commonly available in any store. The outside play area was adequate, but scattered with riding toys and sand equipment. My daughter languished in the beautiful school and, like Rapunsel locked in a tower, began to spend her entire school day sitting on a chair waiting for me to liberate her. Every class photograph I have of her from this period shows a girl with an almost expressionless face, that classic "flat" affect of individuals with NLD. I can see in the neutrality of her expression eyes that are opened a little too wide, eyes tinged with fear, discomfort, and anxiety. Now I am looking at a photograph taken a few months later in the other school. Sara is standing up holding a drawing. There is light in her expression; she is smiling, her body relaxed as she looks directly into the camera.

For the child with NLD, the right environment is everything. Put this child in an environment that stresses her weak areas, and she will respond emotionally by becoming hostile, terrified, anxious, or depressed. However, if the environment supports her and supplies the "psychological safety" she needs to feel secure, she will function at a higher level. When Sara was young I learned how to structure our home so she was comfortable. Gradually, I learned how to compensate for her weak areas without even thinking. Because she could enjoy new experiences if she was prepared for them, I learned the value of rehearsal and practice. I could recognize situations and tasks that would be potentially problematic for her and adapt them. I noticed through trial and error that if she was free to learn at her own pace in an environment that protected her from anxiety and fear, she would grow stronger and learn how to cope better with distressing situations. I could not, however, go to school with her and reorganize the classroom or control what the other children said to her. Therefore, I had to try to figure out the general principles of what she needed in a school setting, and to find a school that supplied as many of these elements as possible.

What was lacking in the first school and how the environment could have been modified

The most important element missing from the Montessori school was the kind of verbal explanation that would have allowed Sara to participate in its daily events. The philosophy of this school espoused that children learn best by observing the teacher and other, particularly older, children demonstrating different tasks. In a Montessori school, the teachers put a great deal of effort into systematically arranging the educational materials in a manner that is spatially logical and consistent. For example, the children are placed in multi-age open classrooms where they are encouraged to choose individual projects such as pouring rice from a pitcher into little dishes, washing cloths, matching picture cards, or completing puzzles. These activities, known as the materials, are logically laid out on shelves in different areas of the classroom. For example, the math materials are located in a specific area of the classroom and are grouped on shelves in a specific order, starting with the most elementary exercises and continuing with the more difficult ones. The children are allowed to work with any material or game as long as the teacher has taught them how to use it. When they have completed a particular exercise, they are required to put the material away in its container and return it to its exact spot on the designated shelf. For Sara, this arrangement created enormous stress on her faulty spatial memory because she could not remember which games she had been taught or where to put the different educational games away when she had completed them. In addition since following the rules was an essential attribute of Sara's character, she became anxious at school when she found she could not locate a required item or remember where on a particular shelf to return it.

Another serious impediment to Sara's ability to learn well at this school was the lack of verbal explanation when teachers gave lessons to either individuals or small groups. They believed that the best way to help children learn how to master certain physical tasks such as how to tie shoes, trace a sandpaper letter, or cut with a pair of scissors, was to demonstrate the movements needed to replicate these tasks while the children carefully watched their hands. However, for individuals with NLD who do not instinctively understand how to make sense of visual cues without accompanying verbal instructions, these lessons were unproductive. Sara could not even figure out that she *needed* to watch the teacher's hand movements in order to follow the lesson. However, she was aware of the fact that she, unlike the rest of her peers, could not figure out how to master the activities in the classroom, and her inability to participate productively added to her discomfort and anxiety.

What kinds of modifications and accommodations could the teaching staff of this school have implemented in order to make this environment a more hospitable one for Sara? It is possible that a Montessori school, which makes such complex visual-spatial demands, simply was not a good choice for a young child with NLD. However, if the school had been willing to modify their teaching style to take into account Sara's way of perceiving the world, her ability to function there most certainly would have been enhanced. For example, Sara needed a teacher who was committed to making sure she received more detailed verbal explanations so she could find her way around the classroom and understand how to operate and use the educational materials. Because students with NLD characteristically become anxious when they find themselves in positions in which they cannot adhere to rules, her teacher would have helped her greatly if the classroom rules about putting items back in the exact place where they belonged, avoiding spilling or dropping them, or generally striving for perfection, could have been adjusted in Sara's case. In this way, she might not have felt her only option was to sit hopelessly on a chair all morning rather than risk making a mistake. She also could have then potentially gained enough practice to learn where items were stored. In order for students with NLD to feel comfortable in any school, teachers must be committed to spending considerable energy providing verbal explanations for all aspects of the school environment and the curriculum. In addition, because children with NLD are particularly averse to making mistakes, they need to be taught by individuals who maintain an unusually flexible, accepting attitude so they feel comfortable enough to ask clarifying questions, take risks, and try new things to get the practice they need to master tasks. For example, Sara would have benefited from repeated verbal descriptions of the classroom layout, encouragement to ask any questions she needed for clarification, and verbal scaffolding from the teacher to ensure that she could eventually function independently. The following model dialogue illustrates good teaching principles at a Montessori school, but the same principles would apply at any public or private school:

Sara (wandering around the room carrying a wooden box): I don't know where this box belongs.

Teacher: Let me help you. Do you know what this work is called?

Sara: It is the movable alphabet.

Teacher: Do you think it belongs with the math materials or the language materials?

Sara: It's language.

Teacher: You're right. Do you remember where the language section of the room is?

Sara: I'm not sure. I think it is those shelves over there under the clock.

Teacher: That's so good. You're right! Let me show you where it goes on the shelf. Look, it goes on the second shelf right here between the green box and the red box. Let's practice later today on finding it and putting it away. I'll get you later and we can try that out.

Children with NLD require an enormous investment of time by caring adults who are committed to using words to explain tasks, then creating opportunities for practice, and finally using questions to encourage and support further independent functioning. In the above example, the teacher could have simply told Sara where to put the box, or even put it away for her. Instead, this teacher builds on Sara's previously mastered knowledge about the classroom layout and her verbal knowledge of categories (language, math) to help her devise a schema to figure out how to put the item away, and to use this schema to put away other items in the future.

Many students with NLD who attend public schools are not given the opportunity to use their language abilities to learn how to master challenging tasks at an independent level. For example, a student's IEP might state that she needs an aide to help her find her way to classes. This recommendation is a good first step. However, just as Sara in the above example will never learn to put anything away if the teacher simply puts it away for her, the student who receives no further assistance than exclusively relying on an aide as a seeing eye dog will find that she makes minimal progress compared to the student who receives further instruction with verbal scaffolding and practice opportunities.

The second preschool: Possible modifications

Sara's next school was a better place for her both psychologically and academically. In addition to having a less complicated physical layout and fewer children and teachers for her to interact with, the teachers were more flexible and tolerant. The structure of the school day contained more activities that the entire class did together, and the teachers explained activities with words more than simply demonstrating them. They also did not encourage perfection, and the students mirrored their values. At the first school, children constantly pointed out Sara's mistakes, avoided her, and pitied her. At the second school, she was included in all social activities, and her peers did not comment on her difficulties.

However, this school was not helpful in teaching Sara age-appropriate academic tasks like how to write her name, put together puzzles, or form numbers. It is particularly essential that children with NLD be taught how to master penmanship before they fall too far behind for several reasons:

- They have the capacity to master this task.
- If they do not receive specific instruction, their writing will stay arrested at the lowest level.
- Written expression, an area of challenge for them, has the potential to open up opportunities for connecting the visual with the verbal (see Chapter 7).

The opportunity for them to make sense of the world they see will be closed to them if they do not learn how to print or write.

An ideal elementary school

An ideal elementary school for children with NLD is one that does not underestimate their intellectual challenges. Because these children frequently are adept at early reading, spelling, and memorizing information, they have the capacity to excel superficially in many of the areas emphasized in elementary school, and it is therefore easy for the adults in the school environment to assume that all is well. Children with NLD need their spatial, social, and cognitive challenges recognized in elementary school, so they can experience the kind of interventions they need in order to reach their potential.

It is unusual for children with NLD to be identified in preschool. However, in preschool, they struggle with many of the activities emphasized in early childhood curriculums such as self-help skills, tasks that involved fine and gross motor dexterity, interpreting pictures, and participating successfully in organized play. Therefore, it is possible that there were questions about some areas of their development. However these questions frequently are silenced in first grade if the child is successfully able to learn how to read. Since the majority of children with LD are children who struggle to learn how to read words, the warning signs of academic failure exhibited by children with less common forms of LD frequently go unheeded. In addition to instruction in the areas already mentioned, these students need specific instruction in the areas described below.

Reading instruction

It is incorrect to assume that children with NLD do not need any reading instruction. They need early reading instruction that emphasizes reading comprehension. They need to be taught how to make connections between the illustrations in children's books and the actual text. Because they usually have good rote memories, they are frequently adept at retelling the plot of a story or novel. Showing them the difference between a "retelling" and a summary, and letting them orally practice both, can capitalize on this skill and improve their comprehension. Children with NLD need to experience rich dialogue and questioning from an adult about character motivation, making predictions and drawing conclusions in order to move beyond the superficial understanding that comes from their facile ability to repeat what happens in a story.

Students with NLD also need specific instruction in vocabulary development, in conjunction with reading comprehension, to improve their pragmatic and semantic language. Even though they frequently have rich vocabularies, their understanding of word meanings is shallow, and they are not naturally skilled at appropriate word choice. Therefore, they benefit from instruction that deepens their understanding of words by teaching them concepts such as the possibility that words have multiple or idiomatic meanings.

Finally, students with NLD are not always natural readers and do sometimes require instruction in single-word decoding. The kind of child with NLD who doesn't seem to be able to figure out how to read from conventional instruction can benefit from programs designed to teach children with reading disabilities how to decode. However, children with NLD benefit from these programs for a different reason. Because they struggle with new concepts, some children with NLD do not automatically figure out how to "break the phonetic code" of English, not because they have difficulty with phonemic awareness but because the task of decoding is too novel for them. Programs designed to teach decoding to children with phonological deficits such as Wilson, Orton-Gillingham and Lindamood-Bell present the steps of reading in a logical sequence, and teach students many rules and generalizations about how words in English are formulated. Children with NLD who do not spontaneously learn to decode can benefit from these kinds of reading programs because they are proficient at figuring out tasks by using rules and logic. When they are shown how decoding can be broken down into small logical steps, they usually catch on quickly to reading without needing the amount of practice typical for students with reading disabilities.

Writing instruction

It is essential that children with NLD are taught the correct way to form letters and are given extensive opportunities to practice and master handwriting. If they receive appropriate instruction, they are generally capable of learning how to print accurately. The ability to write will open up many opportunities for them to use their language skills to advance their learning. They also should learn how to use a keyboard after they have mastered handwriting. Once they are skilled at handwriting, they will also need specific instruction in how to develop a cogent piece of writing, how to take notes, and how to use vocabulary appropriately in written language. Writing instruction can be given in conjunction with reading instruction.

Mathematics instruction

Children with NLD usually struggle with math. One of the first difficulties these children experience is in coping with the spatial demands of copying and placing simple arithmetic problems on the page. They struggle with placing and keeping the numbers in columns, with how to form the numbers with a pencil, and with the meaning of the different mathematical signs such as + and −. Later, they struggle with comprehending mathematical concepts, such as fractions and decimals, and with visualizing the meaning of word problems. They have little understanding of elementary geometric concepts such as size and shape. Therefore, they need explicit instruction in how to use logic and language to understand math.

High school

An ideal high school for students with NLD would be one that not only allows them to flourish academically, but is also committed to helping them have meaningful social and extracurricular experiences. An ideal secondary school would be committed to helping students with NLD, who often find themselves ostracized socially during adolescence, find a meaningful social role through structured activities. This is more likely to occur in a small school where there is an active connection between adults and adolescents, a strong sense of community, and an environment that encourages a high level of acceptance for all school members. Sara was very fortunate to attend a small religious single-sex high school where the staff were actively involved in cultivating an educational environment that emphasized cooperation over competition as well as reflection through language. Sara flourished academically during her four years at this school, but the areas in which she made the most remarkable progress were in her ability to initiate satisfying social interactions, and to learn how to reflect independently about her beliefs and self-image. The positive social environment that existed in her secondary school greatly contributed to her ability to master these areas. An ideal high school for students with NLD would provide the elements described below.

Physical layout

Because of the spatial challenges experienced by students with NLD, the physical layout of their school environment is an important element to consider at every age. However, the complexity of the physical layout is a particularly important issue for high school students with NLD because they differ so strikingly from more typical adolescents who have been able to achieve a high level of independence in their ability to quickly and accurately maneuver their way in complex physical and spatial environments. Since most high schools follow the model where students change classes many times a day, it is important that the school recognizes how challenging this task can be for students with NLD. The following are examples of possible environmental modifications:

- Although a small high school with a simple layout is ideal, if this environment is not possible, try to schedule all of the student's classes in one wing of the school, or relegate classes to the same one or two floors.

- Make few or no changes to the student's yearly academic schedule. It is easier for the student to receive the amount of practice she requires in order to successfully find her way if she has to go to exactly the same classes that are held in the same classrooms for an entire academic year. If class and room changes are necessary at semester breaks, make sure the student knows how to get to her new classes.

- Allow the student extra time for getting to her next class after physical education or studio art where she may have additional physical tasks to accomplish that can slow her down.

- Students with NLD should not be penalized for being late to class.

- Remember the ultimate goal is to assist the students in becoming independent in their ability to travel in the building.

Social environment

A school environment that actively fosters positive social opportunities for students with NLD becomes particularly important during high school when it is assumed that more typical students are able to function socially at a high level of independence. In addition, the role of the teacher and other adults in the high school environment shifts away from active involvement in the social functioning of their students. Teachers now see themselves as specialists in their subject matter, and primarily perceive their role as purveyors of academic knowledge. Students with NLD flounder in this kind of environment because they need much guidance through talking to adults and peers, and also need opportunities to practice their new found skills if they are going to develop the necessary social acumen that will allow them to function independently as adults. A model high school will supply the following kind of social environment:

- The school will have a small student population that stays consistent during the four-year period of high school. This condition is to minimize the number of people with whom your student comes into daily contact so she can learn to recognize and become better acquainted with them. By getting to know a small number of individuals in a deeper way, students with NLD will have a chance to develop and practice friendships. Since many public high schools are large, it is possible to find the small environment these students need by enrolling them in a special program that exists within a larger school. For example, there were about 120 students in Sara's graduating class in high school, but the special academic program in which she was enrolled had only about 30 girls who took the same classes and followed a particular sequence of subjects.

- Students with NLD benefit from receiving instruction from a small number of teachers. Even when students have a different teacher for each class, the number of adults can be controlled if the school has a small teaching staff and the students have many of the teachers multiple times over the course of four years. For example, the high school Sara attended had a coterie of special teachers who were trained to teach IB classes so, although she might have eight teachers per year, she tended to have the same eight teachers during each of her four years of high school. Another way to control the number of adults with whom a student comes into contact on a daily basis is to divide the school day into fewer periods. For example, Sara attended a high school that scheduled classes by blocks instead of periods. So instead of having the traditional six or seven periods of a typical high school, Sara's attended only four 90-minute periods per day. In this way, she had to deal with fewer transitions and a smaller number of individuals on a daily basis than she would have if her school had followed a more conventional schedule. Many public high schools are experimenting with some form of "block scheduling."

- Students with NLD function better in high schools with a highly structured social environment that allows them to experience "ritualized" social interactions like ceremonies and assemblies whose purpose can be easily verbally explained to them. For example, Sara's school had weekly assemblies, monthly religious ceremonies, and yearly retreats that were attended by the entire school and teaching staff. These assemblies were opportunities to give out awards, honor good works of particular students, or listen to a lecture by an invited speaker. The purpose of each assembly was clearly stated to the students beforehand, and students were often assigned specific roles during the proceedings. Students were expected to practice any speaking role they might be assigned for a particular assembly. Participating in social events that have a script, a formal procedure, and opportunities for practice is ideal for students with NLD. For example when Sara was in twelfth grade, she and another girl were chosen to address a local civic organization on behalf of her school. The two girls were asked to write their own address based on a specific set of criteria and then practice their speeches for the principal prior to the event. After listening to the girls' addresses, the principal made constructive comments and later accompanied them to the event, stayed for the entire ceremony, and drove them back to school. After four years of experiencing social events such as this one where caring adults carefully coached her, Sara learned many useful procedures that she could apply to similar social occasions.

- Students with NLD who are naïve, literal, and socially awkward are safest in school environments that have zero tolerance for bullying. Even better are school environments that are successful in creating an atmosphere where students are actively rewarded for practicing tolerance, kindness, and cooperation. Students with NLD frequently flounder in schools that emphasize competition. For example, Sara's school was successful in creating a tolerant attitude in part because all students and faculty members were required to participate in service projects. After these projects, students were required to reflect on how they felt and what they learned through discussion and written journals.

- Students with NLD have a better chance at success in high school environments where adults are personally involved on a daily basis not just with the students' academic concerns, but also with their social and emotional functioning. These students also function more successfully in high schools where there is a high level of parental involvement, since they need a higher level of assistance from their families than is characteristic for more typical adolescents.

Academic environment

The academic expectations of high school place demands on many of the weak areas of students with NLD. These students need assistance in the following academic areas if they are to be successful in secondary school:

- Because these students struggle with comprehending language and completing complex learning tasks that cannot be solved by a memorized solution or rote learning, they require extra academic help in order to benefit from the secondary school curriculum. For instance, students with NLD require many verbal explanations for mathematical procedures and concepts. They need examples of typical problems they can use as models to help them solve similar problems. They need the opportunity to practice problems while a teacher talks them through the logical reasons behind each step. Finally, they need to learn how to apply new learning to variations of the targeted problem and, leading from this, to use new learning to solve new problems. They need verbal mediation to help them with reading comprehension, to understand history books, and to master scientific concepts. They need assistance in clarifying geographic concepts, developing a sense of a historical timeline, and increasing written output. Chapter 10 contains detailed examples of interventions appropriate for high school students.

Sara's high school experience

Sara attended a small, religious single-sex high school. She thrived there even though the staff at her school did not feel that part of their job was to provide specific assistance to students with learning issues. Therefore, Sara received at home the educational interventions she needed to cope with the challenging curriculum. This situation was not always ideal because the staff were frequently unaware of how much pressure she was under, and how granting her basic accommodations like extra time for tests and assignments could have alleviated some of this pressure. In addition, the math and science courses she needed to fulfill the requirements of the IB program were probably unnecessarily rigorous for her. However, the com-bination of successful interventions and a challenging curriculum allowed Sara to move beyond her natural tendency to think about ideas in a concrete literal way, and opened a new world of academic possibilities and intellectual choices for her. In addition, the lack of direct school support for her learning issues had the surprising benefit of inducing me to make sure Sara understood and could recognize what kind of tasks were difficult for her and why. By developing further her ability to be reflective, she learned how to become an expert advocate for herself.

However if Sara's high school believed they could not offer the kind of academic help she needed, they were masters at creating a social milieu that allowed her to flourish socially. The community of the school was close-knit, protective, positive, and hands on, and the staff consciously created an environment where the girls took responsibility for helping each other. Sara found her role in this community by dispensing academic assistance to others. Every night, she fielded phone calls explaining assignments and discussing homework. These discussions undoubtedly helped the other student, but they probably helped Sara even more since she benefited from the process of verbal clarification involved in explaining the different assignments to another person. In return, many of the girls in her classes spontaneously undertook the task of trying to understand some of her unusual behaviors. I was so absorbed during the four years Sara was at this school, trying to develop the right kinds of remedial academic exercises and helping her learn to maneuver through space and develop the ability to advocate for herself, it was not until she almost graduated that I realized what an immeasurable gift her fellow students had given her.

I finally recognized the enormity of what Sara's peers had given her at a luncheon held during her senior year attended by at least 100 of her fellow classmates and their mothers. It was a formal luncheon at a restaurant, and many women were festively dressed in brightly colored clothes and wore a kind of spring hat I had not seen since my childhood. Sara's fellow classmates left their seats and congregated in the middle of the restaurant calling out to friends, meeting their mothers, and forming small groups which continually altered and transformed themselves into new groups, as their end of the year exuberance filled the air with laughter. Sara isolated herself from this happy repartee because she was poor at finding her friends and following conversations amidst all the visual cacophony and movement. Instead, she stayed glued to her chair and resigned herself to talking only to me.

Soon, though, group after group of girls left the center of the restaurant and began to congregate in front of our table. "We have come to talk to you, Sara," they would explain. "Is this your mother?"

Some groups brought their mothers with them to let me know what a fine friend Sara had been to their own daughter. Then they would move away, only to be replaced by another group of giggling girls who demonstrated with such clarity how willing and skilled they were to adjust their social dance to include the one among them for whom the steps were so challenging.

Chapter 7

The Importance of the Family

Home environment

A great deal is required of parents of children with NLD if they are going to be successful in both locating a positive school environment and creating a home environment that enhances the psychological and cognitive development of their child. Parents need to remember they bring many strengths to the table that can help them with what frequently may seem like an overwhelming task. For example, keep in mind that you know your child better than anyone else, and you have access to the most intricate observations about your child's learning and social development. Ultimately you will need to rely on your own judgment to figure out what is best for your child. If you are willing to learn about NLD and to use this knowledge to help you reflect and structure your thinking about how best to fulfill your child's needs, you will find this combination of personal experience, tempered with reflection and acquired knowledge about NLD, to be a sure-fire recipe for success.

Parents can probably best help children with NLD by creating a home environment that provides psychological safety and serves as a refuge from the confusing and exhausting demands of the world and school. Unfortunately, children with NLD expend enormous amounts of effort in order to accomplish most learning activities, as well as the basic tasks of daily living. It is not surprising that children with NLD tire more easily at school when you consider how much energy they need to expend in order to accomplish even simple everyday tasks such as turning on a tap, finding the drinking fountain, or participating in a conversation. Most of their class-mates will be able to do these kinds of activities quickly and automatically, without conscious thought, allowing them to devote their mental energy more exclusively to learning new and complex material. In contrast, children with NLD, who have fewer habitual tasks they can execute on "automatic pilot," are always thinking hard. In addition, the outside world is a constant source of new sights, fresh experiences and surprising happenings. The world is novelty incarnate—an infinitely multifaceted diamond where every day is replete with unexpected events, startling ideas, and unknown people. This is the world we send our novelty-adverse children out to conquer every day. When they arrive home, they desper-ately need down time in order to recharge their batteries in a familiar peaceful place.

In addition, our children need us to serve as guide and interpreter so they can make sense of the world around them. They are at psychological risk because it is difficult for them to interpret visual stimuli in a manner that allows them accurately to make sense of their environment. But they are at even greater risk when no one recognizes their confusion. We cannot tolerate allowing them to stumble along lost, misinterpreting social cues, and missing the deeper meaning of thought and language. We first need to become keen observers of our children's behavior, so we can recognize when they need our assistance and the help of others. We then need to learn how to use words explicitly to convey the kind of information these children need so they can learn to interpret the world accurately. Next, we need to discover ways to give them opportunities to practice different skills and experiences so they can cement their newfound skills into memory.

Our children also have difficulty over the course of their entire lifespan with many daily living tasks that are normally not taught in school, such as dressing, eating, cooking, and using tools and utensils. They need parents who are committed to making sure they master these vital skills. Many of these tasks can best be taught at home by a parent who can carefully observe the exact moment the child is cutting meat with the dull end of a knife, placing the left shoe on the right foot, or trying to thread the wrong end of a needle. In addition, their inability to manage these tasks can be a source of embarrassment to older children. They may be more inclined to ask a trusted parent for assistance than risk potential ridicule at school. As Sara repeatedly told me, "There are a lot of questions I really can't ask other people. They would think I was nuts." Ideally, you will be able to encourage your child to eventually take responsibility for letting you know which tasks are difficult for her to accomplish at school. "This weekend I want to learn how to light a match and crack an egg," Sara announced one Friday in the fall of ninth grade.

Perhaps the most vital reason our children need parents who understand them is because they are psychologically vulnerable and in need of intense parental protection throughout their childhood, and even into early adulthood. Unfortunately, parents who commit themselves to providing the appropriate protection are frequently criticized for being overprotective. When Sara was growing up, I felt as if I had a magnetic field around me that attracted criticism. The nature of this criticism fell into two main categories. First, many friends and teachers were uneasy about the amount of parental involvement and protection I believed Sara needed. Repeatedly throughout Sara's childhood, both professionals and laypersons suggested that I was overinvolved in my daughter's life in a manner that would ultimately interfere with her ability to develop into a self-reliant individual. In addition, I was frequently charged with exaggerating the nature of her difficulties and told my concerns were unwarranted.

Learning how to deal constructively with criticism is one of the many challenges facing parents of children with NLD. Tanguay (2002) points out that "providing the right environment and insisting on an equally appropriate one at school, will likely win the parent of an NLD child the irritating title of 'overprotective'" (p.48). Whitney (2002) reports that 90 percent of parents who are sensitive to their children's difficulties and have an intuitive sense that their children need more protection and care than more typical children are labeled overprotective and overinvolved, and are also accused of exaggerating their children's difficulties. Unfortunately, it is not unusual for parents to hear these kinds of comments from professionals as well as laypeople. Therefore, it is important parents understand the reasons why their children are vulnerable so they can develop the strength to advocate for them. Knowledge is a good antidote to criticism because many of the critical comments parents receive from others stem from ignorance and misconceptions about the nature of NLD. First of all, NLD is a relatively rare learning disorder. For example, it is possible that your child may be the first student with NLD that a particular teacher has ever encountered. By the time your child starts school, you have had many years to develop effective ways to manage many of her baffling behaviors. The teacher, on the other hand, who is more familiar with children with language learning disabilities, may not recognize the challenges your child faces with social relationships, spatial reasoning, or new experiences. In addition, the verbal skills of children with NLD frequently mask the confusion they are actually experiencing. Because they are often adept at using language, people simply believe that they know what they are talking about. It is difficult for people who are not familiar with NLD to comprehend how strongly individuals with this difficulty rely on verbal cues to make sense of the world around them. It is also hard to comprehend why relying so exclusively on language at the expense of processing and integrating visual and tactile cues can result in so many problems for these individuals. Therefore, the greatest gift a child with NLD can have is a parent who truly understands her plight and is committed to throwing her a verbal lifeline when she needs it. The following section lists some suggestions for parents to consider to encourage the healthy development of their child with NLD.

Listen when they talk so you can interpret the world for them

All children benefit from parents who listen to and talk with them. However, for children with NLD, frequent conversation and discussion with a patient individual who is willing to help them learn how to read between the lines is the only way they are going to make sense of the world. Remember your child has a very limited capacity to learn from simply being exposed to different experiences. They do not learn spontaneously by imitation or through osmosis. Yet they need to be exposed to rich experiences and have opportunities to imitate others just as any other child. The difference is that children with NLD need someone who can point out to them through explicit conversation what is important, valuable, or meaningful about these experiences. Children with NLD can become confused and go off course in the spontaneous and normal chaos of their own family's home life where it is common for several simultaneous conversations to compete at the dinner table, where siblings and friends run in and out of rooms willy-nilly, and where ringing doorbells, phones, and TV shows vie for our attention. So even though kids with

NLD have strong verbal abilities, they are actually poor at learning very much from listening to the kind of spontaneous conversation that is common in most households. The reason why these children are unable to glean much meaning from listening to language in authentic situations is because it is difficult for them to process rapidly occurring information. Without mediation, they are poor at following arguments, picking out which information and facts are important, interpreting facial expressions and gestures, and meaningfully integrating the significance of nonverbal stimuli such as doorbells, alarms, and telephones into conversations. Because they struggle with making sense of spontaneous conversations, children with NLD react by becoming passive and withdrawing from social interactions, becoming too verbose and dominating the conversation with verbiage that doesn't quite fit the situation, or by paying attention to some irrelevant stimuli in the environment. Sara often complained that we never kept her informed about topics like our plans for vacation, company we were expecting, or the content of phone calls. "You never tell me anything," she would say. At first, I found her complaints baffling, particularly when I knew our whole family had just discussed that very morning where we were going for vacation. However, families often speak in a "code" that assumes a great deal of implied information. The following is an example of a conversation that seemed crystal clear to me.

> Me (holding a large envelope that I had just removed from the mailbox): The brochure from Canada just came. Where do you want to stay this summer?

> Sara's brother: Let's see it. This sounds like a good place (reading description in brochure). Call, Mom, to see if it is free in July.

Later that evening after school, we get back to a discussion about our summer trip. Sara complains that nobody told her about any trip to Canada in July. She complains that we tell John everything, but we always leave her in the dark. I realize how much we intuit and assume is obvious from the implied meaning of our words, but that Sara needs explicitly stated. The following conversation would have been a better way to tell her about the meaning of the brochure.

> Me (holding the envelope): I recently sent away for a brochure with places to stay in Canada. I am excited that the mailman has finally

brought it, and it is right here in this envelope because we are planning to go on vacation to Canada sometime in July. Sara, do you and John want to help me look through it and see if we can find somewhere we would like to stay. The brochure has pictures of places to stay.

It takes a huge investment of time to make sure your child with NLD understands what is going on and to serve as her mediator. It is time well spent. The following are suggestions to help make this time worthwhile:

- Ask questions to stretch their thinking. (Do you remember where we went for vacation last year? What is your favorite trip we ever took? What are the advantages of traveling in an airplane, a car?)

- Help them to see patterns, and to understand and anticipate routines and schedules.

- Explicitly explain the use of calendars, diaries, checklists, and labels. "Let's write down everything you need to do this week."

- Develop an open nonjudgmental relationship with your child so he or she will confide in you and let you know on an ongoing basis which tasks are difficult for them to accomplish in school. Children with NLD realize pretty quickly that it is mighty strange to be the only child in their grade who cannot figure out how to open the school door, dribble a basketball or use a jump rope. The good news is that our children can learn to master these tasks if someone is aware of their difficulties, teaches them the steps needed to execute the task, and makes sure they receive adequate opportunities for practice.

- Have regular conversations about what is going on in school. Because our children frequently seem more competent than they actually are, you probably will gain information about academic areas in which they are struggling. This knowledge will allow you to more effectively advocate for appropriate educational interventions. You should not have to implement these interventions, but you can help your child's teachers better understand his or her needs.

- Have conversations about your child's social life at school. These conversations can help you determine if your child is isolated or is finding a social place. Again, sharing this kind of information with teachers can help them better understand your child's social needs.

- By talking regularly about the challenges and joys of life, friendships, and schoolwork, you encourage your child to be more reflective. By helping them find solutions to their challenges, you help the children develop a positive, can-do attitude and discourage them from becoming helpless and passive. These are important attributes for all individuals with NLD to acquire, since the ultimate goal for them is to learn to advocate for themselves because many of our children's challenges will persist into adulthood.

Familiarity as an antidote to novelty

One of the reasons why just getting through a day takes so much energy for children with NLD is because they cope poorly with new experiences, thoughts, and concepts. No matter how carefully parents and teachers try to structure their schedule to minimize change, it is impossible to completely shield our children from the unexpected. Although it is desirable to decrease the amount of novelty our children are exposed to at one time, it is probably not only impossible but also to their detriment to try to banish all that is startling from their lives. Parents can best help their children deal with novelty if they expose them gradually to new experiences and ideas. For example, these children need to attend parties and go on play dates, but they do not need to attend six parties and two overnights in one week. Parents can also greatly help their children deal with novelty if they develop a "novelty radar" and can anticipate for their child what aspects of an experience will potentially catch the child off guard. You can greatly neutralize a novel experience if you prepare your child for the experience by describing what she can expect to happen. Over time and as your child builds up her repertoire of experiences, you can help her build verbal schemas that will help her "demystify" the novelty of social experiences. For example, after your child has attended many birthday parties, you can start to help her develop a birthday party "schema." In the car on the way to the party, you can tell your fourth grader:

> I wonder what this party is going to be like? All these parties are a lot the same. For example, there is always a part where the birthday child opens

his presents. Then there is usually a part where all the guests do something fun together. Since this party is at a swimming pool probably everyone is going to play in the pool for a while. Then there is usually the eating part of the party with the lunch and the cake. Finally there is usually the goodbye part where everyone thanks the birthday kid and gets a goody bag.

By verbally pointing out how most events of a related type follow a similar pattern and have identifiable analogous features, you are giving your child a way to manage novelty and learn procedures that can be applied to other comparable situations. If your child finds a new event particularly troubling, make sure you talk to them later, almost like a debriefing, about the disturbing idea or happening.

The following are other ways in which parents can help diminish the effects of novelty for their child:

- Stick to a familiar routine, but make sure the child is cognizant of the routine. Do not assume your child has figured out her weekly schedule simply from experience. For example, if school always ends early on Wednesday, this fact needs to be verbally pointed out to her. It is helpful to regularly review her schedule with her until she has committed it to memory. "Oh today is Thursday. What does your day look like today?" When Sara was in elementary school her class initiated the school day with an exercise where a different child was selected to come to the front of the room and verbally relate the events of the previous day in chronological order. Her school believed this exercise helped all the children improve their memory. For Sara, this exercise allowed her to verbally recall and reflect on the events of the school day and recognize how repeating patterns of activities contributed to the sameness of her weekly schedule. Prepare the child verbally for any changes in routine and exactly what these changes will entail. "There is going to be a change in the car pool this Wednesday. I know Harry's mom usually drives on Wednesday but she has to go to the doctor, so Sophie's dad is driving instead. He has a blue car. Stand with all the usual kids and go with them."

- Limit the number of extracurricular activities the child participates in to those that further her development. Even though it is good for our children to participate in meaningful activities, they easily become overloaded. In addition, they need significant practice mastering skills. Therefore, it is better if they stick to the same activities over the course of a year and do not flit from activity to activity.

- You cannot control everything that happens at school, but you can make your home a psychological haven for your child. Make sure your child has down time to enjoy her home, and time to relax, reflect, imagine, and play.

Dealing with homework

Homework is a difficult issue for most children with learning challenges and their families. Homework is particularly challenging for children with NLD in part because they are slow at processing information. Therefore they can spend an inordinate amount of time completing their assignments, frequently double or triple the time it takes a more typically developing youngster. Since kids with NLD work so hard at school and life, they need time to recoup and recharge their batteries. Parents can work with the school to make sure their children with NLD receive a reasonable amount of homework, which allows them to receive opportunities for enough practice but still allows them to experience free time, social experiences, and time to converse with their families.

Homework becomes particularly challenging for families of children with NLD after the first few grades when not only does the volume of work increase but also the complexity and emphasis on higher order thinking skills. Children with NLD struggle with figuring out what information they need in order to complete written assignments, how to understand the meaning of the books and chapters they are required to read, and how to make sense of the more complex math and science assignments. In addition, their spatial challenges make getting the correct books and papers home difficult, as well as getting these materials back to school. These children frequently go to school with their homework but do not get credit for it because they cannot locate the necessary papers in their backpack. The following suggestions are constructive ways parents can help their child complete her work in a timely way:

- Accept reality. Children with NLD will probably always need to spend more time on homework than other children. The challenge is discovering the appropriate amount of time that allows them to learn but also to have a balanced life. If your child has no time for social experiences, free conversation, or to play or revamp, then she is spending too much time on homework.

- If your child can only achieve a balanced life by limiting the amount of homework she receives, work with the school to make sure your child is doing enough homework to receive the practice she needs to consolidate her skills and understanding. For example, some schools specify that children work only a set amount of time each evening on homework, and then stop working after this time even if all the work is not completed. The problem with this approach for a child with NLD is that it might take the entire two hours of scheduled homework time to complete ten math problems. The child then has no opportunity to practice other vital skills. A better solution for students with NLD might be to have them complete only certain items, like every other math problem or a shorter version of written assignments, so they have the experience of regularly practicing a variety of subjects.

- Since your goal is to encourage your child to become an independent and autonomous learner, supply the kind of help that encourages her to realize this goal. Serve as a verbal mediator for your child. Be available for questions, verbal clarifications, and explanations. Children with NLD have a difficult time getting started on assignments because they often do not completely understand what is required of them. Therefore, help your child start on an assignment and then let her complete the next portion of the assignment independently.

- Children with NLD over-rely on previously learned material when they are asked to learn something new. Use this tendency to help them learn new material. For example, if your child is required to read a particular novel over a period of several weeks, ask her to summarize the previous events in the story before she tackles a new part. Then ask her leading questions to help her connect what she knows with new information. "Oh, now that we know that the main character is trapped in a cave, I wonder what is going to happen next?" Read the beginning of chapters with your child and then let her complete the rest independently. Always have her give you a summary of the sections she read alone and ask questions to further her understanding. "So you learned that the ancient Egyptians used water to irrigate their crops. I wonder where they got all that water from? How would you picture yourself irrigating your garden if you lived by the Nile a long time ago?"

- Curb their tendency to perfectionism while still encouraging a pride in their work and learning. Help them see that they do not have to do everything perfectly all the time. Instead, help them realize the main point of the assignment and encourage them to channel their energy into "the big picture" and not every detail.

- Help them construct drawings, charts, and diagrams. They can tell you what to draw so you are not doing their work for them. Encourage them to use the computer to construct visual representations.

- Watch TV with them so you can talk about what is going on and help them understand the plot.

- Take an interest in what they are reading. Continue to read to them even after they are proficient at this skill. Discuss the ideas and characters contained in the works.

- Help them develop a system of organization so they can locate papers and books. One system employs a series of different colored folders, each used to hold a different subject (math homework in the red folder, etc.) Have the child write the name of the subject on the folder. Keep an extra set of textbooks at home.

When Sara was in high school she spent much of her free time completing homework. Although she tried to complete most of her assignments independently, she sometimes needed assistance from my husband or me in order to get her over the hump of mastering a difficult concept or executing a challenging task. By early adolescence, she was quite adept at knowing when to ask for assistance. Therefore, I frequently found myself acting as her homework facilitator who, with only a few well-chosen words, could clarify an essential point or help her understand an enigmatic concept. Other times she needed me literally to lend her a helping hand so she could cope with the motor and spatial demands of a task. Such was the case one evening when Sara in tenth grade was required to create a map of the world that represented all the places where the crew of the ship, *The Pequod*, had traveled in its search of the white whale. She had spent weeks carefully reading and rereading the novel, *Moby Dick*, in an effort to follow the enigmatic journey of the white whale. She even listened to the story on a series of audiotapes. So she had a good sense of the important elements of the story; she could follow the plot and was acquainted with the characters. However, she became paralyzed with fear as she stared at a blank sheet of paper and a world atlas because she could not figure out how to replicate a map of the world that didn't appear as if it was drawn by a young child and, although she knew the names of every port of call where Ahab's ship sought refuge, she couldn't locate them in her atlas because she had such a poor sense of geography. After an hour of painstaking effort, she had only been able to locate the town of New Bedford where the crew of *The Pequod* had started their journey. It was clear to me it would take her longer to complete the assignment than it had taken the sailors in the novel to locate the white whale. Ironically, she was fabulous at what for me would have been the most difficult part of this ridiculous assignment. Because she had an extraordinary rote memory, she had no trouble keeping track of the exact page and paragraph reference where the author mentioned one of the multitude of places to which the crew traveled. She could also verbally tell me the exact sequence of their journey. "They start in New Bedford, Mom. Is New Bedford a city or a country? Then I know they go here and then here." She rattled off the names of exotic cities and countries and showed me the different pages in the book where she found these references.

I suggested that she might be able to produce a map that she was satisfied with if she used tracing paper, a material with which she was unfamiliar. At first, she was reluctant to try tracing paper because she believed using such a short cut would be a form of cheating. I always found verbal logic to be a good antidote to Sara's literal sense of right and wrong, and she listened to my reasoning on why tracing paper would not be cheating since the objective of the assignment was not to reveal her artistic gifts but to demonstrate that she had read the novel closely. So I introduced her to the marvels of tracing paper, helped her draw a likeness of the map of the world onto a large piece of paper, and agreed to help her locate all the places to which the ship traveled. Sara produced a notebook where she had recorded the exact page number of each of the places the ship traveled on its torturous journey. I could then show her where these places were located on her map. She finished her map in record time and also decided that she could benefit from taking a geography class since she wasn't totally sure if Africa was a country or a continent. She took that class the following year, but she still isn't entirely clear on her geographic categories!

Encouraging autonomy

It is true that children with NLD need vigilant protection and attention from parents who understand their strengths and vulnerabilities, and who are willing to experiment with the power of words. However if our children are going to develop the autonomy they need to live independently in the world, we must courageously step aside and make sure they have experience trying out difficult tasks on their own.

The first time Sara took the public bus home from high school, I asked her if I could drive behind the bus in case she got off at the wrong stop. No, she informed me, that would be a very bad idea. Not only would it be embarrassing if any of her friends noticed me driving behind them, it was totally unnecessary. We had practiced taking the bus route a dozen times, she continued, and she was ready to try it on her own. She would see me at home that afternoon.

I worked in an office in the basement of our house, and the afternoon of Sara's first solo bus trip, I only went through the motions of working with my students. In reality, my attention was focused on our front door, and I felt an enormous rush of relief when I heard Sara's key turn in the lock. Although I had spent an anxious few hours, I realized that it was indeed time for me to step aside and let Sara ride the bus alone—that the trial trips I had supervised were for the sole purpose of ensuring she could ride the bus safely and independently. Later that evening when she triumphantly related how she had remembered to recognize her bus stop, the confidence that she exuded was priceless. Sara rode the bus home from school for the next four years and even learned how to master another adjacent bus route to take when the first one was late.

Because parents know their children better than any one else, they are in the best position to know when their child is ready to try out an experience "solo." Since our need to protect is also strong and appropriate, the following are suggestions to help parents make sure their older children have the coping skills to function in the world independently and safely:

- Individuals with NLD need to become experts in taking public transportation if they live in an area where it is available. Since many people with NLD may never be competent drivers, public transportation will allow them to travel independently. In addition, you do not need to have a good sense of direction in order to take public transportation but can learn how to get from place to place by verbal instructions. "I need to take the orange line of the subway. I get on at the Washington Street stop, go two stops and get off at Jackson Street." Sara now prefers taking public transportation to the convenience of taking taxicabs. I discovered this fact recently when she came home from college for a visit. I suggested that she save time and take a 30-minute cab ride home from the airport rather than ride the subway for an hour. I was surprised when she told me that she found cab rides stressful because the driver usually asked her which roads to take. "He always wants to know if we are close to the house, and I am not sure. The subway is easier because you get on at one stop and you get off at another. There are lots of signs to tell you where to go, and there is only one route and it never changes."

- Make sure your child has a plan and knows what to do in case something goes wrong when she is taking public transportation. For example, does your child know what to do if she misses her bus or subway stop? Does she know what to do if the bus breaks down or is diverted and is forced to take a different route? After your child has first gained some confidence in her ability to successfully take public transportation without mishaps, begin to talk about what to do if a trip does not go smoothly. Since many individuals with NLD are prone to anxiety, you want to make sure they are prepared for the unexpected without frightening them. They need assurance that none of these mishaps is life-threatening and that solutions can be found.

- They should err on the side of asking too many questions and clarification from officials. Because they can be naïve and literal, parents need to spend much time preparing them to recognize who it is appropriate to ask for advice and directions.

- They need to always carry a cellphone programmed with useful telephone numbers, including the number of a reputable cab company. In addition, they should always carry enough cash to pay for a cab if they ever get lost, miss a ride or the last train or bus.

- One of the greatest practical impediments to achieving independence for individuals with NLD is their difficulty in learning to drive. Some individuals with NLD will be able to learn to drive competently, and others will not. If your adult child is not able to drive, she will occasionally need to ask others for rides. Teach her what is entailed in being a courteous passenger, and instruct her always to offer to pay for the gas. Sara is not a good driver. Public transportation has been able to fulfill most of her transportation needs, but not being able to drive has caused her some difficulties. For example, as part of the requirements for her program in speech-language pathology, she is assigned to semester-long internships in various schools, clinics and hospitals in the Boston area. One of her required internships was located in a school in a suburb that was only accessible by car. She was able to find another student who agreed to take her, but the process of making the arrangements was arduous and stressful. Not being able to drive will also put some limitations on the scope of jobs for which she will ultimately be able to apply.

- By the time your young adult with NLD is ready to live independently, make sure he or she can operate all the necessary gadgets and utensils of daily living, such as vacuum cleaners, microwaves, can openers, and so on. Teach them how to cook a small repertoire of nutritious dishes. Make sure they can manage money, use a checkbook, and a credit card.

- Because they have a poor sense of space, they frequently forget to close backpacks, purses, and briefcases. They have a tendency to spread their belongings over too large a space for them to successfully keep track of them and, therefore, tend to lose things more easily than others. This habit also leaves them more vulnerable to pickpockets and identity theft. Help them learn how to better organize themselves, but also teach them what to do if they lose important documents like credit cards. Discourage them from carrying documents that contain their social security number. If they are traveling overseas, encourage them to leave their passport and return airplane ticket in a safe place when they are out and about.

- Help them to understand and accept their limitations. At the same time, point out which accommodations they can use that will allow them to accomplish most things.

- Children with NLD depend on us, much more than other children do, to explain procedures and routines very explicitly because they are unable to figure out how to accomplish these things by simply observing our actions.

Helping the young adult with NLD learn to be a self-advocate

Many parents of children with NLD find themselves cast in the role of advocate for their child. They frequently take on this role through necessity when their child begins school and they discover that educators and other professionals commonly have little practical experience with the workings of their child's rare mind or with their educational and social needs. Sensitive parents realize that their child requires them to serve as a verbal mediator on many levels. First, these children need parents who are committed to using language to explain the everyday workings of the world to them. On another level, children with NLD need their parents to serve as verbal "go betweens" and arbitrators to help them figure out how to communicate effectively with peers and teachers. Although my ultimate goal for Sara was to make sure she had the ability to advocate for herself, I found she still needed me to continue to function occasionally as her verbal mediator well into her early adulthood.

I feel one of the unexpected benefits of being the recipient of frequent criticism where I was accused of being overprotective and giving Sara too much of the kind of help that would ensure she would remain dependent on me, was that I vowed I would never willingly do anything that did not further her independence. The fear that perhaps there was some truth in those critical remarks made me vigilant in making sure that everything I did helped her grow as an independent person. That criticism helped me be a better parent because it gave me the impetus to be more reflective about my actions, my mistakes, and my observations. It gave me the courage to watch her rollerblade repeatedly down a hill that many times ended in two bloody knees, to drive her to the airport so she could board a plane to fly to Bolivia, to hand her the car keys. By the time Sara was old enough to go away to college, I no longer doubted my motivations. I knew in my heart that the only reason I had intervened on her behalf was so she would acquire the skills to live a full and independent life.

It was during her first year away at college that I discovered that if she was going to be able to manage her life without my assistance, she would need to master yet another skill—to understand how to apply for and receive the accommodations she was eligible for in higher education and when she sat for standardized entrance or professional exams. One reason for this is that when she turned 18 and was legally considered an adult, some university officials, psychologists, and other professionals would not speak to me directly about her difficulties. This stipulation may make sense for a typically developing adolescent, but often causes problems for families of students with NLD because our children have difficulties with so many areas of communication, comprehension, and self-reflection. In addition, because they are working so hard to improve their functioning in many areas of development, it makes sense that they may need a few more years than a more typically developing student to reach the same level of independence. I found that we needed to make sure she had the ability to effectively deal with this area of her life not only because of the rules of confidentiality, but also because applying for accommodations would be a recurring theme in her life.

While in college, Sara mastered the procedure she needed to follow in order to file the necessary paperwork that allowed her to receive extra time on her course exams. Her college required her to fill out new paperwork each time she requested extra time on any exam. So at the beginning of each term, she needed to fill out three different forms for each of her classes, and make sure they were filed with the correct office on campus. During her first two years of college, I would frequently receive phone calls at the beginning of the term in which she would ask, "Tell me again,

Mom, how do I explain my problem to someone in 25 words or less. I have to fit this information onto two lines on the form." However, by the last two years college, she filed all her paperwork independently.

After she graduated from college and decided to apply to graduate school, she faced the challenge of applying for the right to receive extra time as an accommodation on the Graduate Record Exam (GRE). This experience introduced her to the workings of bureaucracy and gave her practice in how to advocate for herself in difficult situations. Because Sara has elected to enter a profession that requires both a license and certification, she has needed to take many different standardized examinations and has become highly adept at both receiving accommodations and standing up for her rights. The following suggestions are ways parents can help their students with NLD who elect to pursue higher education achieve independence in this area of their lives:

- Universities usually require your child to submit a diagnostic report either from a private evaluator or from her former school to prove that she is eligible for accommodations. Generally this report cannot be more than five years old. Find out what your student's school requires and make sure your child's records are up to date, so she does not experience a gap in services. Our family knows from personal experience how disruptive and stressful it is to have to schedule a diagnostic evaluation in the middle of a school year!

- Testing agencies such as the college board or Education Testing Service usually do not require your child to submit her actual diagnostic report if the only accommodation she requires is the standard amount of extended time usually granted, and provided your student is currently receiving this accommodation at her school. Instead, the agency requires that the student's current school submit a form stating that they have an up-to-date copy of the student's diagnostic report on file, and that this student does indeed already receive extended time on all her school exams. However, if she requires more extensive accommodations (more time than is typically granted, a reader, etc.), she will need to submit her report directly to the testing agency.

- It is essential that families understand and make sure their student understands that testing agencies partly base their decision to allow accommodations on the fact that the student has received these accommodations in the past. Therefore, it is essential that students do not allow anyone to talk them into taking any standardized tests without accommodations or else the testing agency might claim they do not really require extended time on all future exams. When Sara was in graduate school, she was required to take two certification exams given by the same state agency. A well-meaning professor told her not to bother applying for extra time on the first one because the exam wasn't difficult and because no one else in the program with a learning disability had ever needed extra time on this particular assessment. Luckily, Sara called home to ask my opinion. I wanted her to understand that if she took the first exam without accommodations she might have difficulty when she tried to get them for the second exam. She ended up taking both exams with extended time.

- The professor's advice was inappropriate for an additional reason. Most students with LD have reading disorders. Perhaps the test that he described as simple did not unduly stress the reading skills of these students. However, individuals with NLD have a different set of challenges from those with reading disabilities. Because students with NLD process information extremely slowly, do very little with automaticity, and struggle with novelty and the minor motor challenges of an answer sheet and exam booklet, they will need extra time on all tests. After Sara completed the first exam, I asked her if she was glad she had taken it with extended time. She replied that she would have struggled to complete the questions if she did not have additional time.

- The summer before your student begins college present her with a photocopy of her complete diagnostic report that she can keep at school. Read the document with her. Show her where the information is contained in the report (for example, the date the problem was first diagnosed, the words that describe the actual diagnosis and diagnosis number, a short synopsis of her "problem," etc.). Use this as an opportunity to educate her about her strengths and weaknesses.

- In most cases, it is unrealistic to expect an entering college student to have the maturity to completely understand the nature of their learning challenges in a way that allows them to articulate their difficulties in succinct language to others. However, many colleges do not want parents involved in the process their sons and daughters undergo to receive accommodations. Therefore, let your student know they can phone or email you to answer questions. At first, you may actually have to walk your student through the questions on the form and help them formulate appropriate answers. Ideally, the student should be able to handle this task independently by the end of college.

- Find a private diagnostician you can trust, and who understands the needs of individuals with NLD, so you can refer this person to your student when she is an adult. Even after their formal education is complete, it is a good idea for them to keep their diagnostic records current. First, having a current document makes it easier to receive accommodations in case they return to school or need to take a training program. Second, many more professions and jobs now require individuals to take various tests and assessments throughout their lifetime. Eligibility for extended time will require a current diagnosis.

- Make sure your student understands what accommodations they are legally entitled to and what their rights are in higher educational settings. At the same time, try to prepare them for the possibility that things may go wrong. For example, occasionally students will come into contact with professors who don't "believe" in the need for accommodations, or who feel students with learning disabilities do not belong in their class. Also, since the entire process of applying for accommodations is highly bureaucratic, prepare them for the possibility of problems arising when they sit for standardized tests.

Sara's most challenging experience with accommodations

Although Sara received extended time on all the exams she took in conjunction with her college courses, the first national standardized exam for which she received the accommodation of extra time was the Graduate Record Exam (GRE), an entrance exam similar to the SAT, which is required for admittance to many graduate programs. Because she had honed her advocacy skills in college, she was able to harness her steely determination and extraordinary ability to concentrate to help her cope with the difficult testing situation she faced that day. I also believe she had sufficient mental energy available to advocate for herself because she had prepared very extensively for the exam and the format and kinds of questions she faced that day were completely familiar to her.

Sara was scheduled to take the GRE on a gray afternoon in December. She carried with her a letter from the Educational Testing Service stating that she was eligible for extended time. She had spent weeks jumping through bureaucratic hoops in order to receive this letter—long hours on the telephone and additional hours filling out lengthy forms that could only be processed through the mail and not on-line as is the case for the forms used by more typical learners. She then struggled to find a nearby testing center that was authorized to provide the accommodations she needed. The GRE is now administered via computer at free-standing test centers. In order to provide extra time, the center needs only to reprogram the computer to run for the requisite extra minutes allotted to individuals with LD who receive the standard time accommodation—15 extra minutes on the verbal section of the test, 23 extra minutes on the quantitative section, and 15 extra minutes on each of two essays. However, Sara found that most test centers she phoned stated they did not have the facilities to provide accommodations. When she finally located one center able to provide them, the person with whom she spoke instructed her to arrive early on the day her exam was scheduled, and to bring the letter that stated she was eligible for extra time. On the day of the test, she arrived an hour and a half early armed with her letter. She had also telephoned the test center the previous day to confirm her appointment for the following afternoon, and to remind them she would need extra time.

So when she entered the building, approached the two women sitting at the reception desk and told them she wanted to confirm her accommodations were set up, she anticipated no glitches in her testing experience. The reception area was located in a public area where about a dozen individuals were waiting to take a test. One of the women at the reception desk explained in a voice clearly audible not only to Sara but to everyone else present that this center was not equipped to handle accommodations. Furthermore, they explained that they had received no notification of her need for accommodations. Sara quickly replied that she only needed extended time, not a separate room or any other more elaborate accommodations. She also stated that she had set up her accommodations through the College Board Office of Disabilities exactly as the GRE bulletin had suggested and had a letter to prove it. The receptionist replied that she would have to see if it was possible to "reprogram" a computer. In the meantime, Sara was instructed to fill out more forms.

After Sara had completed these forms and returned them to the receptionist, the woman attached Sara's accommodation letter to this new additional paperwork and placed them in a folder. After ten minutes, Sara was ushered empty-handed through a door into a corridor that led to the testing rooms. Several men sat at desks outside the testing rooms. As Sara approached one of the desks, a man held up her paperwork and accommodation letter, which he apparently must have received from the receptionist, and sternly informed Sara that she shouldn't have brought her accommodation letter into the testing area. "Do you want to compromise your position?" he demanded. Sara was standing there empty-handed and since the man was already in possession of her letter when she entered the testing area, she feared for his sanity. However, she simply apologized and pointed out that the receptionist had said the accommodation letter needed to be attached to the other paperwork. The proctor hissed, "The staff don't really know what they are doing!"

Sara was then directed towards another man sitting at an adjacent desk. This man, the Sir Galahad of the testing center, told Sara that he did not know what the other man's problem was but that she was not to worry. He related to her that the computer currently allotted for her was situated in a noisy corner next to a door. If she waited five more minutes, another computer located in a quiet corner would be available. Sir Galahad would reprogram it himself.

Sara was finally able to successfully complete the exam and receive her scores. Several hours later, she telephoned me from the lobby of a nearby office building. As she recounted the incidents of the afternoon, my heart sank. I assumed that all her months of preparation were in vain, since the day's unnerving events probably caused her to score poorly on the test. As I commiserated with her, I reminded her that she could always take the test over again. "Oh, I did fine on the test," she told me. "I got a 720 on the verbal section and a 730 on the math section. I am just mad that the people in charge of the test can get away with their behavior."

Sara has taken many standardized tests since the day she took the GRE, and she has never again experienced quite as much difficulty receiving her accommodations as she did that afternoon. However, her experiences with standardized testing rarely go smoothly. For example, she once arrived at a testing center to take a certification exam armed with the appropriate letter only to be informed that her name was not on the list of people who needed accommodations and therefore they did not have a seat for her at this center. A relative of one of the proctors then drove her an hour away to another test center where she successfully completed her exam.

The reason Sara occasionally experienced difficulties securing accommodations was not because the individuals who staffed the test centers were deliberately trying to make the testing process difficult for her, or in any way doubted she had learning challenges that made her eligible for extended time. No, her difficulties were a direct by-product of that kind of bumbling bureaucracy that seems to gather around human endeavors where people are required to fill out and process a multitude of forms and follow rigid procedures. Nonetheless, incidents like the ones Sara experienced do make the testing process more arduous, particularly for someone for whom test-taking is already more stressful and complicated. It is ironic that this stress on occasion has been magnified by the very act of trying to obtain accommodations designed to make the test more equitable for her. However, it is a fact of her life, and her only defense against its negative effect is an understanding of how the system operates, a sense of humor, and an immutable sense of her self-worth.

Parents can make all the difference

Children with NLD go through life skating on thin ice. Parents are frequently the first to see below the ice and observe how the eloquence of their child's words actually masks a flimsy and insubstantial understanding of the world. The casual observer watching from the shore assures us that the ice on which they skate is firm enough to hold them. We know this is not true and our instinct is to protect them. We need to protect our children, but we also need to find ways to teach them how to shore up the ice on which they skate.

What parents are capable of doing for their children with NLD is invaluable and irreplaceable. I know a number of diverse factors have contributed to Sara's success. She has been blessed with a deeply optimistic nature and a strong sense of intellectual curiosity. She is a resilient fighter who simply will not give up, and who when given support, recovers quickly from failures and mishaps. Her almost superhuman ability to concentrate is ideal for someone with NLD because she has always had the patience to put in the never-ending rehearsal and practice she needs to master tasks. However, none of these psychological attributes would have done her as much good if my husband and I had not nurtured them.

Moreover, we would not have been as successful at helping Sara if we had not learned as much as possible about the challenges she faced. Although there are many things we parents can do best for our children, we will not be successful in helping them skate through life more securely without the expertise and support of professionals who can help us figure out practical ways to assist our children.

Chapter 8

Charting Sara's Language

Children with NLD depend almost exclusively on language to understand the world around them. They gravitate to the magnetic pull of words and futilely try to create their entire consciousness by speaking and listening. We have seen in previous chapters the hazards of relying solely on language to fashion a deep conceptional framework of the world. In order to develop meaningful concepts, individuals need more input than can be supplied by simply knowing the labels of the objects in their environment. They need the extra raw material that is supplied to them from visual images and tactile experiences.

In addition to over-relying on language, individuals with NLD also depend too heavily on rote memory to construct meaning. It is extraordinarily easy for them to commit words to memory and then to repeat back this memorized material verbatim. Few children with NLD experience the agony more typical students feel when they are assigned the drudgery of memorizing the preamble of the constitution, a long list of dates, or lines from a Shakespearian sonnet. However, the ability of students with NLD to memorize verbal material can be a dubious strength for two reasons. First, their virtuosity obscures the fact that these children frequently have a startlingly shallow understanding of the words they glibly memorize. They sound so well informed, so on the ball, as they blithely recite the date and site of every battle in the Civil War. But probe deeper, and you might find that these "experts" on the Civil War commonly are unaware of the reasons why the war was fought, or even that the battles they recite so convincingly took place in the United States. When children with NLD inadvertently dupe their parents and teachers with their verbal wizardry, we respond unintentionally by neglecting to lead them out of this world of narrow understanding.

Second, rote memory is a poor conduit for forming abstract ideas. As Thompson (1997) points out, a typical learner rarely attempts to memorize information, but "instead...integrates his experiences and then forms corresponding concepts and principles" (p.76). In the process, the typical learner observes patterns, tests hypotheses, notices relationships and frequently comes up with creative solutions and novel thoughts. "In contrast, the child with NLD starts by memorizing rote verbal information and acquires a tremendous store of general knowledge through his accumulated verbal interpretation" (Thompson 1997, p.76). Children with NLD rarely use their extensive font of knowledge as a scaffold to increase their conceptional understanding. They have acquired this information with too little effort and without the need for deep contemplation or mental manipulation. They are perfectly content to do what comes naturally to them—memorization without reflection.

When Sara was young, she placed all her trust in her ability to conquer the world through a combination of language and memory. She was like someone walking on thin ice; she could not distinguish the grave cognitive and emotional danger that lurked just under her feet. Every time my daughter came to breakfast with her shoes on the wrong feet, or her shirt on backwards, I could see the ice develop a hairline fracture. Frequently, I could see the brackish water under the membrane of ice when I tried to make sense of her puzzling renditions of movie plots or her literal interpretations of conversations. I knew that if Sara did not learn how to better understand the physical world, the ice would break and along with it my heart.

It took Sara many years of work before she was standing on solid ground. Words served as a lifeline for her. However, she learned to move beyond words and to figure out ways to connect words with visual stimuli in order to better understand her environment and to deepen her emotional responses. In the process, she learned how to overcome many of her social difficulties.

Sara first started to release herself from the worst symptoms of NLD when she was a young child and found solace and liberation through wordplay. At the Waldorf school, she was introduced to classic stories through storytelling, artistic activities and play-acting. Her natural inclination was to commit these narratives to memory. However, I was able to design interventions that capitalized on her natural penchant to memorize. These interventions allowed her to move beyond the limited understanding of language and concepts she would have gained from simply memorizing words. Although she attended an unusual school with a unique curriculum, there are universal lessons about the value of stories and developing the imagination for individuals with NLD that can be drawn from her experiences. By analyzing the process Sara underwent to strengthen her understanding of language and emotion, it is possible to develop intervention principles that can be applied to all children with NLD.

The first principle is that children with NLD must be taught how to write at a young age when it is still possible for them to develop fluent handwriting, or else they will lose access to a valuable learning conduit. Although it seems as if legible fluent handwriting is an impossible goal for them, individuals with NLD are capable of learning how to print and write if they receive enough practice at an early age (see Chapter 10, Intervention 2). Sara was seven when she finally mastered the required movements that are crucial to form legible letters. For the first time, the physical ability to write allowed her to document in a tangible form the thoughts that were in her imagination. Initially, the stories Sara composed were simply culled from her rote memory. They were literal replications of the stories and poems she heard every day at the Waldorf school, such as the narrative and accompanying illustration below of an Old Testament story she learned in the third grade.

Nov. 3

And God said: Let there be lights in the firmament to divide the day from the night. And let them be for seasons and years.
And God made two great lights. The greater light to rule the day and the lesser light to rule the night. he made. the stars also.
And God saw that it was good. And the evening and the morning were the fourth day.

The second principle is that children with NLD benefit greatly from exposure to imaginative stories with descriptive language and vivid visual images. Traditional fairy and folk tales contain many elements that make them ideal vehicles for expanding the understanding of children with NLD. For example, traditional stories tend to follow a recurring story structure these children can be taught to recognize and imitate. Second, traditional stories where goodness is rewarded and evil is punished appeal to these students' literal sense of right and wrong. Finally, the strong visual images and symbols described in the stories can be used to expand their ability to imagine, respond emotionally to the plight of characters, and think abstractly.

When Sara was in first grade, the school curriculum of her elementary dictated that the children listen exclusively to aural renditions of fairy tales. In the second grade, Sara added folk tales and fables to her story repertoire. These stories deeply captured her imagination. Every afternoon, she would come home from school and relate to me using the same words as her teacher the exact story she had heard that day. Over the course of that year, I heard dozens of magical tales in the simple, stark version of the Brothers' Grimm, very different renditions from the Disneyfied versions with which most American children are familiar.

The third principle is that students with NLD need to hear and discuss many similar examples of each type of story if they are to acquire the background knowledge that serves as raw material for more advanced thinking. By listening to different stories, all of which had related plot constructions and similar types of characters, Sara was able to receive substantial practice internalizing the elements that make up a story and the characteristics that were typical in villains and heroes. In addition, by hearing many renditions of similarly constructed stories, Sara was able repeatedly to identify emotionally with the struggles and triumphs of the main character. These stories were particularly useful to her because they all had a consistent form. One reason why children with NLD do not spontaneously discover patterns and relationships is because they do not process novelty well. However, if an adult points out key patterns and relationships to the child and then gives them much practice finding similar patterns in a parallel setting, the child with NLD can learn how to recognize the patterns and relationships they have practiced.

The fourth principle is to encourage children with NLD to capitalize on their talent in rote memory by encouraging them to retell the stories orally and write them down. When Sara listened to stories at school, it was natural for her to commit them to memory, and it was easy for her later to write down verbatim the words she had memorized. After she had related the story to me orally, she would excuse herself and escape to her room where she would commit the same story to writing. The words poured out of her pencil or crayon as she filled scores of pages over the course of that year. "Once upon a time there lived a man and woman they had every thing they wanted a sept for one thing it was a child! They lived in a hut by the river." After she learned to be a more fluent reader, she would read me her transcribed stories, and we could discuss them.

The fifth principle is to encourage students with NLD to form visual representations of linguistic concepts through artwork or other means and discuss the meaning of these works. At school, the children in Sara's class not only listened to these tales, they also drew pictures to illustrate the actions of the stories, and sculpted figures from modeling materials to represent the characters. I believe these activities helped Sara deepen her understanding of the concepts and emotions behind the words that she could memorize so easily with her extraordinary rote memory.

In the early years, when Sara was in the first three grades, she would race into the house after a day at school barely able to contain her excitement for whatever story she had learned that day. It was as if the floodgates of her imagination would open and words would pour from her. She would recite for me the stark stories of the German fairy tale in almost identical words to those her teacher had used earlier that day. In time, after having numerous experiences with both writing and illustrating the words she spoke, she began to demonstrate more understanding of the emotions of the characters. For example, one of the first stories she committed to writing and illustrating was the folktale, the Hare and the Tortoise, and she chose to capture this story on paper because she so identified with the protagonist in this old tale.

Sara was in second grade when this occurred, and her handwriting, through laborious practice, had only recently become serviceable enough to be quick and fluent. She raced into the kitchen that afternoon, her clothes askew, her brown hair escaping from the rubber bands that held her braids. Her eyes were bright and her cheeks flushed as she told me that she had heard the most wonderful story that day and did I want to hear it. Without waiting for a response, she began to recite the words of the comical old folktale about how a turtle against great odds beat his favored opponent, a rabbit, in a race. "Could such a thing be possible?" she demanded. "Could a very slow animal like the tortoise really beat a rabbit? Isn't it wonderful to think this could happen?" She then told me that she never imagined stories like this one could be true. She entertained the possibility that she was perhaps a tortoise who could win races if she worked hard enough. She decided that she liked the story so much she would go and write it down. She disappeared into her bedroom for an hour and, as became her habitual pattern for many years to come, recorded the words that she had just recited to me into a notebook and drew matching illustrations underneath her words. Through this process, my tortoise began training for the marathon that life had placed in her path.

When Sara listened to stories at school, it was natural for her to commit them to memory, and it was easy for her to write down the literal words she had memorized. By committing these stories to memory, she was learning in a fashion typical for someone with NLD. If she had done nothing else with these stories, she probably would have gained little more than a superficial understanding of them. However, by first writing out the words of the story, then illustrating the words in some fashion and discussing her images with me, she connected the words with visual images, and in the process created opportunities for her to link sensory experiences with the meanings of words.

It may seem inappropriate to encourage children with NLD to use drawing as a means to connect the visual to the auditory, since they are generally poor at art. Their pictures resemble the very primitive drawings of a preschool child. However, the goal of translating words into visual images for these children is not to produce beautiful works of art, but to help them "see" the world more clearly. Through discussing their pictures with them, teachers can glean much information about how these children are seeing the world and, through careful questioning, can lead them to a deeper and more accurate understanding of the meaning of words.

One important caveat is that since the drawings produced by these children are usually primitive, it is essential that no one comment on how "bad" their drawings appear. If students are reluctant to draw, they can use stamps, stickers or pictures cut from magazines to serve as visual representations as in the following example from Sara's early story about dinosaurs.

The sixth principle is that after students with NLD have received extensive practice in recording and illustrating their literal retellings of a particular type of story (biography, fairy tale, etc.), encourage them to invent a story that closely resembles the original one. Students with NLD will be surprisingly successful at creating derivative written passages when they can work from a mental model. About a year after Sara began writing daily literal renditions of fairy and folk tales, she advanced to writing original illustrated stories that were highly derivative of the kind of stories she heard at school and at home. As the stories she was exposed to deepened, so did her own stories.

Interestingly, each time she was required to produce a new type of written work, her writing regressed back to literal retellings. For example when she wrote her first book reports, she was only capable of producing a careful retelling of the plot. *The seventh principle is to encourage students to move beyond derivative writing and literal retellings to experiment with more reflective styles of writing, such as journal writing.* By the time Sara was in fourth grade, she had received extensive practice writing tales just like the ones she heard at school. Her stories then began frequently to mirror the stories she was reading herself, or mirrored events from her daily life. Here is an excerpt and accompanying illustration from one of Sara's first original stories, a tale about the adventures of a tissue named Ned the Napkin.

Later, Sara began to keep journals that recorded her thoughts and feeling as well as literal retellings of the day's events. By middle school, she occasionally began to produce more reflective pieces. For example, she wrote the following entry in her journal after returning from a trip to the zoo where she heard a zookeeper speak about the poaching of elephants for their ivory. "Let elephants live. Only elephants should wear ivory. That what it said on the zoo keepers pins that's right. I wrote this in a elephant that I got from the zoo."

In this passage, she demonstrates an emerging sense of justice and real empathy for the fate of wild elephants. She is additionally working out the figurative meaning of the idiomatic saying, *only elephants should wear ivory*, which the zookeepers had inscribed on buttons they wore and showed to the audience. It is interesting to note that after Sara understood the hidden meaning of the saying—*only elephants should wear ivory* meant that hunters should not kill elephants and use their ivory to make jewelry—she felt a need to record the words of the saying on an actual plastic replica of an elephant. As you work with your child, their entries might at first only be literal retellings of the days events. Lead them to deeper reflective thinking by asking them to answer questions such as: How did that make you feel? Why do you think that person said that? and so on.

Sara learned to connect words to visual stimuli by means of a physical activity at the Waldorf school. At home, we discussed the connections between the visual and the auditory to make sure that her understanding was accurate. Since she found this technique a useful method to aid her in making sense of the many puzzling expressions and experiences she encountered each day, she began to use this approach outside school. As a result, most of the stories, diaries, and written thoughts she produced were accompanied by some kind of visual illustration—usually pictures that she drew herself, but sometimes images cut from magazines, gummed stickers of animals or figures replicated in ink from wooden stamps. She would paste these images collage-like on her paper and write her words underneath. She continued for many years this pattern of recording what she heard, then illustrating the meaning of the words pictorially, gradually acquiring a more sophisticated understanding of language.

The eighth principle is to show the student how to construct original written work such as essays, book reports, and essay questions. Sara learned how to produce more sophisticated writing by being exposed to more complicated models or schema, such as how to compare and contrast, how to write a definition, and how to use examples. However, just as earlier she had focused on one type of story at a time, she now concentrated on mastering one type of essay. For example after she learned what the literary term *symbolism* meant, she wrote many papers for her English class where she discussed how symbolism was used in a particular piece of literature. By sticking to one idea or model, she was able to obtain the practice she needed to master a particular concept. Then she could try combining two models such as using "compare and contrast" with her understanding of symbolism by writing a paper where she compared the use of symbolism in several different literary works.

Using language to improve drawing and perception

Teachers and parents can help their children with NLD "see" the world with more precision by helping them become more accurate illustrators. I discovered this one summer when I tried to improve Sara's ability to draw. By the end of third grade, most of her classmates had developed a facility with drawing, painting, and sculpture. Sara's drawings remained primitive and stood out even more starkly in an academic environment that emphasized artistic work and where the drawing ability of most children in her class was above average. No one at school had ever commented on the primitiveness of her artwork, and Sara continued to enjoy drawing, seemingly unconscious of her limitations. I worried, though, that as the children grew older someone might tease her, and she would abandon the artistic habits that seemed to aid her perception so much.

In order to help her draw in a more mature fashion, I first compared her drawings with those of other children and tried to figure out why their drawings appeared more realistic and adult-like. I noticed one of the major differences was that Sara persisted in making everything in her drawings the same size. People, houses and trees were all the same height. As shown below, the mushroom and flower are about the same height as the children and the tree.

"Which is bigger," I asked her. "A tree or a flower?"
"Well, a tree obviously," she responded.
"How about a dog and a cat?"

She wasn't as sure about that so we went for a walk and observed different dogs. She noticed for the first time that dogs came in different sizes, some large and some small. We had two cats of our own, and concluded that generally dogs were larger than cats, but that there were exceptions. After we had discussed the gross differences between many objects and animals, I tried to get Sara to see the proportional differences between objects. For example, we examined the blades of grass in our lawn in an attempt to understand that although trees were larger than bushes, they were substantially larger than a blade of grass. We spent many hours that summer observing and discussing the world from the point of view of size and proportion.

After a few weeks, I took out some of Sara's drawings and explained that her drawings might be more interesting if they mirrored the sizes that she observed in real life. Through discussion, she saw that a flaw in her approach to drawing was her tendency to make every object the same size. The following examples show Sara's newfound understanding.

Drawing served an additional purpose for Sara. It gave her a means to gain some control over space and time. One of her weakest areas was her inability to understand spatial concepts. She got lost easily and struggled to organize her desk and keep track of her possessions. Even though she attended the same school for the first eight grades, she still was unable to locate many common rooms in her school building when she completed the eighth grade. By illustrating the stories that she learned and composed, Sara could create miniature worlds that were logical and accessible in ways the real world was not. I do not know for certain why she was so preoccupied with spending time recording what she saw and heard into the written word. However, one possible explanation was that in addition to

having NLD, Sara had an articulation disorder of significant severity. Until she completed three years of speech therapy, this disorder made it very difficult for people to understand what she was saying. Our family could understand her of course, but even I occasionally struggled to comprehend her words when we were rushed or when she recited long stories she had heard at school. I have always thought Sara turned to writing as a substitute for speech. Because she struggled so mightily to make herself understood, and because words were the strongest asset she possessed to make sense of the world around her, her pencil became her voice.

One of the differences between speaking and writing is that writing takes longer and encourages more reflection. Individuals with NLD are prone to glibness and verbosity, since they have a propensity for both rote memory and producing words. Sara could also be glib and verbose as a young child. However, since speaking clearly was not an area in which she excelled, she met with discouraging results when she tried to speak with others. Her peers, other adults, and even strangers commented endlessly on how difficult it was to understand her. She learned to speak very little outside her home. Instead, she turned to writing down her words and, perhaps in the additional time the process required, learned how to reflect more deeply.

Experiencing how others feel through play-acting

By listening to archetypal stories and writing them down, Sara learned how to create similar stories in her own voice. Writing supplied her with a means to reflect more deeply about language. She also had many opportunities to experience fairy tales, legends and myths through play-acting while she was a student at the Waldorf school. By taking on the persona of the character in a story, Sara was able to increase her understanding of how others feel.

It was at the Waldorf school where she learned "how to live in her experience." Waldorf education believes it is the "teacher's tasks to transform all that the child needs to know about the world into the language of the imagination" (Barnes 1997, p.151). For Waldorf educators, the elementary school years are a time when children need to develop their ability to feel. Therefore, children in Waldorf elementary schools are immersed in a curriculum of imaginative stories. The children then experience these stories through different media such as art, music, and play-acting. Waldorf teachers do not ask the children to understand these stories intellectually by comparing one legend to another, or to state the main idea of a particular myth. Rather, these teachers hope to make stories so vivid for students that they develop the ability to enter imaginatively into the hearts and minds of the characters and to experience the stories as if they were happening to themselves, almost like a heightened form of empathy. Waldorf teachers call this ability "living in your experience."

The following story is an example of another child "living in her experience." When Sara was ten and her brother was seven, we took one of Sara's classmates to an event at a natural history museum. Sara's friend, who was two years her junior, did not yet know how to read since the Waldorf school encourages late reading. The school believes an advantage of late reading is that children who are not using their mental energy to learn to read will have a greater capacity to interpret the world through imagination and feelings. The event at the natural history museum was a yearly affair where the museum opened up rooms and labs normally closed to the public. That evening scores of adults and children traveled through long corridors, stopping in different rooms to peer into boxes of stuffed birds and jars of creatures preserved in formaldehyde. There was always one room set aside to serve as a dissection site where several scientists dissected a large animal that had been found along a highway. This particular evening, the scientists were dissecting a large black bear. Parents hesitated at the door reluctant to expose their young children to such a grisly sight, but most children were drawn to the side of the table to peer into the innards of the huge shaggy creature suspended from the ceiling. The three children with me were no different. Later, as we continued to move through the museum, we seemed to stumble on bears everywhere we went, such as a Mexican dance group clad in bear masks acting out an ancient folkloric dance of the bear spirit.

Finally, we entered the main hall where museum staff had set up an educational display about bears. Children, obviously bright and literate, circulated among the stations reading the captions under artifacts, photographs, and dioramas that depicted various aspects of the lives of bears. Diana, our guest from the Waldorf school, was the only child present who could not read. Both of my children forged ahead of their friend and joined the crowd of other children around the display tables. Diana followed behind, bored, not fully able to participate in the activities. Suddenly, I heard my son hiss in my ear, "Mom, we have to get Diana out of here. She is turning into a bear." I turned around and watched as my children's friend, a tall and beautiful child, transformed herself into an ungainly bear, walking with a lumbering gait—a bear that soon was going to overturn all the display tables. We moved her away before the other people noticed the human bear in their midst. As we drove home that night, I realized that both Diana and the literate group of children had learned a lot about bears that night. They just learned different lessons. The literate group had learned many facts about the diet, habitat, and biology of bears. Diana, on the other hand, gathered all the sensorial impressions that she gleaned about bears and had used her imagination to transform herself into a real bear. Most of the children at the museum that night learned a lot *about* bears; Diana learned to *be* a bear.

For Sara, the ability "to live in her experience," which she learned through experiencing language transformed by artistic media, helped to deepen her understanding of language, human motivation, and empathy. For example, when she was in the seventh grade, her class put on a play about the life of Joan of Arc. Seventh grade in the Waldorf curriculum is when children learn about the lives of heroes and heroines who have been transformed through heroic events. The class worked on this play over the course of several months. Each girl in the class got to play one small chronological part in the life of Joan of Arc. For example, my daughter performed a ten-minute segment where she was transformed into Joan of Arc as a young girl. As Sara repeated the archaic language of another era, it was clear by the expression in her eyes and the poignancy in her voice that she understood every word she was reciting. For a short time, she experienced what it must have been like for this mystical French legendary figure to hear voices and see angels.

Moving beyond a literal interpretation

Individuals with NLD have a proclivity towards literalness. Sara was no different. So when she turned 12, I began to think about possible ways to help her move beyond her natural inclination to adhere to a strict interpretation of what she heard and read. My goal was to get her to recognize there was room for interpretation and elaboration beneath the literal meanings of words.

I discovered that the traditional way to help literal individuals is to teach them the meaning of common idioms such as "barking up the wrong tree" or "stop pulling my leg." Perhaps this approach has benefits for children with a mild inclination to a literal interpretation of language. However Sara's propensity to interpret language literally was so pervasive, I felt that teaching her how to interpret only selected idioms would not supply her with any general principles that she could use to decide when she was being too literal in other situations. I felt she needed considerable practice comparing her own literal interpretations to examples of more flexible interpretations if she was ever to acquire the ability to self-monitor.

I was able to develop an approach to teach Sara how to see the nuances of language based on the sound advice of her speech therapist. Sara attended several sessions in the summer after sixth grade conducted by the same speech therapist, Debbie, who had formerly taught her how to speak clearly. Debbie taught Sara the meanings of common English idioms, but she was still concerned about how literally Sara interpreted much of what she heard and read. I asked Debbie what could be done about this problem. She suggested that first I needed to teach Sara what it meant to be literal. Then every time I heard her interpret a word, passage, or phrase in an inappropriately literal fashion, I needed to explain to her why her interpretation was incorrect.

When I first heard this advice, I remember feeling completely overwhelmed by the enormity of such a project. There seemed to be an infinite number of instances in everyday conversation where Sara's interpretation or use of language was too literal. How was I going to hear and monitor all these errors of judgment? It seemed to me this task was analogous to raking up a yard full of leaves while new leaves constantly kept falling. However, I decided to heed Debbie's advice and teach Sara what it meant to be literal. It took considerable time and many examples before she could adequately judge for herself when she was being too literal. However, by acquiring the skill to recognize when her interpretation of words was too literal, Sara was able to learn how to self-monitor her own errors and to make more sound judgments about the meaning of the new words she heard, spoke, and read.

After Sara adequately grasped the meaning of the concept of *literalness*, we turned the task of discovering specific examples of her literalness into a family game. Every time one of us heard Sara using or interpreting language too literally, we would let her know. Sara, then, would try to figure out what was wrong with her interpretation. The game became a family affair as three pairs of ears lent themselves to the task of discovering examples of inappropriate interpretation. Even her younger brother, who had an extraordinary sense of language, turned his eagle ears to the task. However, the game had certain rules. No one was allowed to ever embarrass Sara by pointing out any literal mishaps in public or in front of her friends. Instead, we saved up these public examples of literalness and spoke about them later in private. Six years later, when Sara was a senior in high school, she picked up a novel that was lying on a table. It was entitled *The Page Turner*, a story about a failed pianist who made a career turning pages for other more successful musicians. "If you were literal you might think this book is about someone who turns pages, say of music," Sara told me. "But if you were not literal," she continued, "you would figure the title of the book means that this is an exciting book, one that you want to read fast, like a bestseller. What is the title referring to—the literal interpretation or the expression *a page turner*?" I told her that, in this case, the literal interpretation was the correct one.

It dawned on me how much she had learned in the six years our family had dissected every literal example we heard come into our house. It was summer when this happened, and leaves rarely fall in summer. When autumn arrived, I knew Sara would know how to catch any new leaves without our help.

Chapter 9

Some Final Thoughts

The process of writing this book has deepened my admiration for individuals with all forms of learning disabilities. We really know so little about their difficulties, and yet we feel qualified to make predictions about their future. We define their difficulties as both immutable and permanent. In the process, we close the door to the possibility of discovering which obstacles are fluid and surmountable. Through my work with numerous students who struggle with many of Sara's challenges, I have come to believe that all individuals with nonverbal learning disabilities can improve their situation, and that the focus of educational research should move beyond diagnosis in order to concentrate on developing meaningful interventions to assist them.

As a professional, I have been fortunate to know many individuals with learning disabilities and I have been deeply privileged—privileged beyond words—to be able to serve as a guide for my daughter as she has explored the world with her inexhaustible optimism in the power of language. However, if it is imprudent to underestimate the potential of these students, it is equally foolish to romanticize nonverbal learning disabilities and define them as simply another interesting form of consciousness. There is no doubt in my mind that NLD is truly a disability, an irritating condition that makes life unnecessarily arduous. If I had a magic wand and could release my daughter from the spell of NLD, I would free her without hesitation. There is little room in the current definition of learning disability for the grief of parents—for the inexhaustible well of tears that can never be completely shed as parents realize that NLD will certainly deny the possibility of an easy life for their child. Helen Keller (2004), writing about a more concrete disability, blindness, asserted, "The calamity of the blind is immense, irreparable. But it does not take away our share of the things that count…service, friendship, humor, imagination, wisdom" (p.56). The greatest gift I have received from trying to comprehend what it is like to have NLD is that I can understand the sadness as well as the joy of this mysterious condition.

When Sara started graduate school in Boston last year, the initial difficulties that she faced caught our family off guard. We had falsely assumed that after four successful years in college she had all the basic skills she required to quickly adjust to this new educational experience. We honestly thought that graduate school was going to be a piece of cake for her because we had so completely vanquished NLD. We were wrong. NLD is like a monkey on the back of the person with this difficulty; it never goes away even if its intensity fades for a time. When my husband left Sara in front of her new apartment as he prepared to return home, they both could not stop crying because they simultaneously realized how difficult this new challenge was going to be. Two weeks later on the day before Sara started classes, she spent eight hours riding a shuttle bus back and forth from her apartment to her school trying to make sense of the maze of one-way streets that were once winding, twisting cow paths. When I called Sara that evening to see how things were going, she told me that she was preparing to ride the bus several more times after dark since many of her classes would end in the evening, and everything looks different at night. She did manage to get to her classes the next day and, despite all the additional challenges that she faced, has been able to thrive in this new educational environment. However, her success belies the extraordinary effort she has put forth. I can only begin to imagine the depth of courage that individuals like my daughter must call on on a daily basis.

We need to better understand nonverbal learning disabilities. Otherwise, we should hang over the doorway of every school a sign that says "enter at your own peril" because, for these children, school is a maze of confused perceptions. If we are able to understand their difficulties and discover ways to help them, we will open a door of hope, and in doing so we will also enrich ourselves by increasing our understanding of how all children learn and prosper.

Seeing the third dimension

When Sara started graduate school in speech-language pathology, she was caught off guard by how much anatomy she was going to need to learn. Anatomy is a particularly challenging subject for her because it requires translating two-dimensional pictures into three-dimensional mental images. At first, she did the best that she could by relying on her excellent rote memory. She spent hours memorizing the verbal labels for different organs and nerves and then tried to attach these labels to the corresponding location on each visual image she encountered. The first time she was required to demonstrate her anatomical knowledge in a lab, she was lucky to find a compatible lab partner. The purpose of the lab was to use toothpicks to mark the areas on a sheep's brain that corresponded to the labels on a printed diagram. Sara found a fellow classmate with a fabulous sense of visual perception, but with an intense visceral reaction to dissection. If her lab partner stood too close to the sheep's brain, she would instantly faint. Sara and the fainter made an ideal team as lab partners. The fainter with the fabulous visual-spatial sense stood at a distance and gave Sara verbal directions. Sara, with steady hand and stomach, inserted toothpicks into the sheep's brain, and they both successfully completed their labs.

The following semester, Sara was required to take a neuroanatomy class. She had heard from fellow students that this was a very difficult class, and she was worried that her rote memory would not serve as an adequate means to learn the material. She decided to try a different tactic and began to construct three-dimensional models from play dough in an attempt to improve her spatial understanding of the brain. After her second exam in the course, she sent me the following email:

> I wanted to share the good news that I got a 101% on my neuroanatomy exam, and the best part was that I got all the pictures correct, including novel ones in strange views. I am really starting to understand this stuff now. J. [her roommate] helped me by cutting up an apple to look at the different views, and it was so much easier to see it in three dimensions as opposed to two. I am not really worried about neuro anymore, and it is nice not to have to memorize a picture for every view now…

When Sara was in the third grade, we decided to visit her former kindergarten teacher at her old school. Sara wanted to say "hello" and show her former teacher how she had learned to read. Her teacher was a kind woman, but she felt that I had unrealistic expectations for a child with Sara's difficulties. Although she felt that Sara was a lovely child, if you pressed her, you could see that she did not expect Sara to be particularly successful in school or life. When Sara entered the classroom that day, she brought a well-known children's novel with her. "Can you read that book?" the former teacher asked her. Sara opened the book to the page where her bookmark lay. She read a paragraph. The teacher looked away, perplexed, and busied herself with other small children in the room. "It was good to see you, Sara," she said. She did not acknowledge the reading, and yet I know that she would only wish the best for my daughter. I longed to tell her that none of us have a crystal ball, and how I have discovered that no one can totally predict what another human being is capable of attaining. At that moment, I want to reassure her by telling her that she had been completely accurate in her observations about all the things Sara couldn't do. "You were correct," I want to say, "in sensing what an uphill battle learning was going to be for her." But what this teacher did not correctly predict were all the techniques I had discovered to make that uphill battle easier. In addition, she had greatly underestimated the grit of the little girl standing before her who possessed so much of that capacity of human beings to change their situation when they are shown how. But I say nothing, smile, and exit the room.

Chapter 10

A Sampler of Interventions

Introduction

In Colonial America, schoolgirls created decorative pieces of needlework called *samplers*. These samplers might contain an example of each letter of the alphabet embroidered in one of the many representative stitches a girl would need to know in order to become an accomplished seamstress. Samplers were not designed to be exhaustive or complete but gave prototypical examples from which individuals could form generalizations. The following sampler of interventions includes only a taste of the ways teachers and parents can better assist individuals with NLD to adapt academically and in the outside world.

When Sara was young, and I first began developing ways to help her through what seemed a baffling morass of unrelated difficulties, I sometimes felt as if I was trying to clean out an enormous messy attic. I didn't know where to start cleaning because I was overwhelmed by a seemingly chaotic untidiness. But when I started helping her in one area, like teaching her how to form a letter, I noticed that this clutter was not as random as I had first believed. As I found a way to order one area of the attic, I saw that I could use the same techniques to clean up another area and, by moving back and forth between clean and cluttered areas, could restore order.

The mind of someone with NLD can seem as disorienting as the jumble of a neglected attic, and at first it seems impossible to believe there can be a system to restore order to this disarray. Unlike the difficulties of an individual with verbal learning disabilities that usually only affect one domain and a few related academic subjects, the challenges faced by the individual with NLD affect many domains and diverse academic subjects. Therefore, the learning profile of a typical individual with NLD does not lend itself to strictly linear interventions (do this step first, and then this next step will follow logically, etc.). The following sampler contains diverse examples of interventions that can be used at different ages to help individuals with NLD. From these examples, I hope teachers and parents will uncover a logic they can use to develop other interventions to help their special children, and to make the process of cleaning up the attic seem less random, chaotic, and overwhelming.

As you begin to develop interventions, it is important to keep in mind the following principle. It is not possible for these students to "bypass" the visual if they are going to make sense of their world. At first, it might seem logical to restrict their exposure to visual materials such as charts and maps or to discourage them from participating in writing, drawing, or copying because they are not visual learners. By taking this course of action, we hope to shield them from unnecessary frustration and failure. We also believe they can learn all they need by participating in activities that capitalize on their verbal and auditory strengths. Unfortunately, the logic behind this kind of thinking is well-meaning but faulty. Individuals with NLD must be taught how to understand the visual precisely because they are not natural visual learners and, unless explicitly taught, will not otherwise spontaneously learn how to make sense of our highly visual world. Unless we provide them with meaningful ways to interpret what they see, they will be excluded from important information about their environment that often provides the keys to independent thought and social acumen.

An analogous situation occurred in the past in teaching reading to children with reading disabilities. These children have great difficulty learning how to read because they fail to grasp that spoken words are made up of individual sounds. Consequently, they cannot spontaneously figure out how the individual sounds of spoken language work together to create words, or how letters correspond to these sounds. As a result of this weakness, some authorities erroneously believed these children would not benefit from phonics instruction. Instead, they believed the best way to teach children with reading disabilities how to decode was by capitalizing on their strong visual skills. They felt it was possible for these children to read if they memorized what the words on the page looked like, and in this way they could completely bypass their weak areas in phonemic awareness and phonics. Research has since found this thinking untenable. Children failed to learn to read successfully unless they were explicitly taught how to analyze the sounds in words.

We cannot expect students with NLD to learn spontaneously how to interpret visual materials. We need to show them explicitly how to connect the visual with the verbal, so they can learn to deepen their understanding of what they see. The following general principles are important to keep in mind when developing interventions:

1. The first principle is always to use language to explain every learning experience. The way to "show" someone with NLD how to accomplish a task or understand a concept is by using words. Language is the medium through which these individuals gain understanding.

2. Always clarify the basic visual "vocabulary" of the task before you start teaching any concept. For example, before teaching a high school student how to get to her classes, make sure she knows what a *floor* in a building really means. Explain how the numbering system of the building frequently matches the number of the floor on which the room is located (all the rooms in the 200s are found on the second floor). If you are teaching a student how to use an elevator, do not assume the student understands that the numbers she must push in the elevator car match the floor where she wants to exit. Before your student attempts to find a solution to a geometry problem, make sure she understands the vocabulary of every diagram or drawing, such as *line, angle, corner, side*. Assume nothing. Keep in mind how often the verbal skill of these individuals masks their confusion with elementary concepts. They can use words like *floor, angle, corner,* and *diagonal* convincingly when they speak. However, if you ask them to identify an angle in a complex figure or guess on which floor room 343 is found, you will find they frequently have the ability to use words without a clear understanding of their meaning. Fortunately, if you make sure they have enough experience through clear verbal explanations to match a verbal label to the visual object, they will eventually gain a conceptual understanding of the term.

3. Introduce the idea early to the student that words can have multiple meanings, and look for every opportunity to teach these

multiple meanings. Individuals with NLD are both logical and spectacularly literal. This combination results in individuals who try to make sense of what goes on around them by employing a curious logic that is frequently difficult for others to decipher. For example, if you were to ask a student with NLD who is not familiar with the multiple meanings of the word *floor* how many floors were in her school, she might respond by counting all the classrooms, bathrooms, and closets because each has a floor.

4. Remember these are students who respond well to logic. Employ clear, logical verbal explanations when explaining complex concepts. You want them to understand that the world is not totally random even though visual stimuli often seem that way to them. Moreover, if they understand the logic of how things work, they will not need to over-rely on rote memory.

5. Teach them generalizations. In order for them to master a task or concept, they need extensive practice with a specific model. However, after they have mastered a specific concept, they need help in forming useful generalizations they can use to judge new situations. For example, Sara learned how to monitor her tendency to literalness when she could judge what it meant to be literal.

6. Encourage flexibility of thought. Individuals with NLD do the best they can with the mind they have been given. They are not naturally flexible, and generally try to make sense of the world by rigidly applying rules. Counter this tendency by discussing and giving examples of how rules have exceptions and limitations.

7. Work simultaneously on interventions to improve students' academic, social, and motor challenges.

8. Have realistic expectations for these students. Individuals with NLD vary greatly in their cognitive abilities, drive, and capacity to learn.

9. However, don't sell these students short. If teachers and parents can successfully figure out how to explain educational tasks using language, there is not one area—not algebra, reading comprehension, or social acumen—that cannot be taught to individuals with NLD. They can learn anything if they are taught appropriately.

Each of the interventions that follows will be presented in a similar format, with the following sections:

    (a) problem

    (b) strengths available to the student

    (c) proposed intervention solution

    (d) how the solution can be generalized to other situations

    (e) ultimate goal of this intervention

    (f) resources available to parents and teachers.

The Appendix illustrates how the previously described strategies can be combined to form lessons that address or reinforce multiple learning goals.

Intervention 1: Common motor skills

(a) Problem

Difficulty learning how to do up/undo buttons, brush teeth, open a door, or related everyday tasks that require making sense of simple motor movements.

(b) Strengths

Sensitivity to verbal cuing, strong desire to learn, strong rote memory for verbal information.

(c) Solution

Observe the child carefully, and directly teach each motor task with which she is struggling. The teacher needs to break the targeted motor skill into each discrete step required to complete the task. Do this by practicing the task yourself before you demonstrate the steps to the student. When you are able to isolate each component step of the motor task, directly demonstrate each step to the student and, at the same time, explain with words exactly what you are doing. The following is a sample dialogue to teach a student with NLD how to fasten a button. First, make sure that the student is looking in the direction of your hands and the actual button. This may seem obvious, but many children with NLD are not aware of the particular direction or spot towards which you want them to look. After you have ascertained that she is looking at your hands and the button, repeat the following directions orally, while you slowly execute the necessary movements required to fasten a button:

First, pinch the button with your thumb and first finger. Open up the buttonhole with your other thumb and first finger like this (pause). Push the button through the hole, and grab the button with your other thumb and first finger (pause). Pull the button through the hole with your fingers, and at the same time grab the cloth around the buttonhole while you pull the button through.

Immediately after you have demonstrated how to fasten a button, have the child try to replicate the necessary movements for doing this. You will need to continue to repeat the oral directions for each separate movement at the exact time the child is executing the movement. Then have her practice fastening a button several more times. You should include fewer words in your oral directions with each subsequent repetition. By the time the child is almost proficient at independently fastening a button, your directions should be reduced to "pinch, (pause or snap your finger), grab, (pause or snap finger), pull through." Particularly with younger children, it helps to snap your fingers or make another sound between each command. This seems to help the child with the rhythm of the movements.

(d) Generalization

This procedure can be adapted to teach any motor task. Remember, if students with NLD extensively practice a motor task, they will become proficient at it. However, you will need to repeat this procedure with each new motor task the student encounters, such as opening and closing an umbrella, operating a microwave, and so on. Also keep in mind that this procedure will need to be repeated with every new variation of an already learned task. For example, even when a student has mastered opening one umbrella, they will need instruction on how to use another umbrella that opens with a different mechanism. Consult an occupational therapist if you need advice on how to figure out the steps for more complex motor tasks like riding a bicycle or skipping with a rope.

(e) Goal

Ultimately, you want the student to be able to recognize when she is unable to complete a motor task and to ask for help. For example, you want her to be able to come to you and say, "I cannot complete this lab because I don't know how to turn on the Bunsen burner. Will you show me how?"

(f) Resources to help with motor skills

Infancy

1.   Purchase a British-style wooden baby walker. This device is completely different from an American baby walker. An American-style baby-walker has a seat with openings for the baby's feet and four metal legs with wheels. The baby sits in the seat and moves the walker with her feet. A British baby walker is a low wooden wagon with a high erect handle that the baby holds while she walks. The device is designed not to tip. It will aid a baby who has poor balance when she first tries to walk. One model is available from Galt Toys (www.galttoys.com).

2.   Do everything possible to encourage exploratory behavior. For example, bring interesting objects with various textures to your child and encourage her to feel them. Let her play with water, soap bubbles, and sand. Respect her dislike of novelty by slowly introducing her to new experiences. The publication, *Growing Child*, is a monthly newsletter that contains developmental information about infancy. Although the newsletter concerns itself with the development of "typical" infants, it contains many creative suggestions for developmentally appropriate activities that encourage exploratory behavior. As always, a parent or therapist will need to add language to these activities to make them meaningful for the child with NLD. "Feel this piece of sandpaper. Oh, it feels so rough."

Preschool

1.   *Helping Children Overcome Learning Difficulties* (1979) by Jerome Rosner has an excellent section on improving the motor skills and visual perception of preschool children (pp.310–323). The book is not specifically written for children with NLD, so remember to add verbal instructions to all the exercises and games.

2.   The National Lekotek Center maintains centers with "toy lending libraries." These libraries contain high-quality toys designed for children with a broad range of disabilities, including physical disabilities. Many of the games and toys make wonderful tools to help children with NLD increase their understanding of visual-spatial concepts. When Sara was a preschooler, our public

library contained a small toy lending library with educational toys from Lekotek. I remember borrowing many expertly designed puzzles for Sara. By showing Sara how to use these educational tools, she was able to learn many important concepts about classifying size and shape. I remember one particular wooden toy that came in two large wooden boxes. Sara loved this toy, and we took it out many times when she first became interested in trying to print letters. The toy was a series of 52 inlay puzzles, one for each upper- and lower-case letter of the alphabet. Each letter of the puzzle was carved from hardwood and fitted into a matching wooden form. Sara used to fit the letters into their matching inlay and lay the 26 puzzles out in alphabetical order across our living room. Sometimes she would experiment with different ways to classify the upper- and lower-case letters. The letters were large, and she needed to move around a great deal in order to lay out the puzzles. To learn more about locations with toy libraries contact Lekotek Center, 3204 W. Armitage Av, Chicago, IL, 773-276-5164, www.lekotek.org

Elementary school

1. *Helping Children Overcome Learning Difficulties* (Rosner 1979) has an excellent section for improving motor and visual perceptional skills for K-3 students (pp.119–126; pp.82–89).

2. Ark Institute of Learning (www.arkinst.org) offers a product called the Learning Window, which is a frame covered with a transparent piece of plastic. The frame allows the teacher to demonstrate drawing in a position where she is facing the student. In this way she can more accurately guide the student's movements.

3. Keep your elementary-aged child involved in appropriate activities that encourage fine and gross motor skills. Encourage your student to continue to develop gross motor abilities by remaining physically active. Children with NLD do not need to participate in conventional sports in order to fulfill this goal. Encourage physical activities that combine movement with language. For example, encourage your student to start and maintain a collection of leaves, rocks, feathers, or shells. Since children of this age are frequently interested in collecting, they

may enjoy activities such as hiking if the purpose is to find more objects to add to their collection. Have them display collections in interesting containers and label items with gummed labels.

4.   Encourage games and play that develop fine motor skills and visual perception. Many contemporary toys are too visually busy to be helpful. Seek out well-designed games with simple graphics. Some possible choices are the following:

(a) Hama or perler beads (www.perlerbeads.com, www.makingfriends.com, www.beadmerrily.com)—these are plastic beads that fit on a pegboard to make interesting objects; the beads are then fused together with an iron to make a permanent keepsake.

(b) Rubber stamps—since drawing is difficult for children with NLD, they can create interesting pictures, cards, and stories using stamps as illustrations.

(c) Collage—another art form that does not rely on drawing ability; the student can use paper, photographs, postcards, ripped paper, and so on.

(d) Elementary-age children can have some success working with modeling materials such as clay, play dough, and so on.

(e) Encourage them to memorize skipping rope songs, riddles, and other verbal nonsense that children enjoy. They memorize this kind of information easily, and it can give them a role to play in games if the corresponding physical activity is too demanding. For example, Sara never learned how to skip with a rope well, but she was the champion at knowing the verses of every skipping rhyme. So when the girls in her class went through a stage where they spent recess skipping with ropes, she learned how to turn the rope and provide all the right words.

High school

1.   *The Source for Visual-Spatial Disorders* (2002) by Neff, Neff-Lippman, and Stockdale has a section on how to teach a

teenager with Turner's Syndrome how to drive. Turner's Syndrome has many similarities to NLD.

2. Enroll the student in a beginner's photography course if she has an interest. By learning how to capture visual images on film, the student can learn to better observe her environment. There are many books explaining basic photographic principles, such as *The Absolute Beginner's Guide to Taking Great Photos* (2002), by Jim Miotke.

Intervention 2: Penmanship
(a) Problem
Difficulty forming any letter or numeral legibly due to challenges in understanding how to analyze patterns into their component parts, how those parts fit together, and having no visual concept for terms like straight, curved, diagonal, and so on.

(b) Strengths
Sensitivity to verbal directions, good vocabulary, strong interest in stories, motivated to learn to write.

(c) Solution
Before showing the student how to form a letter, show her how to analyze patterns. Rosner (1979) has an excellent program called the *Visual Perceptual Skills Program*, where the child copies patterns using geoboards and rubber bands (pp.75–82). The child learns how to stretch rubber bands over pins to form shapes and lines. In order to form these shapes, the student copies the increasingly more complex patterns that the teacher models. The program does not emphasize language and must be modified to include verbal cuing to ensure it is meaningful for students with NLD.

Teach the language of patterns and lines (straight, curved, top, bottom, half-way down, slanted, etc.) concurrently with teaching the student how to copy patterns. Do this by systematically asking the student questions after she copies a specific pattern. For example, the first pattern in Rosner's program is a square. Point to the square, and ask the child questions such as, "Can you show me a side of this shape? Let's count the sides, and see how many sides this figure has? Are these sides straight or slanted?"

To ensure that the child is not relying solely on rote memory to learn these concepts, offer many opportunities to deepen her concept by combining language with experience. For example, have the student form a curved line out of clay or with a piece of yarn, while she verbally explains the important features of a curved line. Help the student compose an illustrated dictionary of terms describing spatial concepts.

When the student has a good understanding of the kind of lines that make up basic patterns and can successfully analyze elementary patterns, you can begin teaching her how to form specific letters. You can use the following approach to teach either cursive or manuscript writing. However, remember to emphasize that all lower-case print letters start at the top and go down, and all lower-case cursive letters start at the bottom of the line and go up. Begin with an easy letter to form like an *i*. Analyze the letter in the same manner as you would analyze a pattern. Say:

> Look at this letter. It is made up of two parts—a straight line that is standing up, and then a little dot on top of the straight line. Watch me make an *i* (speak at the same time as you are writing). When we make this letter, we start right here, and move our pencil down. Then we pick up our pencil and make a little dot on top of the line. Now you try it. I will tell you what to do while you make it.

When the student is able to make several of the less complex letters without the help of verbal cuing, divide the alphabet into "families of letters." Determine which letters go in each family by the similarity of stroke that you need to use to form the letter. For example, you make the following six letters, *c, a, o, g, q, d* using the same beginning stroke. Identify these letters with a descriptive name like the "c" family. The letters *i, t, l, b, h, k, j, p,* and *r* form another family, because they are all formed with the same initial straight line. They could be called the "line family." Have the students practice all the letters in one family so that they learn the movements needed to form similar letters. Include verbal cuing until the student can form the letters correctly and has committed the shapes to memory. It is not necessary at first to emphasize the relative sizes of different letters. Allow the children to make their first attempts at forming specific letters on unlined paper, so they can make their letters as large as they need to.

After the children can legibly form all lower-case letters, help them make smaller letters that can fit on conventional lined paper. Next show them how various letters have different relative sizes. Divide the letters of the alphabet into groups by size. Explain and demonstrate to the student that some letters are tall (b, h, k, t, etc.), and take up the whole space between the lines on a piece of paper. Others are short (a, c, e, m, etc.) and take only half a space. A third group of letters hangs down below the line (p, j, g, etc.). Have the students practice making letters while they consider the size and position of the letters on the paper.

Develop ways to increase the sensorial and kinesthetic feedback to the hand. One way to accomplish this is to make a "writing screen." To construct a writing screen, purchase a 10 inch by 20 inch (approx 25 cm by 50 cm) piece of screening used to repair screen windows. Then frame the perimeter and back of the screen with sections of wood so there are no sharp edges of the screen visible. Place a piece of unlined paper on top of the screen. The teacher then forms a particular letter on the paper using a crayon. The student is instructed to copy over this letter many times. The teacher should talk to the student while she repeatedly copies the letter to make sure she is moving the crayon in the right direction. If the student uses a different colored crayon each time she copies, she will create an interesting effect by producing a multicolored letter with a bumpy surface. When the student has completed her letter, she can trace over it with her fingers. This exercise works particularly well with Stockmar stick beeswax crayons (available from www.waldorftreasures.com/artsupplycraftkit/artsupplies/stockmar/stockmar.htm) because the different colors blend together to form interesting shades.

When the student is skilled at forming letters, ask her to write from memory all the letters in a particular class; for example, write all the letters in the "c" family, or all the tall letters. Ask her questions to help cement the visual image of the letter into her memory. For example, ask her questions such as the following: How many letters are there in the "straight-line" family of letters? How many letters in the alphabet hang down below the lines? Can you make each of them?

Other ways to increase visual memory of the form of letters are to ask the student to write them with her eyes closed, to write letters on a chalkboard using a large paintbrush and plain water, to use chalk on the sidewalk, or to use a marker on a white board. Make up riddles such as the following: "Write the letter that is a tall letter and is in the line family and looks like a cross." Remember students with NLD need to experience an exorbitant amount of practice copying letters if they want to attain legible handwriting, so you want to develop fun and varied ways for them to practice. After the students have mastered the form of each individual letter, they can start to practice making each letter in alphabetical order.

When the students are proficient at forming letters, they can begin writing words and sentences. Encourage as much writing as possible because, through repetition, the handwriting of students with NLD will become highly legible. Since they have strong verbal abilities, written expression is a possible vehicle for self-expression. Writing can become an area of strength, if they also receive assistance in concept-building and semantic language. Sara was even able to cultivate certain social skills that were difficult for her by learning to write emails to her high school classmates that allowed her time to reflect on her interactions with them.

In addition to handwriting instruction, students with NLD need instruction in keyboard skills during middle school. Learning to type requires less fine motor control than learning penmanship, and as a result is an easier skill for these students to master. However, students with NLD will initially find using a keyboard a challenge and will require specific verbal directions from a teacher. Acquiring keyboard skills will aid the writing of these students by giving them access to word processing programs and electronic organizers.

(d) Generalization

The same principle of using words to analyze patterns can be used to help students with NLD understand how to interpret maps, charts, graphs, visual organizers, pictures, or even how to improve their drawing if they are interested in art. Constantly teach the increasingly more sophisticated language of space and size that students will be exposed to as the curriculum becomes more complex (e.g., parallel, perpendicular, angles.) Give the students concrete experiences to make sure they have the conceptual basis for understanding these terms, and are not relying on their rote memory simply to parrot back a definition.

(e) Goal

Students will create accurate and specific internal pictures or images to match their language and be able to apply this knowledge in similar situations.

(f) Resources for handwriting

All ages

The sooner a student receives help in handwriting the better her chances are for mastery. However, the same procedure is appropriate for any age, and these resources can be modified to teach any student to write. Since these are not resources specifically developed for students with NLD, the teacher must make certain that she is adding verbal instructions.

1. "Teaching Handwriting" in *Multisensory Teaching of Basic Language Skills* (Birsch 2005) is a useful chapter by Beverly J. Wolf on teaching handwriting to students with dyslexia. With modification, many of the same approaches are relevant for students with NLD.

2. *Writing Skills for the Adolescent* (1985) by Diana Hanbury King has an excellent section on learning cursive handwriting. Specifically written to teach adolescents with serious spelling and reading problems, the information on teaching handwriting is relevant to younger students and to students with NLD.

3. *Loops and Other Groups: A Kinesthetic Writing System* (1999) by Mary Benbow is probably the best writing method for children with NLD. It is written from the point of view of an occupational therapist, and emphasizes the motor movements needed to form a letter. The system only covers cursive letters, but the principles in the book can be adapted to teach manuscript writing.

4. The grotto grip is a highly effective plastic grip that can be attached to a pencil to help the student learn the correct way to hold the pencil. (See www.grottogrip.com.)

5. The following resources are helpful for teaching typing:

    (a) *Keyboarding Skills* (1986) by Diana King is an excellent program for teaching students with NLD how to type. The program emphasizes verbal cuing and presents a way for a student to learn the whole keyboard in a very short time.

(b) *Read, Write & Type Learning System* is a computer program to teach children with reading difficulties how to read and type (www.readwritetype.com). Most children with NLD do not need the reading portion of the program but can benefit from the massive amount of typing practice provided by the program. In addition, the program is developed for young children (ages 6–9).

(c) There is lightweight inexpensive "typing machine" called the Type-Right II. It resembles a toy typewriter and is easy to transport, making it ideal to use for extra practice in the car, in waiting rooms, and so on.

Intervention 3: Finding one's way
(a) Problem
Difficulty finding their way around even in familiar places like school and home, tendency to get lost, difficulty remembering and picturing what familiar places look like. No internal compass to make sense of the space around them.

(b) Strengths
Memory for factual material, even nonverbal material, if it is strongly coded into memory with words. Excellent rote memory such that if they practice a task simultaneously with verbal cuing and the task becomes overlearned, they will remember it.

(c) Solution
Many individuals get lost easily. However, the difficulty that students with NLD experience when they try to go from point A to point B is much more debilitating than many of us can imagine. Much of the anxiety experienced in school by students with NLD comes directly from this difficulty. Older students are often unable to concentrate in school because they are worrying about how they will find their next class. The inability to find their way around frequently results in these students isolating themselves and limiting their physical activity. Individuals with severe NLD can be directly across the street from a building they are looking for and not be

aware of it. Luckily, they have strengths that can be harnessed and used to help them learn how to travel independently.

By using a combination of verbal mediation and rehearsal, students with NLD can learn how to find their way around. It is best if a teacher or parent can show them how to find their way to specific places before they experience failure and the resulting anxiety. Since the problem of getting lost is not magically going to vanish, it is safe to assume that every new environment will be a challenge for them to maneuver. Therefore, it is a good idea for the student to practice going to all new important places. For example, before the school year begins, an adult should help the older student, who will need to change classes, find her way to each of the rooms where her classes are held. This includes pointing out the spatial logic of the school—for example, the numbering system of the rooms, the number of floors, where staircases are located. For the first few times, a person with a good sense of direction should accompany the person with NLD, giving verbal instructions on where to go. Then, let the student try to find the way on her own with the helper standing a distance apart. Finally, allow the student to try to find her way totally on her own. This procedure may sound time-consuming, but there are actually a finite number of places that make up an individual's daily routine. Once the individual with NLD has mastered her routine, she will not need your assistance.

Parents can use the same rehearsal procedure to build up a repertoire of places that the child with NLD can draw on successfully to get around her community. Explain the spatial logic of your community to your child. For typical U.S. towns, for example, explain what a block is, and then practice walking one block. Play games where you write out instructions like, "walk for two blocks in the direction of H.'s house. Then turn left, and continue walking for three more blocks, and I will be waiting there for you." The important thing is to anticipate the difficulty that students with NLD are going to experience when traveling to new places, and to rehearse a route with them for getting there before they experience failure and anxiety. The time that teachers and parents spend doing this kind of rehearsal is well worth the trouble and will give the student the skills needed to become independent.

(d) Generalization

The same rehearsal with verbal cuing technique can be used to teach individuals with NLD how to use public transportation systems.

(e) Goal

Since this will be a life-long problem, it is essential that adults with NLD learn how to rehearse independently getting to and from the places where they will need to travel in every new situation in their life. They need to learn how to ask for direction, and whom it is safe to ask. They need to have a plan about what to do if they find themselves lost. Consequently, they need to know how to use and carry a cellphone at all times.

(f) Resources

1. *The Source for Visual-Spatial Disorders* (2002) by Neff *et al.* has some information about finding one's way around. This book concentrates on the experience of someone with Turner's Syndrome.

2. The article "Helping the Learning Disabled Adolescent Learn to Drive" has useful suggestions for students with NLD (Brown 2005). Available from www.ldaamerica.org/aboutld/parents/help/drive.asp.

Intervention 4: Vocabulary and reading comprehension

(a) Problem

Difficulty with reading comprehension particularly after the third grade when text becomes less concrete, difficulty understanding the "deeper" meaning of words, an emptiness to their understanding of words, a tendency to use words inappropriately.

(b) Strengths

Sensitivity to and strong interest in language, familiar with many words, excellent decoders, adept at reading text, good rote memory for verbal information.

(c) Solution

Even though students with NLD are facile at reading words, they have difficulty understanding the underlying meaning of text. These students have excellent rote memories and are adept at answering questions that require them to recall facts about a text. They are also good at giving a literal retelling of a story plot. However, they are not proficient at seeing the big picture, so they struggle with essential reading comprehension tasks such as understanding the main idea, forming inferences, drawing conclusions, making predictions, and devising judgments. The most powerful way to improve the reading comprehension of students with NLD is to teach them how to visualize through a formal program called *Visualizing and Verbalizing for Language Comprehension and Thinking* (V/V) by Bell (1986). In this carefully structured program, students are taught a series of steps to learn how to transform the words they hear and read into corresponding mental images. For example, the student might read the sentence "*the cat is under the table.*" The student would then be instructed to describe to the teacher in specific detail what these words made her see. If the student replied that the words made her see a black cat sitting on a metal chair next to a wooden dining room table, the teacher would ask her to reread the original text and check to see if her picture matched what the words in the sentence were saying. Through questioning, the teacher would guide the student to the realization that her picture did not quite match the text. The student would then adjust her image by moving the cat from the chair to under the dining room table. By carefully leading the student to visualize more complex chunks of text (sentences, paragraphs, whole pages of text), the V/V program increases the student's ability to experience text and words in an accurate and meaningful way. The program strives to help students become adept at linking written language with mental images through the process of verbally describing and evaluating their internal mental pictures. By verbalizing their responses, and learning how to modify their words to match what the text really says, students learn how to self-monitor and self-correct their own thinking.

The program has particular benefits for students with NLD because it relies heavily on language to teach comprehension. In addition, the V/V program taps into the strong rote memories of these students by requiring them to formulate oral summaries of what they have read or heard. By having them answer questions posed by the teacher, the program then strives to move students beyond simply memorizing what happens in a passage to a more profound understanding of the text. The teacher decides which questions will best elucidate the text for the student by listening carefully to the student's summaries. In this manner, the teacher can see exactly where the student's logic and understanding break down, and can design individually directed questions to help the student get back on track. The program is particularly beneficial for students with NLD because it supplies the massive amount of practice and repetition these students need to master a task.

Once students become skilled at the technique of visualizing, they can use the same procedure to gain a more accurate understanding of specific vocabulary. Volden (2004) cites the following example to illustrate a typical vocabulary error made by some students with NLD. The student here is talking about the experience of going to a grocery store and uses these words to describe exiting from the store: "after you're finished then you go to the cashier. Then you go out the door. If it's at the *beginning* then you can go to the mall" (p.135). In this example, the student uses the word *beginning* to mean *entrance*. Students with NLD have a tendency to use synonyms inappropriately, frequently substituting one word haphazardly for another word that has a somewhat similar meaning.

In addition, they frequently select an inappropriate synonym that results in too dramatic a meaning to be suitable for the particular context they are using it in. In the sentence, *I am liberated from school everyday at 3:10*, the writer was not trying to be facetious or ironic. She did not fully understand that the word *liberate* is usually reserved for setting people free from more spectacular circumstances. Individuals with NLD may be prone to these types of errors because they are so literal. It is difficult for them to understand why two words with identical meanings cannot be used interchangeably. In addition, their proclivity for using the more dramatic form of two synonyms aligns with their tendency to florid writing and speaking.

So even though students with NLD frequently are familiar with many words, they do not always have enough understanding of each word to use it appropriately. It is essential to teach them how to deepen their understanding of words, and develop the ability to know when a word best fits a particular context. During elementary school, Sara used V/V to learn the meaning of new words. Whenever she encountered a word she did not know, she made a special vocabulary card. On the front of each card was printed a specific word. On the back of each card was a definition, a sentence describing how she visualized the word, and a simple drawing that illustrated her sentence.

Two years ago, when she was studying for the GRE, an exam similar to the SAT and required for admittance to some graduate schools, Sara decided to commit to memory some difficult words recommended by a preparatory guidebook. She did this by using the same V/V technique. Every night she would leave a pile of cards on a shelf. I was to read the cards and point out to her the places where she did not use a word appropriately. Sara and I referred to this more subtle meaning of a word as its connotation. I needed to make sure Sara was visualizing not only the literal meaning of the word, but also the connotation. When I discovered a card where a word was used in a fashion that did not match its connotation, Sara adjusted her internal picture of the word and wrote a new sentence to match her new picture. She not only received a high score on the verbal part of the exam, but also learned a great deal about the subtlety of words.

In addition to helping students improve their ability to understand text and vocabulary, V/V is also useful in helping students improve their comprehension of math and visual-spatial concepts. Lindamood-Bell Learning Processes, the developers of the visualization program, have developed a math program, *On Cloud Nine* (Tuley and Bell 1997), to teach students how to use visualization to clarify basic math concepts, and a program called *Drawing with Language* (refer to information about this program p.224) to teach individuals how to picture visual-spatial concepts.

As students become more skilled in comprehending text and language, they need to be constantly encouraged to engage actively in text, to draw on background knowledge, to highlight important passages, and to reflect on their understanding as they read. They need to be exposed to a wide range of texts, both expository and narrative. Finally, early readers can learn a lot about important literary elements, including plot, setting, and conflict, by using well-designed graphic organizers such as story grammars. More advanced readers can gain knowledge of many terms and abstract concepts found in expository texts by using visual organizers such as Venn diagrams, charts, and diagrams. Students with NLD respond best to simple visual organizers that are not cluttered with extraneous visual detail. As always, it is essential to explain the visual logic to these students, to give them a model of a completed visual organizer before they attempt to try one on their own, and continually to ask questions and offer clarifications to make sure they comprehend the point of the assignment.

Students with NLD can also increase their understanding of character motivation by acting in plays. The experience of pretending they are another person can help these students understand multiple points of view if an adult asks them appropriate questions (e.g., What do you think the character is feeling?, What does she say that makes you believe she is sad, happy, etc.?, Would you solve this problem in the same way if you were really your character?). Because students with NLD have an extraordinary memory for verbal material, they can memorize the lines of plays with little effort. However, they may find the physical demands of imitating a character's movements and facial expressions challenging. Therefore, Reader's Theater where students are only required to speak the words of their character is a good choice for them.

Finally, students with NLD need instruction in reading comprehension in both the early and the later grades. Do not assume they understand what they are reading simply because they can accurately read the words on the page. Constantly challenge them to think more deeply about what they are reading as soon as they are able to read fluently.

(d) Generalization

The same techniques can be used to enhance concept understanding in science, math, and history. Also, students can use their new deeper understanding of language to become more reflective and to reach a better understanding of their own learning style. Improving reading comprehension and vocabulary through visualization can also improve the student's ability to write more meaningful essays.

(e) Goal

The student will be able to understand and use words in a meaningful way. At first, the teacher or other adult verbally guides the student to an understanding of the text and language. The ultimate goal is to help students internalize this ability so they can verbally mediate their own learning and gain the metacognitive ability to study, write, and understand concepts independently.

(f) Resources for vocabulary and reading comprehesion

1. *Bringing Words to Life* (2002), by Beck, McKeown, and Kucan, is one of the best sources for creative ways to enhance a student's vocabulary. The suggested exercises are particularly ideal for students with NLD because the authors demonstrate ways adults can engage students in meaningful verbal dialogue about the nuances of word meanings.

2. *Vocabulary Development* (1999), by Stahl, is a thin volume that contains excellent suggestions for teaching students semantic categories. This book gives many helpful ways to use visual organizers to show how different words fit into meaningful categories.

3. *Vocabulary Instruction: Research to Practice* (2004), edited by Baumann and Kame'enui, contains excellent suggestions for ways to deepen the vocabulary understanding of young children during read alouds (Chapters 3–5). Chapters 11–13 have

suggestions on how to encourage word play among students, such as giving "formulas" for how to make up riddles and puns.

4. The manual with instructions on how to teach a student to visualize is called *Visualizing and Verbalizing for Language Comprehension and Thinking* (1986), by Nanci Bell. The Lindamood-Bell Learning Processes gives training workshops throughout the country for all their programs, including *Visualization and Verbalization.* They also hold summer clinics where students of any age can receive intensive individual instruction. (See www.lblp.com or call 800-233-1819.)

5. *Improving Reading Comprehension: Research-Based Principles and Practices* (2002), by Carlisle and Rice, describes many strategies students can use before, during and after reading a text.

6. *Reasoning & Reading* (2000), by Carlisle, is a series of workbooks that teach important reasoning skills such as how to understand analogies, synonyms, antonyms, and definitions, and how to form generalizations, make inferences, and draw conclusions. This series of books can be used with a variety of ages (available from EPS, 800-225-5750).

7. *From Talking to Walking: Strategies for Scaffolding Expository Expression* (2002), by Jennings and Haynes, is written for students with language-learning disabilities, but many of the strategies are useful for students with NLD. The visual organizers included in the book give students with NLD (who do well with rule-based strategies) categories and models they can use to generate cogent writing. The techniques can also be modified to use in teaching reading comprehension.

8. "Nonverbal Learning Disabilities and Remedial Interventions" (1991), by Foss, is a scholarly article that contains practical teaching suggestions. It has a good section on reading comprehension and how to teach students to internalize verbal mediation so they are able to direct their own learning.

9. *The Reading Teacher's Book of Lists* (2000), by Fry, Kress, and Fountoukidis, has numerous examples of common idioms and metaphors that can be used to demonstrate figurative language. *Semantically Speaking—advanced edition* (1989), by Krassowski, is a board game that includes decks of cards of common idioms,

words with multiple meanings, and other semantic classifications (available from Proed, 800-397-7633).

10. The following websites have useful information and sample lessons:
www.manatee.k12.fl.us/sites/elementary/palmasola/readcompin dexa.htm
http://www.literacy.uconn.edu/compre.htm#strategy
http://www.readingrockets.org/articles/105

11. A good source for well-designed graphic organizers is the series called *Organizing Thinking* by Parks and Black (1992). The lessons in these books are also available as computer software.

12. Speech-language pathologists are professionals who are trained to help individuals with their semantic language.

Intervention 5: Interpreting words and phrases literally

(a) Problem

Tendency to interpret words, phrases, and situations very literally. Contributes to their naïveté and over-trusting nature. Contributes to their difficulty with reading comprehension and social skills.

(b) Strengths

Sensitivity to and strong interest in language, familiar with many words.

(c) Solution

Young children tend to interpret language and conversation in a concrete and literal manner. We find their errors charming and delightful. We also expect them to grow out of this tendency and learn how to read between the lines. Individuals with NLD do not grow out of their tendency to interpret language literally. Although the errors they make may seem amusing to a listener, their problem with literalness causes them much painful confusion and contributes to the perception by others that individuals with NLD are "weird" people. It is possible for these individuals to learn how to be less literal, but as always they need a massive amount of practice in order to become proficient at self-correcting their literal interpretations of language. It took Sara many years of work in order to reach this goal.

However, she is now able to recognize and adjust her thinking for almost every literal situation in which she finds herself (see Chapter 8).

In order to ensure that individuals with NLD learn to be less literal, it is important to do more than teach them the meanings of English idioms. The first step is to teach the student what it means to be literal. Say:

> When someone is literal they don't always get what the other person is trying to tell them. To be literal means you believe exactly what you hear and see. Let me give you an example. What if I asked you to tell me how many stories our house has? What do you think that would mean? [The child might tell you that she doesn't know exactly because she would need to count all the books your family has.] I can see why you might think that, but actually what you are thinking—that a story means a book is too literal. The word *story* has another meaning that makes more sense in this question.

Explain the alternate meaning of *story* and discuss why this other meaning makes more sense in this question. Give several other examples of literalness. The most effective examples are authentic ones you can gather from your child's own speech and daily experiences. When the child has a fairly secure concept of literalness, explain to her that many words have more than one meaning. Tell her if she is going to escape from being too literal, it is important for her to figure out how to match the correct meaning of the word to the context of the sentence. Say:

> Most words have more than one meaning. As a matter of fact some words can have six different meanings. Let's look in the dictionary to see what I mean. [Show child a word in a dictionary with many different meanings.] Wow, that sure makes understanding sentences tricky. Let's play a game and see if we can figure out if we are being too literal. Remember last night when we were reading *The Little House in the Big Woods,* and we read about how Pa scooped up a handful of earth. I wonder, does that mean Pa broke off a chunk of the whole earth, or what? I wonder which word in that sentence has two confusing meanings. Yes, the word *earth* has two meanings. It can mean the whole planet or it can just mean dirt. For example, you could say, "I filled the flower pot with earth and planted some seeds." Which meaning of earth makes more sense in the sentence about Pa? If Pa scooped up a handful of earth, what would you picture him doing?

An adult then needs to listen very carefully to detect examples of the student's literal interpretations that occur in her daily conversation. Next, "dissect" these examples with the student so she understands why she is being too literal. Because parents are in an ideal position to observe their children in a wide variety of situations, they may need to take a leadership role in helping their children in this area. However, they can work in conjunction with a speech therapist who can assist them with this process. Remember the process of helping a student with NLD combat their literal tendencies may take several years.

(d) Generalization

The same technique can be used in other situations where students need to form judgments. Helping students learn how to monitor their own errors with literal interpretations will aid them to become more reflective and insightful. Students will be able to form more sound opinions, make better decisions, and make more reliable guesses. In addition, this process will give them more confidence in social situations and make them appear less gullible.

(e) Goal

Students will be able to understand what it means to be literal, and ultimately to learn how to recognize and correct their own errors independently. At first, the teacher or other adult verbally points out real-life examples of their literalness. The ultimate goal is help students internalize this ability so they can verbally mediate their own speech and interpretation.

(f) Resources for combating literalness

1. Speech-language pathologists are professionals trained to help individuals develop a less literal outlook.

2. Visualization will help students with NLD learn how to make important judgments about both written and oral language. Asking students to visualize their literal interpretations of situations can help them understand why certain interpretations do not make sense. See information under Intervention 4 about how to obtain material for the V/V program.

3. There are many resources for teaching multiple meanings of words, idioms and metaphors. Some of these include: *The Reading Teacher's Book of Lists* (Fry *et al.* 2000), *Semantically Speaking—advanced edition* (1989) by Krassowski, a board game that includes decks of cards of common idioms, words with multiple meanings, and other semantic classifications (available from Proed, 800-397-7633), *Multiple Word Meanings* (2002) by Lattyak and Dedrick, *Multiple Meanings for the Young Adult* (1995) by McCarr, *Picture This* (2002) by DiPerri, and *Idioms Delight* (1990) by Arena (www.buttepublications.com).

Intervention 6: Social development

(a) Problem

Difficulties in social situations, poor social judgment and perception, poor understanding of the nonverbal aspects of communication (facial expressions, body language, gestures), difficulty understanding pragmatic language (understanding the function of language, and how to use language appropriately in social situations).

(b) Strengths

Verbal abilities, an acute desire to please.

(c) Solution

The social difficulties experienced by individuals with NLD stem from a complex interaction of weaknesses. In addition to the obvious difficulties of misreading nonverbal social cues and pragmatics, all of their other weaknesses conspire to increase their social shortcomings. For example, difficulties with semantic language and with understanding concepts make it difficult for them to understand language in a deep way. This weakness leads to social problems as much as academic ones. Social judgment relies, in part, on the ability to understand language and effectively form sophisticated determinations about situations. Difficulties with visual-spatial concepts may cause them to get lost, or have trouble forming letters or lining up numbers in a math problem. But this same core difficulty might also result in poor social judgments, such as standing too close to someone in a social interaction. Social situations are frequently novel experiences, so problems adapting to novelty also contribute to their social difficulties.

A more positive way to view this interplay of weaknesses is to recognize that when individuals with NLD receive interventions in any single area, they are indirectly working on improving their social difficulties. When you help them with semantic language, reading comprehension, or show them ways to get around their school or neighborhood, you are making sure that they are gaining the skills to be more socially adept. As students with NLD receive interventions that increase their perceptual base in one area, this improvement will lead to gains in social acuity because you are working with a stronger, more knowledgeable student.

It is also important to realize that students with NLD have important strengths on which parents and teachers can capitalize in any effort to improve social perception. First, they are strongly motivated to be socially competent. They are keenly aware of situations in which they are experiencing social difficulties, and they want to change their situation. One could argue that a reason why individuals with NLD may isolate themselves is because their situation makes them so unbearably unhappy. They want to be a good friend if only someone would explain to them exactly how to go about doing this. One of the principles of teaching students with NLD is that they can learn anything if only they are taught properly.

The earlier one intervenes to improve the child's social competence the better chance that the child will become socially able. While there is little research to support this assertion, I believe it is true based on my personal experience as a parent of a young adult with significant NLD who functions well socially. Every intervention that Sara received helped her to improve her social skills. Learning how to visualize improved Sara's reading comprehension, but also improved her reasoning powers in ways that could be useful in developing better social acumen. The following suggestions are specific ways in which teachers and parents can help students with NLD improve their social skills:

1.   · Because individuals with NLD do not care for novelty, they frequently react with alarm in early childhood to new social situations with alarm. It is important to introduce the child gradually to positive experiences with other children. In this way, they can build up a rich repertoire of social experiences. In addition to exposing them to varied social situations, it is

essential that adults discuss social situations with the children in an explicit way so they understand that social interactions have rules and protocols. Through experience and practice, they will learn to master their social milieu.

2. Teach the "rules" of behavior that govern events like birthday parties or family dinners. Gives the child an overview of what will happen at an upcoming social event before the child ever gets there. Since most birthday parties have the same structure, the child who attends frequent birthday parties will build up enough social experience to recognize this structure.

3. However, the child with NLD will not develop an understanding of social events simply by attending them. Use verbal mediation to clue them in about what to expect and how to respond. Discuss words or actions they might use so they have general prototypical examples of dialogues or appropriate behavior, and give them opportunities to practice in many authentic social situations so they learn to generate their own personal, but socially astute, responses.

4. Have a family member or adult attend social events with the child until she has enough successful social experience to function comfortably on her own. Later, discuss the social event with the child to help clarify any social skills that seem mystifying to her.

5. Encourage repetitious social experiences with the same group of people by joining ongoing playgroups or classes. In elementary school, choose only one or two extracurricular activities that she is interested in, and concentrate on making these activities successful.

6. Once she reaches school age and it is no longer possible for an adult to accompany her to activities, help your child cultivate stable friendships with a few children and send them to activities together. For example, I found that Sara formed positive friendships with kind, but bossy, verbal girls who liked to be in charge. They kept a running commentary of the day's events that served as a perfect verbal map for Sara ("OK, Sara, let's go in this door. This should be a good art class. I heard the teacher was nice. I am looking forward to learning how to use clay, aren't you?") Sara was a good listener and a loyal friend, and these relationships enriched both children. Help solidify positive

friendships at home by getting to know the other child's family, and take an active role in volunteering to drive in the carpool, inviting other children over, and so on.

7. Encourage the child to have social experiences with mixed ages. The social dynamic changes in helpful ways when children with NLD interact with groups of mixed-aged children, or when they play near groups of adults. For example, Sara had some of her most meaningful social experiences in elementary school with groups of children made up of her younger brother's friends as well as friends her own age. At these times, she could experience what it was like to take a leadership role when she explained the rules of games to younger children.

8. At the same time that you are providing positive social experiences for the child, have many conversations with her about what constitutes a positive friendship. In this way, you are encouraging your children to form values and generalizations about how independently to create positive social situations for themselves as they get older.

9. Capitalize on the child's interest in books and language to further social understanding. Read stories and novels with her and discuss the motivations of characters. Ask the child why she thought a character acted or responded in a particular way. Use stories to teach her about emotions.

10. Encourage imaginative play by supplying appropriate toys and props such as dress-up clothes and puppets. Through imaginative play, children re-create situations in their own words and get a chance to practice social situations from many points of view. Encourage the child with NLD to put on plays with other children.

11. Pragmatic language can be taught. Speech-language pathologists are skilled in teaching individuals the meaning of the nonverbal signals of communication. Children with NLD should receive direct instruction in the meaning of facial expressions, gestures, and how to initiate and end a conversation. Then provide opportunities to practice these skills in authentic social situations, so the child with NLD can learn independently to form generalizations and apply her understanding to new situations in the future.

12. Encourage independence and a sense of personal competency in high school. Rehearse how to get to every new place and how to get around school so they do not spend mental energy worrying about getting lost. Teach adolescents to use public transportation, how to get places by rollerblading or riding a bicycle. Do not assume they understand the logic of traffic lights or the flow of traffic, and make sure for their physical safety that they do.

13. Continuously build on the skills and strategies they already have in order to increase social perception.

14. If they want to participate in an organized sport, encourage one that requires the least amount of complex movements, such as running, or possibly volleyball.

15. Make sure the adolescent is cognizant of all the social rules that govern high school life. Find out what kinds of clothes are fashionable.

16. Encourage extracurricular activities that help them become part of a positive social group, and also capitalize on their verbal strengths (writing for the newspaper, participating in theater groups, groups that perform dramatic readings, foreign languages). They are most comfortable in structured activities. Encourage service work as children with NLD have a strong sense of justice. If they are attracted to music, remember that many children with NLD have extreme difficulty with rhythm so they will probably not become highly adept at a musical instrument. Seek out a music teacher who does not emphasize perfection. The clarinet and saxophone are two instruments that, relatively speaking, require less physical dexterity to achieve moderate proficiency.

17. Structured overnight summer programs can give high school students with NLD opportunities to practice independence in a safe environment.

(d) Generalization

Explicitly teach the child how to function in every social situation. Do not be afraid of hurting her feelings by giving direct instruction on how to behave in social situations. Remember she strongly desires social acceptance.

(e) Goal

To carefully expose students to many social situations in a positive way. To increase pragmatic language. To explicitly teach students the "rules" of social interaction.

(f) Resources to increase social perception

1. Two resources to help students interpret facial expressions are the computer software program called *Mind Reading: The Interactive Guide to Emotions* (Baron-Cohen 2004) (available from www.jkp.com/mindreading), and a book written for art students called *The Artist's Complete Guide to Facial Expressions* (1990), by Gary Faigin. *Mind Reading* is an interactive program that demonstrates the facial expressions that correspond to 400 different human emotions. In addition, the program has an "emotion library," where individuals can collect their own examples of people expressing various emotions by using photographs of family members or friends. The *Artist's Guide* is a low-tech way of introducing students to the different facial expressions that people use to express different emotions.

2. Speech-language pathologists can help develop ways to aid students with NLD simultaneously with both semantic and pragmatic language.

3. The following books have excellent suggestions for improving students' social acumen: *It's So Much Work to be Your Friend: Helping the Child with Learning Disabilities Find Social Success* (2005), by Lavoie, and *How to Start Conversations and Make Friends* (2001) by Gabor (helpful suggestions for older adolescents and adults).

4. A resource to assist individuals choose an appropriate musical instrument is *The Right Instrument for Your Child: A Practical Guide for Parents and Teachers,* by Ben-Tovim and Boyd (1985).

Intervention 7: Mathematics instruction
(a) Problem

Difficulty understanding mathematical concepts and procedures. Particular difficulty matching what they can memorize verbally (e.g., an acute angle has less than 90 degrees) with the correct visual representation (e.g., picture, diagram). Poor at "word problems."

(b) Strengths

Ability to understand verbal logic.

(c) Solution

If students with NLD plan on increasing their mathematical understanding, they need simultaneously to increase their reading comprehension ability (see Intervention 4), and their ability to understand visual-spatial concepts. *Drawing with Language* (www.lblp.com or 800-233-1819), a structured program developed by Lindamood-Bell to improve visual-spatial skills, is not available in a published form. However, students can receive instruction in this program at their summer clinics. Students first learn how to visualize a concept (such as the length of an inch) and then learn how to draw it. By helping students increase their ability to comprehend concepts, teachers will find they are more able to tackle math. The following suggestions are specific ways in which teachers and parents can help students with NLD improve their math skills:

1. Put particular emphasis on teaching the meaning of place value. Elementary students with NLD have great difficulty lining up the correct numbers for arithmetic problems. Allowing them to use graph paper with large squares will help this problem, but verbally explaining how place value works will give them a deeper understanding of why certain numbers need to go in specific columns. After the child understands the meaning of "place value," the teacher will have a verbal way to talk about where numbers are placed. Say:

   > We have a gigantic math problem to do, and we want to make sure we put all the numbers in the correct column or else we will not be able to get the correct answer. Place value can help us know where to put the numbers. Let's first mark our sheet to show the right places.
   >
   > Now let's look at the first number we need to copy onto our paper. It is 243. How many units are there in 243? How many tens? Hundreds? The next number we need to copy is 597. This number also has a number in the units place, one in the tens place and one in the hundreds place. Let's copy these three numbers and make sure we keep all the units in the units column, all the tens in the tens column, and all the hundreds in the hundreds column.

$$\begin{array}{r}
\text{hundreds} \quad \text{tens} \quad \text{units} \\
2 \quad 4 \quad 3 \\
+ \, 5 \quad 9 \quad 7 \\
\hline
\end{array}$$

2. Students with NLD need to see a model of how a particular kind of problem is solved, hear a verbal explanation on how to proceed and why, and then receive an enormous amount of practice solving many examples. In order to make sure they are not learning only how to solve these problems in a rote fashion, ask them questions that require active thinking, such as: When you divide, should your answer be smaller or larger than the amount you start with? Which fraction is larger, $\frac{1}{2}$ or $\frac{1}{4}$?

3. Write out cards that contain examples of each type of math problem the student is currently learning. Next to each example, write out in words the steps needed to solve the problem. Store these cards in an index card box that the student keeps with her. When she has to solve a particular kind of problem, such as long division, have her find the card from her box that matches it.

4. Encourage verbal logic. For example, if your student cannot answer a question about which fraction is larger, say:

    Imagine you are eating a chocolate cake. Picture the cake in your imagination [or actually ask the student to draw the cake]. What if you ate $\frac{1}{2}$ the cake? Now picture yourself eating $\frac{1}{4}$ of the cake. Which piece would be larger?, etc.

5. Although these students need to experience a great deal of practice on each specific type of problem, they cannot accomplish all the necessary practice in one sitting. They will tire after much copying, but still need the experience of copying because

physically setting up the problem will help cement procedures in memory. So, instead of giving them 20 long division problems to do in one evening, have them do this amount of work over four evenings, for example, by assigning only five problems at any given time.

6. Use flash cards containing the symbol, a verbal explanation, and a picture to help illustrate difficult visual-spatial concepts. Have the students keep these definition cards in their index card box to use for clarification.

7. Use manipulatives judiciously. Choose well-designed manipulatives that are not visually overwhelming. Students with NLD will not figure out how to use manipulatives without explicit verbal explanation. Assume nothing and explain in words every important aspect of the manipulative and the corresponding concept.

8. Clarify important concepts by helping the student visualize the concept in both two and three dimensions. For example, if trying to get the student to understand the concept of $\frac{1}{3}$, first show the student a concrete example of this fraction by using a manipulative, or cutting something such as a pizza into three equal parts. After explaining in words what $\frac{1}{3}$ means, have the student draw a pizza and illustrate $\frac{1}{3}$. Ask clarifying questions to make certain the student completely understands the concept (e.g., If you were going to eat $\frac{1}{3}$ of this pizza, how many pieces would you eat, if I color two pieces of the pizza that you drew, would that be $\frac{1}{3}$?).

9. Teach students how to estimate, because they are prone to make wildly incorrect guesses to answer problems. Have them check work with a calculator, and discuss any answers that are wildly different from the results on the calculator. Always encourage them to think, does this answer make sense?

10. Have students use clay or play dough to build models of concepts. Discuss the essential elements of the concept. This approach works particularly well with geometric concepts, such as acute, right, and straight angles. For example, have a student build a model of a right angle with clay, then move the vertical side of the angle to create an acute angle and show her how this angle is less than 90 degrees.

11. Teach students how to use a highlighter to emphasize which information is essential in word problems.

12. Encourage students to write essays about mathematical concepts to capitalize on their ability to grasp concepts better when they are encoded into language. The following excerpt is from an essay Sara wrote about geometric symmetry when she was in the tenth grade:

> The simplest type of symmetry is bilateral or mirror symmetry. Bilateral symmetry is when two halves of a whole are the mirror image of each other. In order to determine if an object contains bilateral symmetry, you can imagine a mirror down the middle of the object. If the object contains bilateral symmetry the original object should be recreated. Usually our eyes are the best tool to determine if an object has bilateral symmetry. One example of bilateral symmetry in the world around us is in butterflies. If a butterfly was cut down the middle, the right and left halves would be identical. [Here she inserts an illustration.]

(d) Generalization

The same principles apply to teaching higher-level math skills such as algebra and statistics if the student wants to learn about these subjects. Students will need an enormous amount personal initiative and one-to-one assistance in order to master more advanced math concepts. You need to decide based on the student's future educational and vocational goals if the massive amount of effort required to master upper level math is worth it.

(e) Goal

To understand fundamental mathematical concepts, to think logically about mathematical problems, and to be able to tell when a solution is based on unsound reasoning.

(f) Resources

1. The math program, *On Cloud Nine* (1997), by Tuley and Bell, is an excellent program developed to accompany the visualizing and verbalizing program. The program recommends effective

manipulatives to use with the verbal explanations provided in the manual. The program teaches basic arithmetic concepts through decimals.

2. *Teaching Mathematics to the Learning Disabled* (1989), by Bley and Thorton, has some excellent suggestions. The book contains good information on teaching students how to solve word problems.

Appendix

Example of How to Combine Strategies to Develop Lessons

Since students with NLD need to receive simultaneous interventions in many diverse areas, teachers will find it valuable to create lessons that bolster several areas at the same time. The following is a sample lesson where a teacher can use the visualization strategy, which has already been presented to the student in the context of improving reading comprehension, to teach her how to deepen social perception, increase pragmatic and semantic language, and practice writing.

Teacher: Let's make a list of all the emotions we can think of. An emotion is a feeling like *sadness*. (Write down all the emotions that the student can list.) Well, this is a good list of feelings. Some of these are positive feelings like *kindness*, and others are negative feelings like *meanness*. (Discuss which emotions on the list are positive, which are negative, and which are neutral. Next, show her a picture of an individual with an astonished expression on her face. Use a picture from *The Artist's Complete Guide to Facial Expressions* (Faigin 1990) or the *Mind Reading* (Baron-Cohen 2004) (software.) One emotion that people can feel is astonishment. People feel astonishment when they are surprised in an amazing way. Just like *huge* is bigger than *big*, *astonishment* is more surprising than *surprise*. For example, when I was in high school, my family went on a trip to Mississippi and Louisiana. We stopped for a picnic outside, and I was astonished to see dozens of green chameleons walking around in the grass. I had never seen a chameleon in the wild before so the sight of seeing so many bright green creatures was astounding to me. Have you ever been astounded? I was wondering how you would picture *astonishment* if you tried to visualize it?

Student: Well, this is how I picture astonishment. I see a girl sitting at a table with a big present in front of her. She rips off the wrapping paper and opens the box. A large, green parrot flies out of the box. She looks up at the parrot with an expression like this on her face. (Student makes an expression that shows surprise.)

Teacher: Wow, that is a good picture for astonishment. I would be really astonished, too, if a parrot flew out of a present.

After the teacher is certain that the student really understands what *astonishment* means, use the following types of exercises to extend the student's knowledge into other subjects. Read passages from stories where a character experiences something astonishing, and ask the student to explain what emotion the character is feeling, and why this character feels the way he or she does. Have the student write sentences or paragraphs illustrating different emotions. Ask questions like, "Which would be more astonishing—a farmer who grew a thousand oranges on his farm in California, or a girl who bought a thousand oranges at a grocery store in a city? Could you ever be bored and astonished at the same time? How does surprise compare with astonishment?"

References

Arena, J. (1990) *Idioms Delight*. Novato, CA: Academic Therapy Publishing.

Badian, N. (1992) "Nonverbal Learning Disability, School Behavior, and Dyslexia." *Annals of Dyslexia 42*, 159–178.

Barnes, H. (1997) *A Life for the Spirit: Rudolf Steiner in the Cross Currents of Time*. Hudson, NY: Anthrosophic Press.

Baron-Cohen, S. (2004) *Mind Reading: The Interactive Guide to Emotions*. London: Jessica Kingsley Publishers.

Baumann, J. and Kame'enui, E. (2004) *Vocabulary Instruction: Research to Practice*. New York: Guilford Press.

Beck, I., McKeown, M., and Kucan, L. (2002) *Bringing Words to Life: Robust Vocabulary Development*. New York: Guilford Press.

Bell, N. (1986) *Visualizing and Verbalizing for Language Comprehension and Thinking*. Paso Robles, CA: Academy of Reading Publications.

Ben-Tovim, A. and Boyd, D. (1985) *The Right Instrument for Your Child: A Practical Guide for Parents and Teachers*. New York: Quill.

Benbow, M. (1999) *Loops and Other Groups: A Kinesthetic Writing System*. San Antonio, TX: Psychological Corp.

Berg, M. (1999) "Nonverbal Learning Disorder: The Hidden Disability." Paper presented at the annual meeting of the International Dyslexia Association, Chicago, IL.

Bigler, E. (1989) "On the Neuropsychology of Suicide." *Journal of Learning Disabilities 22*, 180–185.

Birsh, J. (ed.) (2005) *Multisensory Teaching of Basic Language Skills*. Baltimore, MD: Paul H. Brookes.

Bley, N. and Thorton, C. (1989) *Teaching Mathematics to the Learning Disabled*. Austin, TX: Proed.

Brown, D. (2005) "Helping the Learning Disabled Adolescent Learn to Drive." Retrieved May 21, 2006 from www.ldaamerica.org/aboutld/parents/help/drive.asp.

Buka, S. (1998) "A Researcher's View: Learning-Disabled Children Get Lost in Definitions." *Brown University Child & Adolescent Behavior Letter 14*, 1–3.

Burger, N. (2004) *A Special Kind of Brain: Living with Nonverbal Learning Disability*. London: Jessica Kingsley Publishers.

Carlisle, J. (2000) *Reasoning & Reading*. Cambridge, MA: Educators Publishing Service.

Carlisle, J. and Rice, M. (2002) *Improving Reading Comprehension: Research-Based Principles and Practices*. Baltimore, MD: York Press.

Diferri, K. (2002) *Picture This: Multiple Meanings in English Context*. Hillsboro, OR: Butte Publications.

Dombrowski, S., Kamphaus, R., and Reynolds, C. (2004) "After the Demise of the Discrepancy: Proposed Learning Disabilities Diagnostic Criteria." *Professional Psychology: Research And Practice 35*, 364–372.

Earle-Cruiskshanks, J. (2000) "Nonverbal Learning Disabilities: A Physician's Story." Retrieved September 14, 2004 from www.nld.com.

Faigin, G. (1990) *The Artist's Complete Guide to Facial Expressions.* New York: Gupill Publications.

Fletcher, J. (1989) "Nonverbal Learning Disabilities and Suicide: Classification Leads to Prevention." *Journal of Learning Disabilities 22*, 176–179.

Fletcher, J., Coulter, W., Reschly, D., and Vaughn, S. (2004) "Alternative Approaches to the Definition and Identification of Learning Disabilities: Some Questions and Answers." *Annals of Dyslexia 54*, 304–331.

Forest, B. (2004) "The Utility of Math Difficulties, Internalized Psychopathy, and Visual-Spatial Deficits to Identify Children with Nonverbal Learning Disability Syndrome: Evidence of a Visualspatial Disability." *Child Neuropsychology 10*, 129–146.

Foss, J. (1991) "Nonverbal Learning Disabilities and Remedial Interventions." *Annals of Dyslexia 41*, 128–140.

Fry, E., Kress, J., and Fountoukidis, D. (2000) *The Reading Teacher's Book of Lists.* San Francisco, CA: Jossey-Bass.

Fuchs, D., Mock, D., Morgan, P., and Young, C. (2003) "Responsiveness-to-Intervention: Definitions, Evidence, and Implications for the Learning Disabilities Construct." *Learning Disabilities Research & Practice 18*, 3, 157–171.

Gabor, D. (2001) *How to Start Conversations and Make Friends.* New York: Fireside.

Green, D. (2002) *Growing Up With NLD.* Albuquerque, NM: Silicon Heights Computers.

Greenham, S. (1999) "Learning Disabilities and Psychosocial Adjustment: A Critical Review." *Child Neuropsychology 5*, 3, 171–196.

Jennings, T. and Haynes, C. (2002) *From Talking to Walking: Strategies for Scaffolding Expository Expression.* Prides Crossing, MA: Landmark School, Inc.

Johnson, D. (1987) "Nonverbal Learning Disabilities." *Pediatric Annals 16*, 133–140.

Johnson, D. and Myklebust, H. (1967) *Learning Disabilities: Educational Principles and Practices.* New York: Grune & Stratton.

Keller, H. (2004) *The World I Live In.* New York: New York Review of Books.

King, D. (1985) *Writing Skills for the Adolescent.* Cambridge, MA: Educators Publishing Service.

King, D. (1986) *Keyboarding Skills.* Cambridge, MA: Educators Publishing Service.

Klin, A., Sparrow, S., Volkmar, F., Cicchetti, D., and Rourke, B. (1995) "Asperger's Syndrome." In B.R. Rourke (ed.) *Syndrome of Nonverbal Learning Disabilities: Neurodevelopmental Manifestations.* New York: Guilford Press.

Kowalchuk, B. and King, J. (1989) "Adult Suicide versus Coping with Nonverbal Learning Disabilities." *Journal of Learning Disabilities 22*, 177–179.

Krassowski, E. (1989) *Semantically Speaking.* Tucson, TX: Communication Skill Builders.

Lattyak, J. and Dedrick, S. (2002) *Multiple Word Meanings.* Hillsboro, OR: Butte Publications

Lavoie, R. (2005) *It's So Much Work to be Your Friend: Helping the Child with Learning Disabilities Find Social Success.* New York: Touchstone.

Levine, M. (2002) *A Mind at a Time.* New York: Simon & Schuster.

Levine, M. (2003) "Celebrating Diverse Minds." *Educational Leadership 61*, 12–18.

Little, S. (1993) "Nonverbal Learning Disabilities and Socioemotional Functioning: A Review of Recent Literature." *Journal of Learning Disabilities 26*, 653–665.

Lyon, G., Fletcher, J., Shaywitz, S., Shaywitz, B., Torgesen, J., Wood, F., Schulte, A., and Olson, R. (2001) "Rethinking Learning Disabilities." In C. Finn, C. Hokanson and A. Rotherham (eds) *Rethinking Special Education for a New Century.* Washington, DC: Progressive Policy Institute.

Matte, R. and Bolaski, J. (1998) "Nonverbal Learning Disabilities: An Overview." *Intervention in School & Clinic 34*, 39–43.

McCarr, D. (1995) *Multiple Meanings for the Young Adult.* Hillsboro, OR: Butte Publications.

Miotke, J. (2002) *The Absolute Beginner's Guide to Taking Great Photos.* Roseville, CA: Prima Publishing.

Molenaar-Klumper, M. (2002) *Non-verbal Learning Disabilities: Characteristics, Diagnosis and Treatment.Within an Educational Setting.* London: Jessica Kingsley Publishers.

Mooney, D. (2004) "Nonverbal Learning Disabilities: Interventions for Home and School." Paper presented at conference in Oakbrook, IL sponsored by Maple Leaf Center.

Neff, B., Neff-Lippman, J. and Stockdale, C. (2002) *The Source for Visual-Spatial Disorders.* Moline, IL: Linguisystems.

Palombo, J. (1994) "Descriptive Profile of Children with Nonverbal Learning Disabilities." Retrieved September 14, 2004 from www.nldline.org.

Parks, S. and Black, H. (1992) *Organizing Thinking: Graphic Organizers (Book I).* Pacific Grove, CA: Critical Thinking Press and Software.

Parks, S. and Black, H. (1992) *Organizing Thinking: Graphic Organizers (Book II).* Pacific Grove, CA: Critical Thinking Press and Software.

Roman, M. (1998) "The Syndrome of Nonverbal Learning Disabilities: Clinical Description and Applied Aspects." *Current Issues in Education 1*, 1–21. Retrieved September 14, 2004 from http://www.ldonline.org.

Rosner, J. (1979) *Helping Children Overcome Learning Difficulties.* New York: Walker.

Rourke, B. (1987) "Syndrome of Nonverbal Learning Disabilities: The Final Common Pathwway of White-Matter Disease/Dysfunction?" *Clinical Neuropsychologist 1*, 209–234.

Rourke, B. (1989) *Nonverbal Learning Disabilities: The Syndrome and the Model.* New York: Guilford Press.

Rourke, B. (1995) *Syndrome of Nonverbal Learning Disabilities: Neurodevelopmental Manifestations.* New York: Guilford Press.

Rourke, B., Ahmad, S., Collins, D., Hayman-Abello, B., Hayman-Abello, S. and Warriner, E. (2002) "Child Clinical/Pediatric Neuropsychology: Some Recent Advances." *Annual Review of Psychology 53*, 309–339.

Rourke, B., Young, G. and Leenaars, A. (1989) "A Childhood Learning Disability that Predisposes those Afflicted to Adolescent and Adult Depression and Suicide Risk." *Journal of Learning Disabilities 22*, 3, 169–173.

Rubinstien, M.B. (2005) *Raising NLD Superstars.* London: Jessica Kingsley Publishers.

Shaywitz, S. (2003) *Overcoming Dyslexia.* New York: Alfred J. Knopf.

Stahl, S. (1999) *Vocabulary Development.* Cambridge, MA: Harvard University Press.

Stein, M., Klin, A. and Miller, K. (2004) "When Asperger's Syndrome and a Nonverbal Learning Disability Look Alike." *Pediatrics, 114*, 5, 1458–1463.

Sternberg, R. and Grigorenko, E. (1999) *Our Labeled Children.* Reading, MA: Perseus Books.

Tanguay, P. (1999) NLD on the Web. Accessed 12 February 2007 at www.nldontheweb.org.

Tanguay, P. (2001) *Nonverbal Learning Disabilities at Home: A Parent's Guide.* London: Jessica Kingsley Publishers.

Tanguay, P. (2002) *Nonverbal Learning Disabilities at School.* London: Jessica Kingsley Publishers.

Telzrow, C. and Bonar, A. (2002) "Responding to Students with Nonverbal Learning Disabilities." *Teaching Exceptional Children 34*, 8–12.

Thompson, S. (1996a) "Nonverbal Learning Disorders." Retrieved October 18, 2004, from www.LDonline.com.

Thompson, S. (1996b) "Nonverbal Learning Disorders Revisited in 1997." Retrieved October 18, 2004 from www.LDonline.com.

Thompson, S. (1997) *The Source for Nonverbal Learning Disorders.* Moline, IL: Linguisystems.

Thoreau, H. (1989) *Henry David Thoreau: A Week on the Concord and Merrimack Rivers/Walden; Or, Life in the Woods/The Maine Woods/Cape Cod.* New York: Library of America.

Trapani, C. (1990) *Transition Goals for Adolescents with Learning Disabilities.* Boston, MA: A College-Hill Publication.

Tuley, K. and Bell, N. (1997) *On Cloud Nine.* San Luis Obispo, CA: Gander Publishing.

Vacca, D. (2001) "Confronting the Puzzle of Nonverbal Learning Disabilities." *Educational Leadership 59*, 26–31.

Volden, J. (2004) "Nonverbal Learning Disability: A Tutorial for Speech-Language Pathologists." *American Journal of Speech-Language Pathology 13*, 128–141.

Whitney, R. (2002) *Bridging the Gap: Raising a Child With Nonverbal Learning Disorder.* New York: Perigee.

Subject Index

Author Index